the
bartender's
GIN
compendium

With that's a love
from

(handwritten signature)

the
bartender's
GIN
compendium

gaz regan

Library of Congress Control Number: 2009906970
ISBN: Hardcover   978-1-4415-4688-3
                   Softcover   978-1-4415-4687-6

Ten-percent of all revenue received by Bar Rags, LLC for this book will be donated to charity. At the time of writing we're donating to WinetoWater.org, a 501 (c) (3) non-profit aid organization focused on providing clean water to needy people around the world. Doc Hendley is the founder and president of Wine To Water. In 2003 he dreamed up the concept of the organization while bartending and playing music in nightclubs around Raleigh, North Carolina.

This book was printed in the United States of America.

To order additional copies of this book, contact:
Xlibris Corporation
1-888-795-4274
www.Xlibris.com
Orders@Xlibris.com
60992

Contents

This book is dedicated to every bartender on the face of the earth. God bless each and every one of you.

Acknowledgements

Thanks to all the members of The Worldwide Bartender Database for sending all those fabulous recipes for inclusion in this book, and thanks, also, to everyone in the gin business who helped by sending information my way.

I'll forget to mention everyone's name who helped with this project, but I do want to make sure that I thank Jonathan Pogash, The Cocktail Guru, for helping get this book off the ground, Martha Schueneman, for such a fabulous editing job, and Louise Owens from the Windmill Lounge in Dallas—the Best little Cocktail Bar in Texas—for kicking me in the pants and telling me to get to work on this.

Hugh Williams, Master Distiller Emeritus for Gordon's, Tanqueray, and Booth's gins in London, contributed his fabulous array of knowledge to this book, as you'll see in the Dry Gin chapter. Thanks, Hugh. You're a grand old friend.

Words are inadequate when it comes to expressing how I feel about the fabulous cover that the incredible Anistatia Miller designed for me. Thanks, thanks, thanks, thanks.

I'd better mention David Wondrich, too, I suppose. Thanks go to Dave for writing *Imbibe*, a book that taught us lots about the foundations of our craft, and a book from which I stole lots of information that you'll find peppered throughout this compendium. Dave: It's your round, I believe.

Thanks, too, to Lynn Moore, Gwen Campanero, Michael Cabahug, Marian Lumayag, Jill Marie Duero, Jake Muelle and everyone else at Xlibris.com who have made my first attempt at self-publishing so very easy. Your hard work and professionalism is very much appreciated.

Thanks, too, to President Obama. He didn't help with this book, but he helped me feel great about living in America—something that was missing from my life for a few years.

The rest of you, and you know who you are, thanks for putting up with all my bullshit. I've said it before, and I'll no doubt say it again, this is one of the weirdest lives I've ever had. And I'm loving every second of it.

Picture Credits

The picture on the back cover of this book was taken at the Beefeater Distillery, 2008. Photograph by Jim Ellam.

Lots of the other pictures in this book were donated by various gin companies, God bless 'em, and unless otherwise noted, the rest are from my personal collection.

Cover Design

As noted above, the inimitable Anistatia Miller, co-author with Jared Brown of *Spirituous Journey: A History of Drink*, and director of Exposition Universelle des Vins et Spiritueux, is responsible for the cover of this compendium. I hope that you agree with me when I say, "It's F***in' Fabulous," right?

Introduction

You walk into a saloon, belly up to the bar, and ask for a Dry Gin Martini, straight-up, no garnish, water on the side, no ice. The bartender asks if you want a particular brand of gin. You make your choice. You give it to her straight. "Brimelow's Gin, please. The high-proof bottling if you have it, or . . ."

"Oh, we have the high-proof Brimelow's alright," the bartender tells you. "Good gin, too. Been a best seller since it hit the shelves back in 2003. Not that far back in gin terms, but the Brimelow family's been in the gin biz since 1794, you know. Arthur Brimelow started the company. Bastard to work for, they say . . ."

You take a barstool, you sip your ice-cold elixir, you observe your problems being cleansed from your very soul, you watch as your focus sharpens, and the bartender, who has been waiting for this exact moment, says, "They added sage to the original recipe to make this bottling. That's where you're getting that sense of peace. It's the sage." Or maybe that's not what she says at all. Maybe she tells you that the gin you chose is the only gin in the world that's made in an Austrian hybrid still, and that each botanical is distilled separately. Or perhaps the bartender will tell you all about the origins of gin. About Dutch Courage. About Gin Lane. About Dr. Sylvius, the seventeenth-century Dutch professor who created the world's first gin. Or did he?

Some bartenders might quote from Casablanca when you order your Dry Gin Martini: "Of all the gin joints in all the towns in all the world . . ." Other bartenders might recite the old Ogden Nash poem, instead: "There's something about a Martini . . ." and every now and then you'll meet a bartender who tries to get you to switch your brand of gin. "If you usually drink Brimelow's Gin, I'm going to suggest you try this new one, Hopewell's Gin. It's not quite the same, but it it's sort of in the same family if you know what I mean . . . lots of my regulars are switching to it."

There are bartenders in this world, and God bless each and every one of them, who won't just try to get you to switch gins, they'll try to change the whole damned cocktail. "How about trying a Martinez instead of a Martini? Different drink, that's for sure, but she's sort of the Martini's mother. You might want to take her around the dance—floor once or twice. She's got a mean pair of gams." And the same bartenders, you can bet your bottom dollar, will eventually turn you on to Aviation cocktails. And you'll be oh so glad you found the Aviation.

While some bartenders will teach you about classic gin cocktails, others might introduce you to brand spanking new twenty-first-century drinks. If you're lucky enough to be seated across from Jonny Raglin who, at the time of writing, holds forth from behind the stick at Absinthe in San Francisco, you might be able to persuade him to fix you a Bengali Gimlet, providing he made up some of his incredible Curried Nectar before showing up for his shift, of course. Audrey Saunders, Queen of New York's Pegu Club, could suggest that you try an Earl Grey MarTEAni, one of her most fabulous gin-based potions—and Audrey has given birth to lots of fabulous new gin drinks.

This book, then, is hopefully for all the bartenders we just met, and it's for their customers, too. And it's for amateur mixologists, and it's for the pros. It's for gin tipplers, gin connoisseurs, gin lushes, gin swiggers, gin aficionados, and this book's for people who don't like gin, too. I'm in the mood to change some minds out there.

The Bartender's Gin Compendium, with a bit of luck, attacks gin from all angles. I'm hoping that this will be the book you reach for if there's anything at all you need to know about gin. I've detailed how it's made, where the flavors come from, and you'll find chapter on the history of gin and gin-based drinks here, too. There are recipes here, new and old, from all over this wonderful world of ours, many of them complete with words of wisdom from today's very best cocktailian bartenders, and there are all sorts of historical quotations, poems, and trivia here, too. And if you need to find details on all of the best gins on the market, this is the book to look at.

Here's Jonny Raglin, Bartender Extraordinaire from Absinthe,
San Francisco, and creator of the Bengali Gimlet. Look like he's playing
with some No. 209 Gin, a local product in Jonny's neck of the woods.

A Word to the Wise and a Nod— not to mention a Wink—to the Past

In the tradition of nineteenth-century bartenders such as Christopher Lawlor author of *The Mixicologist* (1895), I have inserted paid advertisements into this book. But they're nowhere near as blatant as were the ones that Lawlor took money for—I've been far more devious than he . . .

Here's what I did: You'll find descriptions of and information about lots and lots of brand-name gins in this compendium—the proof of the spirit, the web sites, lists of the botanicals their producers use, and so on, and not a penny has changed hands for this content. If, however, producers wanted to insert images of their bottles or labels or logos, etc., I've charged them a premium for that. And in some cases I've even written some personal flashbacks about specific brands, too. I think that you'll find that the images serve to make the book a lot prettier, and my essays, when all's said and done, are just bar stories. Stuff that's gone down while I was working in the bar business that makes me think of this gin or that gin. Tales that I'd tell you if we were hanging out at the end of the bar together.

I'll bet that Lawlor is looking down right now wondering why he didn't think of that.

The Label of One Billy Pitcher

"With the coming of June it was again time for me to cross the ocean once more. The day before I betook myself to the good ship Parthia, the maid handed me a package with 'Something for you, Miss!' It was a quart bottle of gin cocktail! Within an hour another bottle arrived, and later on yet another! They all bore the label of one Billy Pitcher—known to the male sex as a famous expert in cocktails. What did it mean? Why should I be the innocent recipient of all this compromising liquor?" *Memories of a Musical Career* by Clara Kathleen Rogers. Published by Little, Brown, and Company, 1919.

Chapter 1

Thoughts from a Gin Mill

Gin's a spirit unto herself. She's a loner. Gin can gnaw on the back of your neck till she nigh-on draws blood, and she can just as easily kiss you softly behind each ear, stroke the back of your shivering hand, and make you know that everything's going to be okay. And it will, you know. It really will.

Gin can be sort of sneaky, too. Many a Ramos Gin Fizz has been served to a supposed gin hater, for instance, and the glass has been refilled more than twice before they discovered what was being poured. And who the hell would have thought that gin would walk out quite so well with chocolate? But if you've ever had a Twentieth Century Cocktail—gin, creme de cacao, Lillet Blanc, and lemon juice—you know for your own self that these two make quite a lovely couple, especially when Lillet and lemon juice tag along as chaperones.

Gin is for thinkers and doers alike, but she won't be seen dead with the loud, brash braggart down the end of the bar. Gin likes a little foreplay before she commits to going all the way. Tease gin with elderflower cordial, for instance, and she'll flirt for a while before she takes her blouse off. There's no doubt in anyone's mind that the blouse is coming off, but Gin takes her own good time.

Gin makes her own statement, too. She doesn't need a sleek black dress and screw-me pumps to make her presence known at the party. She can just sit quietly at the end of the bar, faded jeans and a plain white T-shirt, secure in the knowledge that only the guys and gals who know exactly what they want, how they want it, and how they're gonna go about getting it, will ever approach her. And when they sidle over to her side, they know that they'd better treat her with some respect, too. Don't mess around with gin. She's been known to take off her earrings . . .

Here's Ada Coleman, early twentieth-century bartender at London's Savoy Hotel, and creator of the Hanky Panky—you'll find it in the recipe chapter.

Chapter 2

A Brief History of Gin and a Look at the Evolution of Gin-Based Cocktails and Mixed Drinks

An Agreeable Beverage

"The use of the juniper for flavouring alcoholic beverages may be traced to the invention, or perfecting, by Count de Morret, son of Henry IV of France, of juniper wine. It was the custom in the early days of the spirit industry, in distilling spirit from fermented liquors, to add in the working some aromatic ingredients, such as ginger, grains of paradise, &c., to take off the nauseous flavour of the crude spirits then made. The invention of juniper wine, no doubt, led some one to try the juniper berry for this purpose, and as this flavouring agent was found not only to yield an agreeable beverage, but also to impart a valuable medicinal quality to the spirit, it was generally made use of by makers of aromatized spirits thereafter." *The Encyclopædia Britannica: A Dictionary of Arts, Sciences, Literature and General Information.* Published by The Encyclopædia Britannica Company, 1910.

When it comes to history, gin's got a bit of everything. Monks and monarchs, mischief and mayhem, misery and melees—and, of course, the Martinez and the Martini. And the dawn of the twenty-first century gave gin a most fabulous rebirth, complete with new styles hitting the market, and old styles—think Old Tom, think genever—finding themselves sitting proudly, once more, on the backbars of some of today's fanciest gin mills. Gin is as hip and as flash as can be.

When we look back at the origins of gin though, and this, unfortunately, seems to be the case with most spirits, we head into murky waters. Oh, sure, we can point to certain years when we positively know that this happened, or that went down, and we might know that gin was the culprit, or at least the excuse, but when it comes to pinning down the birth of gin, we have to make do with clues instead of definitive answers. If we take a quick look at the history of distillation, though, we'll find a few clues about the origin of juniper-flavored spirits.

The Monks from the Black Friars monastery, where Plymouth Gin
is now made, are celebrated on the labels of these old gin bottles.

Distillation, a process that's described in more detail in the *Dry Gin* chapter (look for "Dry Gin Production"), involves separating individual components of a liquid from each other, and although it was known to folk before the Common Era, their methods of distillation were inefficient to say the least, and it wasn't until Gerber, aka Jabir ibn Hayyan—a Persian alchemist, astronomer, and physicist who lived circa 721 to 815 C.E.—invented the alembic still that high-proof spirits became relatively easy to produce.

The next step on our journey to discover the origins of gin takes place in Salerno, Italy, around 1100 C.E., a time when Salerno boasted the greatest medical school in the world. It was so good, in fact, that a scholarly character by the name of Constantine the African called Salerno "The City of Hippocrates." Quite a compliment. Documents from this medical school contain mention of *aqua ardens*, meaning "burning water," or "ardent spirits," and this was the they term used to describe high-octane booze. Liquor. Hooch. Was it gin, though?

Well, it could have been. These guys were making medicines—this *was* a medical school, after all—so it's possible, or more like probable, that when they learned how to distill spirits, they would have added some plants to their stills. Plants that were known to have medicinal qualities. Plants such as juniper, which had long been known to be a diuretic, and which happens to grow very well indeed around Salerno, so, well, it's possible . . .

This copy of the 1757 book, *The Complete Distiller*, by Ambrose Cooper, hows images of early alembic stills. The book is resting in The Museum of the American Cocktail in New Orleans.

Black Death

We don't hear much about juniper-flavored spirits again for quite some time, but there's a chance that when the Bubonic Plague hit Europe, some sort of crude gin might have been used to combat it. The Plague started in China in the 1330s and made its way to Europe by the late 1340s, killing, oh, around 25 million people between 1347 and 1352. The Bubonic Plague didn't mess around. This horrendous disease attacks the lymph system, thus causing swelling, especially around the groin area, and this symptom of the Black Death is what makes us think that gin could have been used as a medicine during this period.

Juniper, as we already noted, was a known diuretic and during this very frightening time people were using juniper berries in all sorts of ways to try to escape from the plague—there are records of people burning juniper wood to fumigate houses against the disease, for instance. A few centuries later—after the Great Plague of London in 1665-66—a recipe for "Plague Water" was detailed in the 1784 book, *The Art of Cookery*, by Hannah Glasse. It called for a total of 20 roots, 16 flowers, and 19 seeds, juniper berries among them: "Mix all these together . . . then fill them in an alembic with a slow fire, and take care your still does not burn," the book instructed. Chances are decent, then, that Europeans could have been swigging juniper-flavored spirits during the plague period of the 1300s, and that would explain how a precursor to gin made its way north from Italy, and became known in Northern European countries such as the Netherlands—the place where, just a couple of centuries later, genever, the mother of all modern gins, would make an appearance.

The Works of Francis Bacon

"The plague is not easily received by such as continually are about them that have the plague; as keepers of the sick, and physicians: nor again by such as take antidotes, either inward, as mithridate, juniper-berries, rue, leaf and seed, &c." *The Works of Francis Bacon, Lord Chancellor of England* by Basil Montagu, 1859.

Courage in a Bottle

Until recently most people were pretty much certain that Dr. Franciscus de la Boe, aka Dr. Sylvius, a seventeenth-century professor of medicine at the University of Leyden in the Netherlands, was the first to document a recipe for a grain-based, juniper-flavored spirit, but it turns out that this simply isn't true, and there's a good chance that the story was conjured up by some marketing maven a few decades ago. There are Dutch manuscripts from the 1500s that refer to a beverage called *genever*—the Dutch word meaning "juniper"—so we now know for sure that the drink was readily available in the Netherlands long before Sylvius took the job at the Uni. And not long after gin officially made an appearance in Holland, it took a trip to England where it was very well received, indeed.

In 1568, the predominantly Protestant Dutch revolted against their Catholic rulers from Spain, and in 1585 Queen Elizabeth I of England sent Robert Dudley, Earl of Leicester, to help her friends in Holland in their quest. It's thought that Dudley's soldiers returned from these battles with a new habit that they'd picked up from their Dutch buddies—they had learned that it was far easier to charge into battle with a few shots of genever under their belts. They called it "Dutch courage," but it wasn't long before the term referred to courage summoned up by any sort of liquor. "Mr. Blunt took a pretty heavy draught of the Dutch courage, which was, indeed, the very best French cognac," wrote author/journalist George Augustus Sala in his 1864 book, *Quite Alone*.

Genever Takes a Trip

By the mid-1600s upwards of 5,000 Dutch men and women lived in London, and by this time the English, in their inimitable fashion, had shortened genever's name to gin. Some Londoners started to wonder why they had to go back to the Netherlands to get some, and no matter what you have to say about the English, no one can deny that they seldom miss a chance to make some money. It wasn't long before gin distilleries opened up in Bristol, Plymouth, Portsmouth, and London, and some of these enterprises were making a pretty penny, too. Can you guess what happens next? That's right—the politicians got involved. Wouldn't you just know it?

Strong Water Made Of Juniper

"Sir J. Minnes and Sir W. Batten did advise me to take some juniper water, and Sir W. Batten sent to his Lady for some for me, strong water made of juniper . . . but whether I shall grow better upon it I cannot tell," Samuel Pepys, 1663.

In the late1680s William of Orange, a Dutchman descended from Charles I of England, took over the English throne from James II. He didn't do this for the sake of gin, mind you, but gin ended up figuring into the picture. In a nutshell, this was yet another of those Catholic-Protestant things. James II was the Catholic, and as such he wasn't very popular in the oh-so-very Protestant England. William, a man of the Protestant persuasion whose prime objective in life was to annoy the French—France had invaded the Netherlands in 1672 and William had gotten proper vexed with them—seized what seemed like a decent opportunity. He simply sailed into England and took the place over. Then, once he was King of England, he banned all French imports into England. Chalk one up for William.

Although the English loved their gin, they were also fond of French brandy, so when their brandy was taken away from them they had to start making even more gin to fill the gap. It wasn't long before the country was producing around half-a-million gallons of gin each and every year. Oh, those Englishmen and their gin. The period known as the Gin Craze was about to begin.

> **Foursomes at Four**
>
> "One Saturday, in March of 1736, William Bird left his house in Kensington
> in the care of Jane Andrews, his maid. Once Bird was out of sight she, too,
> left the house and went to a gin shop she often visited. There she met 'a
> Drummer of the Guards of her Acquaintance,' a chimneysweep, and an
> individual described only as 'a Woman Traveller.' Andrews invited all three
> back to her employer's house, where they continued to drink from ten in
> the morning until four in the afternoon. It was at this point that Andrews
> 'proposed to the Company . . . that they, and she, should go to Bed together,'
> upon which all four 'stript, and . . . went into one bed.' Wishing privacy,
> Andrews had taken the understandable precaution of closing both the doors
> and windows of the house; even so, it was not long before 'a Mob,' hearing
> of this affair, surrounded the Door and disturbed the happy pairs . . ." *Craze:
> Gin and Debauchery in an Age of Reason*, Jessica Warner, 2002.

When William died in 1702, Queen Anne, his sister-in-law, took over the
gin-soaked country, and she made it legal for anyone in England to make their
own gin—no license required. By 1727, around six million English people were
drinking five million gallons of gin a year. You may have read that the government
intervened at this point and enacted laws designed to protect the people from
the evils of gin, but that doesn't tell you the whole story. It's more likely that,
since all the poor folk were way too drunk to do all the hard work necessary to
keep the country running, the high and mighty were a little concerned that their
profits were starting to dwindle. Something had to be done lest the rich folk lose
their money.

In 1736, the Gin Act was introduced, effectively making it illegal to either
make gin without a proper license, or to sell the stuff in quantities of less than
two gallons. Licenses cost 50 pounds sterling—very expensive in 1736—so not
many people in England could afford a license to make gin, and only the wealthy
had enough cash to buy two whole gallons of the stuff at one time. You might
think that the poor had been painted into a pretty sober corner, but poor isn't
stupid.

The government's big mistake with the Gin Act was to specify *gin*, so the
common folk came up with new names for the stuff, and they carried on distilling,
selling, and drinking spirits that they referred to as, for instance, "Parliamentary
Brandy." But this liquor wasn't brandy at all—it was the same stuff that Londoners
had been calling gin prior to the new laws taking effect. And truth be told, it's
doubtful that we'd recognize most of these spirits as being gin, anyway. Much

of the homemade "gin"—though perhaps not all of it—was low-grade fuel at best. There's a chance that if we brought this "gin" into the twenty-first century, it would be akin to poorly-made moonshine. Whatever its name was, though, Londoners were pounding it down at an enormous rate. By 1743, it's estimated that enough gin was being consumed in London for every man, woman, and child to get 18 ounces—over half a liter—of gin per day.

Although kids did drink gin back then, it's more than likely that the adults were guzzling more than their children, so the imagination runs wild when thinking about how drunk everyone must have been in those days. So drunk, in fact, that plays were commonly canceled because of unruly audiences, actors who were too drunk perform, or both. By the middle of the century, ruination at the hands of gin had become so commonplace that artist William Hogarth put his hand to *Gin Lane*, a street scene depicting the gin-induced horrors of the time.

No book about gin is complete with an image of Hogarth's *Gin Lane*.

Hogarth's work was described by John Nichols in his 1785 book, *Biographical Anecdotes of William Hogarth*, as a "genuine narrative of the horrible deeds perpetrated by that fiery dragon, Gin; the wretched and deplorable condition of its votaries and admirers; the dreadful havock and devastation it has made amongst the human species; its pernicious effects on the soldiers, sailors, and mechanicks of this kingdom; and its poisonous and pestilent qualities in destroying the health, and corrupting the morals of the people."

And a certain Rev. James Townley came up with a poem to go with Hogarth's picture:

Gin Lane by Rev. James Townley, circa 1751

Gin, cursed fiend, with fury fraught,
Makes human race a prey;
It enters by a deadly draught,
And steals our life away.
Virtue and Truth, driven to despair,
Its rage compels to fly;
But cherishes, with hellish care,
Theft, murder, perjury.
Damned cup, that on the vitals preys,
That liquid fire contains;
Which madness to the heart conveys,
And rolls it through the veins.

One of London's most famous small-time gin producers of this period was a certain Captain Dudley Bradstreet, a government agent who tattled on illicit distillers but was himself an illicit purveyor of gin. In his book, *The Life and Uncommon Adventures of Captain Dudley Bradstreet*, 1755, Bradstreet described exactly how he went about selling small quantities of gin during the time when such sales were illegal: "I . . . purchased in Moorfields the sign of a cat and had it nailed to a street window. I then caused a leaden pipe, the small end out about an inch, to be placed under the paw of the cat, the end that was within had a funnel to it . . . . When the liquor was properly disposed, I got a person to inform a few of the mob that gin would be sold by the cat at my window next day, provided they put money in his mouth . . . at last I heard the chink of money and a comfortable voice say, 'Puss, give me two pennyworth of gin!' I instantly put my mouth to the tube and bid them receive it from the pipe under her paw."

That's right—he invented a vending machine to dispense gin, God bless his little cotton socks.

The 1736 law proved to be both unreasonable and unenforceable, and the act was repealed in 1743. As Philip Henry Stanhope, aka Lord Mahon, wrote in his 1853 book, *History of England*, "The duties imposed by that Act, and amounting nearly to a prohibition, had only afforded encouragement and opportunity to fraud. Informers were terrified by the threats of the people; justices were either unable or unwilling to enforce the law; and it was proved that the consumption of gin, instead of diminishing, had considerably augmented . . . Liquor continued to be sold at all corners of the streets; nay, we are even assured that the retailers of it used to set up painted boards, inviting people to be drunk at the small expense of one penny . . . To check these frightful disorders; and at the same time prevent the loss to the Revenue, the Ministers had framed a new Bill, by which a small duty per gallon was laid on the spirits at the still-head, and the price of licenses reduced to twenty shillings."

Eight years later, in 1751, the Tippling Act was introduced, and this law added a few more restrictions onto the sale of gin—distillers were no longer allowed to also be retailers, for one thing—and the general drunkenness of the masses began to subside. For a while.

The Foundations of Some Gin Dynasties

1740 According to *The Kindred Spirit—A History of Gin and the House of Booth* by Lord Kinross, the Booth's distilling business started in 1740, though it wasn't until 1778 that the firm of Phillip Booth & Company had grown large enough to be included in the *Directory of Merchants* as owners of a distillery.

1769: Alexander Gordon of Gordon's Gin founded his distilling business in the Southwark area of London.

1793: Mr. Coates founded the Plymouth Gin Distillery in Plymouth. (Records show that the building was a mault [malt] house in 1697, distilling a number of common spirits.)

1830: Charles Tanqueray established a distillery in Bloomsbury, London.

1863: James Burroughs purchased 23 Marlborough Square in London, the site of the first Beefeater distillery, though he developed his first gin recipe in 1820.

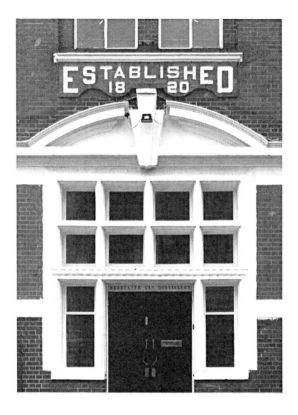

The doors of the Beefeater Distillery today—the date reflects the year
in which the recipe for Beefeater gin was first conceived.

Of Mills and Factories and Palaces to Boot

Toward the end of the 1700s, the Industrial Revolution began to take hold
in England, and by the 1820s lots of people from rural areas had moved to the
cities looking for work at the factories and mills. They needed somewhere to
hang out of an evening, and it wasn't long before ornate pubs that came to be
known as gin palaces began to appear in the cities. The working class was back to
pounding the gin again, and after a law was introduced that lowered the taxes on
distilled spirits, the consumption of liquor in England more than doubled in one
year, jumping from 4,132,263 gallons in 1825 to 8,888,644 gallons in 1826.

According to Edward Hewett and W. F. Axton, authors of *Convivial Dickens:
The Drinks of Dickens and His Times*, the crime rate in London rose drastically at
this time, and the general consensus was that gin was the culprit. Temperance
movements began to spring up, and many of the temperance leaders blamed
gin for the widespread urban misery and poverty. A certain chappie by the
name of Charles Dickens disagreed: "Gin drinking is a great vice in England, but

wretchedness and dirt are greater; and until you improve the homes of the poor, or persuade a half-famished wretch not to seek relief in the temporary oblivion of his own misery, with the pittance which, divided among his family, would furnish a morsel of bread for each, gin-shops will increase in number and splendour. If Temperance Societies would suggest an antidote for hunger, filth, and foul air, or could establish dispensaries for the gratuitous distribution of bottles of Lethe-water, gin-palaces would be numbered among the things that were," he wrote in his 1836 book, *Sketches by Boz*.

Dickens also noted that the gin that had once worn the "Parliamentary Brandy" label was now masquerading under even more fanciful names such as Cream of the Valley, The Out and Out, The No Mistake, The Good for Mixing, The Real Knock-me-Down, The Celebrated Butter Gin, and The Regular Flare-up, and he went on to describe the interior of a typical gin palace of the time: "A bar of French-polished mahogany, elegantly carved, extends the whole width of the place; and there are two side-aisles of great casks, painted green and gold, enclosed within a light brass rail . . ." Sounds mighty fine, huh?

You get a different picture of gin palaces, though, when you read the words of a guy calling himself "A. Templar" who, in 1842, wrote, "It is worth while for the snug merchant or other member of what ought to be the comfortable classes in a land like ours, to step into a gin-palace occasionally, as he returns home from the theatre or his club. In one corner he will see some veteran out-pensioner, who has encountered an old acquaintance, sunk down to this class, and, for the sake of former days, has stepped in to take a glass. The old hero has perhaps been at Astley's or some minor theatre, and is eloquent about the absurd manner in which the storming of the fort, amid a blaze of blue or red light, was got up; no general ever dreamed of mounting a breach with cavalry. Near these gossips stand a group of dustmen, with a stray chimney-sweep amongst them, puffing at enormously long tobacco-pipes. These are the more select portion of the assemblage; the vestments of the remainder are indescribable—sex, age, and shape, are scarcely distinguishable. They are ragged as if worn for centuries, and filthy as if gathered from the lay-stalls. They are shouldering and pushing to the counter,—all tongues are loosed, and loud and incoherent is their clatter. But, with the exception of brief angry bursts, all is good nature. The gin-palace is a city of refuge, within which the policeman does not intrude, so long as the noise is not very excessive: the inmates know the precarious tenure of their sanctuary, and have acquired the habit of respecting its conditions. Still, the scene is not over-edifying; and those verging on dishonesty are brought into perilous contact with those who have already sunk into the quagmire. And yet every one of the inmates, if remonstrated with for their indulgence in "Old Tom," or "Cream of the Valley," might urge, and with more reason, the plea which Scott has put into the mouth of Maggie Mucklebackit. [Mucklebackit is a character in Sir Walter Scott's 1816 novel, *The Antiquary*, though we're at a loss to find the plea referenced here.]

"Since we have got to the gin-palace, we may as well hover about a little, for the sake of watching those who loiter round its doors of a Sunday morning. The street-sweeper is the only one whose industry encroaches on the rest of the Sabbath; and even in his case, the bulk of the labourers are casual—mere Sunday sweepers, as has already been noticed. For the rest, however, Sunday is a mere cessation from toil. They have become so inured to their haunts that they cannot leave them. The bashfulness of bad clothes keeps them from emerging into the airy and open spaces of the town; and to wander beyond its limits is an enterprise of which they seem as incapable as the fish of taking a walk on shore. Their rest is a wearisome effort; and to dull their sense of it, they repair for a doze to the gin-palace, and then lounge apathetically about its door, relieved for the time from the tedium of their own existence."

Here's a shot of the interior of a modern-day gin-palace style pub:
The Grapes, Blackpool, Lancashire, circa 2000.

Still Life

While the factory workers hung out in the gin palaces, the guys who produced the gin for them were getting used to a new invention—the patent still, aka the

Coffey still, aka the continuous still. This revolutionary device, introduced in the 1830s, made it possible to produce high-octane spirits fairly quickly and easily, and it wasn't long before gin producers took advantage of this new-fangled gizmo. The best thing about this was—and is—that it can produce very "clean" spirits. Spirits with very few impurities. Spirits such as vodka. So, if the gin producers distilled their botanicals into vodka, their gin would be free from any "off" notes from the inferior spirits that they'd previously tried to hide behind the herbs, fruits, and spices they used as flavorings, and the botanicals could take center stage.

Here's a selection of the botanicals used to make Plymouth gin,
sitting pretty next to a pair of mighty fine looking Martinis.

The continuous still, then, made it possible for the style of gin we know as London Dry, to emerge triumphant by the end of the 1800s, and this, as we shall see, led to the creation of a cocktail that a certain Mr. Bond liked to have shaken, not stirred. Before the invention of the Dry Gin Martini, though, a couple of other gin-based drinks came into being—drinks that are still with us today—and the Brits popularized these drinks worldwide as they went about their business of global colonization . . .

In the early 1800s—around 1825—British soldiers in India started mixing their gin with a quinine-based remedy to stave off threats of malaria. When they added a little sugar and soda water they found the drink to be quite palatable, and the Gin and Tonic was born. Thanks God for that, huh? A man who went by the name of Raul recalled a fascinating G & T scene in India in his 1893 book, *Reminiscences of Twenty Years' Pigsticking in Bengal*: "He got a glass of gin-tonic, and the twinkle in his eyes showed that he was going to enjoy it when, all of a sudden, there were shouts of a mad buffalo charging. I believe it was Gibson who gave the first alarm. The big Judge on the big horse was the first to draw the buffalo's attention, and as he charged, Bainbridge did not wait to look for his glasses or finish his peg, but dropping his gin-tonic he soon cleared out." Those Brits certainly knew how to throw a party, huh?

Pink Gin, a mixture of gin and Angostura bitters, was the drink favored by the officers of the British Navy in the later years of the nineteenth century—the lower ranks made do with rum, of course—and the drink, according to Anistatia Miller, Director of the *Exposition Universelle des Vins et Spiritueux* in southern France, was introduced to Britain at the Great London Exposition of 1862. According to Miller, the original drink, made with gin, bitters, and a little water, was the brainchild of the man who created Angostura bitters in the first place, Johann Gottlieb Benjamin Siegert. Siegert had been the Prussian Surgeon General at the Battle of Waterloo before he took off for South America to help Simon Bolivar liberate Venezuela from Spain, and it was there where he developed the formula for his *amargos aromáticos*, a tonic for Bolivar's soldiers that eventually became known as Angostura bitters.

Gin in the First Golden Age of the American Barroom

Gin and Tonic is a fabulous drink, and Pink Gin's not too shabby, either, but in order to understand the huge role that gin has played in the cocktailian pursuits of the bartender we should probably skip over the pond now. So say, "ta-ta," to the shores of that Green and Pleasant Land, and yell "hi there" to the United States of America.

We'll start out by taking a look at the birth of the cocktail—something that probably occurred a few years before 1800 (1803 is the first printed mention of the word that's been discovered at the time of writing; 1806 marks the year when the word was defined in a Hudson, New York, newspaper). It wasn't until 1862, though—right at the same time that the Brits were starting to quaff their Pink Gins—that Jerry Thomas, the man who most people recognize as being the founding father of the mixology set, published *How to Mix Drinks or The Bon-Vivant's Companion*. By using Thomas's book as a foundation and consulting subsequent cocktail books, we can get a feel for how bartenders have employed gin from the mid-1800s right through the early years of the twenty-first century. It's come a long way, baby.

Luckily for us, shortly before we started work on this book, our good friend David Wondrich, the man who steadfastly refuses to stand his round if Gary is among the sporting party being served, wrote a book by the name of *Imbibe*. It's a groundbreaking work. Wondrich, by way of much original research, deciphered Thomas' and other mixologists' cocktail books from the late nineteenth—and early twentieth-centuries, and he gives us a glimpse into what people were really drinking during the First Golden Age of the American Barroom. Therefore, let us proclaim that if your library does not include *Imbibe*, it is not complete, and with our consciences now clear, we'll proceed to steal David's work and fill you in on the place of gin during the dawning of the cocktail era.

From 1800 until the mid-1880s, if gin was called for as an ingredient in a cocktail, chances are very good that the bartender was using genever, or *Hollands* as it was commonly called at the time. This gin is made from grain, it's flavored with juniper, and it bears some of the grainy, or cereal-y, nuances that we associate with whiskey. Wondrich suggests marrying eight ounces (240 ml) of Jameson's Irish whiskey with 10 ounces (300 ml) of Plymouth gin, and adding 1/2 ounce (15 ml) of his rich simple syrup (2 parts Demerara sugar dissolved in one part water) in order to approximate the style of genever our forebears behind the stick were using, but a few brands of genever are now quite easy to procure, and we suggest that, should you want a sip of yesteryear, you might want to think about shelling out the money and springing for a bottle of the real stuff. Oude—old—genever is the style they were using in the 1800s, quite simply because jonge, or young, genever wasn't created until the twentieth century. And oude genever, as you might deduce by Wondrich's Irish whiskey formula, is very distinctive.

Wondrich then points to the 1887 edition of Jerry Thomas' book, *The Bar-Tender's Guide*, to draw attention to the fact that Old Tom, a sweetened gin, was, by then, being called for by name in drink recipes, so genever was beginning to get pushed out of the picture a little. And our friend David goes on to cite genever's reluctance to harmonize with dry vermouth—a cocktail ingredient that really found its stride in the late 1800s—as the reason for its demise in the latter years of the nineteenth century. We don't argue with Dave. During the last decade of the 1800s, then, genever was starting to fizzle out, Old Tom, was becoming known to American bartenders, and both Plymouth—a distinctive dry gin made in the port town of Plymouth—and London Dry gins were starting to make a big splash behind the bar. The rippling effect of that splash is still being felt today.

In the latter half of the 1800s American bartenders were serving a variety of gin-based drinks. Take the Gin Cocktail, for instance, made with gin, simple syrup, bitters, and perhaps a little curaçao or absinthe. Here's a fabulous example of a minimalistic formula that yields an incredibly complex drink, and at the same time it allows leeway in the form of the optional liqueurs. It's important to understand that the fact that both of these liqueurs appear in the recipes of that time suggests that, should the bartender want to experiment a little further—a little Chartreuse, perhaps?—then that would be fine, too. There's lots to be gleaned between the lines of these first cocktail books.

If you listen to the likes of John Franklin Swift, the Gin Cocktail was also a drink that could sometimes buy favors: "Every journal in the town was represented, not by a single local reporter alone, to be bribed with a gin cocktail and a cheap cigar, but editors and proprietors, in black evening coats and white gloves . . . It was a beautiful sight," he wrote in his 1870 book, *Robert Greathouse: An American Novel*.

Among the other gin-based drinks that crossed the bars of America during the years leading up to the twentieth century: Gin Fizzes, Gin Slings, John Collinses (made with genever), and Tom Collinses (Old Tom), as well as the Martini. Let's take a look at the Martini before we go on.

The popularity of vermouth among bartenders in the late 1800s and early twentieth century made a huge impact on the cocktailian craft, and although the Manhattan—a whiskey-based cocktail created somewhere around 1870—was probably the first drink of its kind to make a lasting impression on the bar world, it wasn't long before the Martinez was born—"make like a Manhattan, using gin instead of whiskey" instructed quite a few late nineteenth-century cocktail books. The Manhattan, then, can be seen as the Granddaddy of this style of drink in which a base spirit has its soul soothed by vermouth, and as we shall see, the Manhattan begat the Martinez, the Martinez became the Martini—made with sweet vermouth—and from the loins of the Martini, the Dry Gin Martini emerged.

Recipes from *The Bar-Tender's Guide* by Jerry Thomas, 1887

The instructions for making these drinks differ only inasmuch as the Manhattan is shaken and strained into a claret glass whereas the Martinez is shaken and strained into a cocktail glass. Both drinks are garnished with a "quarter of a slice of lemon," and Thomas adds in both cases that if the customer prefers it very sweet, two dashes of gum syrup may be added. Only the order in which the ingredients are given has been changed.

Manhattan Cocktail
3 dashes Boker's bitters
2 dashes Curaçao or Maraschino
1 pony of rye whiskey
1 wine-glass of vermouth
2 small lumps of ice

Martinez Cocktail
1 dash Boker's bitters
2 dashes Maraschino
1 pony of Old Tom gin
1 wine-glass of vermouth
2 small lumps of ice

Here's Dan Warner, Beefeater Brand Ambassador, and a lad with whom I've been
honored to share the limelight behind the stick. He's seen here with Anistatia Miller,
the fascinating femme who designed the cover of this book, author,
with her equally intriguing hubbie, Jared Brown, of *Shaken Not Stirred*.

The first printed recipe we can find for a Martini, as opposed to a Martinez,
appears in *New and Improved Illustrated Bartender's Manual or How To Mix
Drinks of the Present Style*, (1888), by Harry Johnson, but this recipe is basically
the same as earlier recipes for the Martinez cocktail—Old Tom gin and sweet
vermouth, as well as gum syrup, bitters (Boker's genuine only), and curaçao.
Similarly, George Kappeler's 1895 book, *Modern American Drinks: How to Mix
and Serve All Kinds of Cups and Drinks*, includes a Martini recipe, and it too,
is made from the same ingredients that other bartenders were using to make
a Martinez. Proof positive that these names—Martini and Martinez—were
interchangeable during the last years of the 1800s. The first drinks to be called
Martinis were actually Martinez cocktails—the name was changing, but the
ingredients were the same.

Old Harry Johnson sported one heck of a moustache, huh?

How did the name change from Martinez to Martini? We can't be sure, but the story that makes most sense to us is that the Martini & Rossi company used the recipe for the Martinez, a deservedly popular drink of the time, to spread the word of their fine vermouths, and they took just a little liberty with the name. Bartenders played around with the formula for the Martini, using dry gin instead of Old Tom, and dry vermouth rather than sweet, and the Dry Gin Martini—the cocktail that has been an icon of sophistication for a century and counting—was born. She was such a beautiful baby.

By and large, the first Dry Gin Martinis were made with equal amounts of gin and dry vermouth with a dash or two of orange bitters, and it didn't take long before people such as Louis Muckensturm, author of *Louis' Mixed Drinks with Hints for the Care and Service of Wines* (1906), were adding items such as curaçao to the mix, and going up a little on the gin—Muckensturm's recipe calls for two parts gin to one part vermouth. And although the curaçao didn't stick around for very long, the orange bitters remained, and the ratio of gin to vermouth was approximately two-to-one until the enactment of Prohibition in January, 1920. Even after the Great Drought came to a close in December, 1933, the Martini remained pretty much unchanged for quite a while.

Here's a fine shot of Louis Muckensturm, straight from his book.
Who would have thought that a man such as this handsome brute
would add curaçao to his Martinis, huh?

DRY MARTINI COCKTAIL ⇌

    Take two dashes of orange bitters,

    One dash of Curacao,

    One liqueur-glass of French Vermouth, and

    Two liqueur-glasses of dry gin.

Fill the mixing-glass with ice; stir well and strain into a cocktail-glass. Squeeze a small piece of lemon peel on top.

And here's Muckensturm's recipe, complete with the curaçao.

One of the first new bartending guides to hit the shelves after Repeal was Patrick Gavin Duffy's *The Official Mixing Guide* (1934), and Duffy's recipe for "Martini Cocktail (dry)" called for two parts gin, one part French (dry) vermouth, and one dash of orange bitters. Two years later, Harman Burney Burke's *Burke's Complete Cocktail & Drinking Recipes* recommended the exact same ingredients and proportions.

As far as we can make out, it was some bastard in the early fifties who decided to take the vermouth out of the Martini. We don't know his name, but he upset the likes of cocktailian mastermind David Embury, and that's all we need to know in order to figure out that the guy was a complete bastard. In the 1952 edition of his book *The Fine Art of Mixing Drinks*, Embury wrote, "Quite recently . . . there has sprung up the vermouth-rinse method of making Martinis. This consists of rinsing the inside surface of the cocktail glass with vermouth, pouring it back into the bottle, and then filling the glass with iced gin." Bastard.

And that bastard begat other bastards, too. One group of wags, calling themselves the "American Standards Association," published the "American Standard Safety Code and Requirements for Dry Martinis" in 1966, a document that was obviously written by people who had a sense of humor. Included in the pages were such definitions as: "Lemonade. A term applied to drinks which have been subjected to the peel of a lemon. There is no place for the rind of any citrus fruit, or its oils, in an American Standard dry martini." Another entry is: "Vodka. A distilled alcoholic beverage made originally from potatoes, but now encountered in grain alcohol versions. It is never employed in a dry martini."

The document goes on to note such things as the maximum olive size for a martini—0.4730 cubic inches for a 3 1/2-ounce cocktail—and on the subject of vermouth, it clearly states, "The employment of vermouth in an American Standard dry martini shall not be mandatory, provided no other ingredient is employed as a substitute." Finally, the work includes instructions on how to mix a Martini by "the radiation method," which involves placing a 60-watt light bulb exactly 9 inches from a bottle of vermouth, and situating a bottle of gin 23 inches on the other side of the vermouth. By illuminating the bulb for a period of between 7 and 16 seconds ("Clear bottles require the shortest exposure"), they claimed that enough vermouth would be "radiated" into the gin to make an American Standard dry Martini.

For the rest of the twentieth century, then, or near-as-damn-it that long, the Dry Gin Martini was little more than chilled gin. There's nothing wrong with chilled gin, mind you, but chilled gin does not a Dry Gin Martini make. Bartenders carried on using the vermouth-rinse method of making the drink, they waved the vermouth bottle over the mixing glass without pouring so much as a drop of aromatized wine over the ice, and even if they did venture so far as to up-end the bottle, it was seldom that Martinis were made with more than the slightest splash of vermouth. The Dry Gin Martini was a cocktail in name only for a few decades, but as we shall see, she's been resurrected recently, and she's looking more fabulous than ever these days.

The Martini isn't the only gin-based classic cocktail to be born prior to Prohibition. Not by a long chalk. And some of the other drinks that sprang up in the late nineteenth and early twentieth century serve to show us just how versatile gin can be. Take the Negroni, for instance, a drink born in Italy to a father of noble blood—Count Camillo Negroni—at a bar in Florence, circa 1920. Here we see Campari snuggling up to gin and sweet vermouth in a perfectly balanced ménage à trois. And switch now to a fabulous Ramos Gin Fizz, a drink that took the 1915 Mardi Gras celebrations in New Orleans by storm after saloon keeper Henry Ramos decided that gin would mix well with cream, and egg white, and simple syrup, and lime juice and lemon juice and orange flower water of all things. And Henry Ramos was right. The Ramos Gin Fizz, according to its creator, should be "snowy white and of the consistency of good rich milk," if made with patience.

The Dubonnet Cocktail, a drink that kept the late Queen Mother in good spirits for many years, dates back to at least 1914 when the recipe appeared in *Drinks*, by Jacques Straub, a "wine steward" at The Blackstone in Chicago who also worked at Louisville's Pendennis Club at some point in his illustrious career. (Straub's recipe called for equal amounts of gin and Dubonnet, and a dash of orange bitters.)

Very Much A Gin Drinker

"As an anonymous Anglican bishop told the Daily Telegraph, 'The Queen Mother was very much a gin drinker. I think it pickled her.' Stories of her prodigious capacity abounded. Like the lunch party where the hostess 'knew she liked a big gin and Dubonnet, so I gave her a whopper, which I suppose amounted to a triple . . . When I came back to her, four or five minutes later, her glass was already empty, so I offered her the same again. 'So delicious', she said, 'perhaps just a little more.' She had three of those triples before lunch and her fair share of wine during it . . ." Neil Pendock, South Africa's *Sunday Times*, May 5, 2002.

"DUBONNET"

The Greatest Tonic and Appetizer

is IMPORTED and SOLD ONLY in BOTTLES

Any one offering for sale "DUBONNET" or a substitute in bulk, imitating or refilling Dubonnet bottles, is committing a

"FELONY"

We offer $500 Reward

for evidence which secures arrest and conviction of such person or persons.

J.B. MARTIN IMPORTATION CO
1182 Broadway, New York

This ad, found in *The New Police Gazette Bartender's Guide*, (1901), shows us that bogus spirited formulas must have been pretty common in the good old days.

The Last Word, a fabulous mixture of gin, maraschino, green Chartreuse, and lime juice, is another pre-Prohibition creation, and it's thought to have been the brainchild of vaudeville entertainer Frank Fogarty, the man who said, "You can kill the whole point of a gag by merely [using one] unnecessary word."

The Clover Club—gin, lemon juice, egg white, and raspberry syrup—dates to around 1910; the Bronx Cocktail, according to *The Old Waldorf-Astoria Bar Book*, first crossed the mahogany prior 1917; and the Gin Rickey, a drink that started out as a whiskey-based potion, was being served in the nation's capital in the 1890s.

Colonel 'Joe' Rickey

"The Rickey owes its name to Colonel 'Joe' Rickey . . . [who] had been a lobbyist in Washington, and as such used to buy drinks for members of Congress in the glamorous days before they had come to depend upon the discreet activities of gentlemen in green hats to keep them wet while they voted dry. The drink was invented and named for him at Shoemaker's, famous in Washington as a Congressional hangout." *The Old Waldorf-Astoria Bar Book*, by Albert Stevens Crockett, 1935.

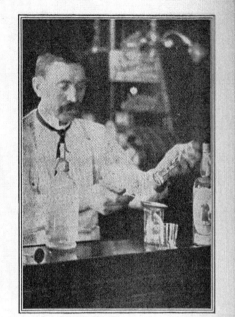

SQUEEZING THE LIME FOR A GIN RICKEY.

This picture appears in *The Hoffman House Bartender's Guide*, 1912.

The Singapore Sling, a drink that might have started life as a drink made with gin, cherry brandy, Benedictine, club soda, and a spiral of lime zest—nothing more, nothing less—was reportedly crossing the bar at the Raffles Hotel in the early twentieth century, though the history of this particular sling is filled with misinformation from a variety or sources—mainly the Raffles Hotel—that leads us to throw up our hands and cry "uncle." But the Aviation cocktail, the very model of everything a great cocktail should be, with grace, charm, balance, simplicity, and yet layer after layer of complexity, can be pretty safely traced back to *Recipes for Mixed Drinks* by Hugo R. Ensslin, a bartender who held forth from behind the bar at New York's Wallick Hotel.

A Parched Throat

Although gin was commonplace prior to Prohibition, whiskey more or less dominated the drinking scene in the early twentieth century, but the Noble Experiment soon put paid to that. When the country went dry, whiskey became hard to come by, and gin's popularity increased as it became the drink of choice. The major advantage that made gin preferable—to the producer, at least—is that whiskey needs to be aged, but gin can pretty much be knocked back as soon as it drips from the still, or as soon as it's siphoned out of the bathtub. During America's Great Drought—January 1920 through December, 1933—plenty of whiskey was smuggled into the country from Canada and some made its way to the USA from Scotland, too, but badly-made gin—basically vodka with flavorings in the form of oils added—was far easier to get your hands on. And it was far cheaper, too. Gary's late stepfather-in-law, John Hilgert, worked behind the bar in a Prohibition-era speakeasy in Ohio, and he used to tell the story of going down to the basement in the club where he worked and watching his boss prepare gin by simply mixing grain alcohol, distilled water, and juniper flavoring.

Prohibition had many long-term effects, even after Repeal. One was that it took decades for whiskey to make its comeback in earnest—the single-malt scotch blast of the late 1980s brought whiskey back into vogue. Gin, on the other hand, remained popular among Americans until vodka toppled it from the top of the heap, a phenomenon that got serious in the sixties. Ever the lady, gin waited patiently on the sidelines for people such as Audrey Saunders to come along . . .

Gin in the Twenty-First Century

Gin has come a long, long way in the first decade of this new century, mainly due to pioneers such as Audrey Saunders of New York's Pegu Club; Simon Ford, the Plymouth Gin man who, at the time of writing, represents Beefeater gin in the USA, too; Dan Warner, Beefeater Brand Ambassador who might just be the very personification of London Dry Gin; and of course Desmond Payne, the man in charge of the Beefeater stills, and the guy responsible for bringing us the fabulous new gin, Beefeater 24. Thanks, Desmond, you're a Gin God if ever there was one. Sean Harrison, the man who mans the stills at the Plymouth gin distillery belongs here, too. He's an ex-Royal Navy man, he makes a damned fine gin, and he's much fun to argue with!

We can't forget Charlotte Voisey, the Hendrick's ambassador in the U.S.A.; Xavier Padovani, the guy who does the Hendrick's thing on a global scale; and Angus Winchester, the Tanqueray chap who roams the world spreading the G-word. In Oregon we have Ryan Magarian, the guy behind Aviation gin; and let's not forget Tal Nadari, the Dutchman who is currently flogging Bols Genever in the U.S.A. Tal, of course, must be eternally grateful to David Wondrich, the guy who unearthed the fact that most mid-nineteenth-century gin-based drinks were made with genever, and thus, almost single-handedly, brought Hollands gin back into vogue. And he still hasn't bought me a Goddamned drink.

Entrepreneur Eric Seed deserves mention here, too: He has not only brought Old Tom gin back on the shelves, he also made sure we could once again get our hands on some fabulous creme de violette so that our Aviations can be authentic once more. There are, of course, many more gin aficionados out there who will never forgive me for not mentioning them. God bless each and every one of you, and God bless all the people who have done their bit for gin whose names I haven't mentioned here.

These people, and lots of other bartenders and gin ambassadors all over the world, have helped to redefine gin. These guys have pushed the envelope of creativity by inventing some fabulous new cocktails, they have helped bring Old Tom and genever gins back to the forefront, they have introduced brand-new styles of gin that are nigh-on impossible to categorize, and best of all, each and every one of them has helped everyone else in the industry, comfortable in the knowledge that whatever is good for one brand must also be good for every brand, and whatever's good for one bar must also be good for all bars.

The history of gin is, indeed, a colorful one, but since the spirit was conceived, there's never been a time like right now in terms of ingenuity on the part of the distillers, and genius at the hands of today's bartenders, for gin to once again make its way to the forefront of the backbar. Hopefully, as you read on, you'll discover the passion that these good folk have brought to the world of great gins, and to the cocktailian craft. It makes my little heart very glad, indeed.

Here are a few new-ish gins, alongside an old genever.

And here we have a few new-ish bartenders with more
than a couple of old-timers mixed in with them.

Picture by Michael Harlan Turkell.

Back Row: Julie Reiner (Flatiron Lounge, Manhattan, and Clover Club,
Brooklyn), Charlotte Voisey (Hendrick's Gin), John Deragon (PDT, Manhattan),
Sasha Petraske (Milk & Honey, Manhattan, among others), Giuseppe Gonzales
(Cotton Club, Brooklyn), Kenta Goto (Pegu Club, Manhattan), Eben Freeman
(Tailor, Manhattan).

Front Row: Leslie Townsend (then at Astor Center, New York, currently Queen
of The Manhattan Cocktail Classic, New York), David Wondrich (author of
Imbibe, Brooklyn), Gary Regan (Ardent Spirits, New York), Audrey Saunders
(Pegu Club, Manhattan), Dale DeGroff (King Cocktail himself), and that's Jim
Meehan (PDT, Manhattan)leaning on Leo DeGroff's (Contemporary Cocktails,
New York) shoulders.

Chapter 3

Dry Gin

Dry Gin Defined

All four styles of gin described in this book—dry, genever, Old Tom, and Plymouth—are are produced using *similar* methods (though genever goes off on somewhat of a tangent), and the following narrative applies, in general terms, to all of them. The specific methods used to produce genever, Old Tom, and Plymouth, are discussed in the chapters dedicated to each one, but you'll understand all of them far better once you get the following information about dry gin under your belt.

The term "Distilled Dry Gin" differentiates gins made with fresh or dried botanical ingredients from "compound" dry gins—spirits that are flavored with oils and essences rather than fresh or dried ingredients. In this compendium, we'll look only at distilled gins. The guys who produce these babies go to incredible lengths to make them. First off, let's take a quick look at distillation—a process that separates different components of a liquid from one other.

To make a spirit you need beer or wine or some fermented beverage that contains alcohol. You make beer by adding yeast to a stew of cooked grains, and wine is made by adding yeast to fruit juice (technically, you could make a beer or wine using beets or potatoes or molasses or any number of things containing sugar or starch, but for our purposes we needn't explore this). The yeast eats the sugar in the juice or the starch—complex sugar—in the grain stew and converts it to heat, carbon dioxide, and many types of alcohol, though ethyl alcohol—the stuff that gives you a buzz—predominates. Now you have a liquid at, for the sake of argument, 10 percent (ethyl) alcohol by volume (abv), and you need to concentrate that alcohol to achieve a liquid that you can put into a liquor bottle.

Armed with the knowledge that water evaporates at 212° F or 100° C, and ethyl alcohol evaporates at (approximately) 172° F or 79° C, you can figure out that, if you heat your beer or wine so it's somewhere between those two temperatures, the vapors that evaporate from the liquid will contain a greater percentage of alcohol than the beer or wine you started out with. Condense those vapors and you have a liquid that has a higher percentage of alcohol. It's nowhere near that simple, but that's just about all you need to know right now. I don't want to keep you away from the bar for too very long.

It's Still a Still

There are many types of stills, but for our purposes you need know only about the two main styles.

Pot stills, sometimes called alembic stills, have been with us for centuries—they look like huge onions with tall necks sprouting from the top. If you add beer or wine to a pot still and heat it up the liquid will start to evaporate. The resultant vapors travel up the neck of the still and are directed into a coil that's surrounded with cold water. The cold water condenses the vapors, and from the end of this coil drips a liquid that has a higher percentage of alcohol than the beer or wine that was poured into the still. It's usually necessary to distill at least twice in pot stills in order to achieve a liquid with enough alcohol to be called a spirit.

Continuous stills—aka Coffey Stills or Patent Stills—were invented a couple of hundred years ago and are still thought of by many as being "modern" or "new-fangled." These are tall chimney-like contraptions that are fitted inside with perforated metal disks. Steam is introduced at the bottom of the chimney while the beer or wine is poured into the top, and when the two meet, the steam turns the liquid into vapors which are drawn off the still and condensed back into liquid form. These babies can turn beer into 96% alcohol by volume (abv) spirits in one fell swoop.

Both of these stills are usually used to produce dry gin, though a few producers might use hybrid stills, or stills with their own peculiar designs built into them. For the most part, though, gin producers get high-proof spirits from a continuous still, then introduce their botanicals—the flavoring agents—to the liquor within the belly of a pot still.

Here's a convenient old picture of a past master distiller at the Bols genever
distillery in Holland. It's convenient because he's sitting in front of some hybrid
stills—the cylindrical tower at the front of the picture is a continuous still,
and the device at its side is a pot still.

Gin is, in a very real sense, flavored vodka. Most, though not all, gin distillers
buy their vodka; very few distill their own. It's made to each distiller's specific
standards, of course, and purchased at high proof from vodka producers. Then
comes the hard part. They have to flavor it so it tastes like gin. No gin distillery
wants their gin to taste like anyone else's gin, so they go to enormous lengths to
differentiate theirs from every other bottling on the market. First off they have
to come up with a list of ingredients that will be used to put the gin flavor into
the gin. Juniper's always top of the list, of course, and you'll usually find some
angelica in there, too, and some citrus zests, a little cinnamon, perhaps, maybe
a pinch of caraway, a teaspoon or three of ginger, and myriad other botanical
ingredients from which these guys can formulate their very own shopping list.
Choosing the ingredients is only part of the recipe. Once the distillers have done
their shopping they have to figure out how much of each one of them to use, and
as a man who has done this, as you can see in the *Plymouth Gin* chapter, I can
tell you that it ain't an easy thing to do. (Following this discussion you'll find a
special treat—Hugh Williams, master distiller emeritus from Gordon's, Tanqueray,

and Booth's gins in London, has provided us with a distiller's perspective of the process, and a run-down on the major botanicals used to make gin. Don't miss this section if you want the nitty gritty.)

The botanicals here are sitting in a pot still waiting
for to be turned into Beefeater gin.

After formulating the recipe—usually by making tiny batches in a laboratory until the right balance is achieved—the distiller has to choose a method of getting the flavors of the botanicals into the vodka, and there are a few different ways to achieve this. You can throw them into the high-proof vodka, let them soak for a while, add some water, and redistill the liquid—that's one way to do it. Some distillers, on the other hand, don't let a second go by between adding the botanicals to the vodka and turning on the still. Their gin works better when it's made that way. Other masters of the craft put their botanicals into a wire basket and hang it in the neck of the still so that, as the vapors rise when they redistill the vodka, they capture the essences of the ingredients in the basket. Each and every distiller has his or her own way of making their gin, and in the "Dry Gin by the Bottle" section that's coming up, each of them will tell you how they do it. If they want you to know, that is. Distillers sometimes have their secrets, you know.

Most gins are made in concentrated form. That is, the distiller uses, say, ten times the amount of botanicals needed to flavor the volume of vodka he or she is re-distilling, and once the concentrated gin leaves the still, more vodka is added to it before it's brought down to bottling proof, usually by the addition of de-mineralized water. Why do it this way? Because gin distillers are fond of using old-fashioned pot stills, and these babies are slow, and labor intensive. Pot stills are also idiosyncratic. If you make gin using exactly the same recipe in two different pot stills, chances are extremely high that they won't taste the same—this has to do with the shape of each still, and if we linger here too long I'll start boring you to death about why the shape matters so much. Just take it from me, please, that the only way for the brands that sell best to make enough fabulous gin in a pot still to keep the whole world supplied with their Dry Gin Martinis each and every evening at 5:24 in the p.m., is to start out by making a gin concentrate.

Another aspect of distillation that's important to understand is that the first burst of spirits to leave the still—known as the heads or the foreshots—are not good. And neither are the dregs that come off the still at the very end of the run—the tails or feints. The distiller, then, takes what's known as the heart of the run, and that's what ends up in your gin bottle. It's the good stuff. Knowing when to make these cuts is a major part of the distiller's craft. Next up, we'll take a look at what's been happening to gin in the recent past.

Dry Gin in the Twenty-First Century

The powers that be in the European Community saw fit, in 2008, to redefine gin, and they didn't do a bad job of it, but they weren't bloody wizards when it came to gin, either. You can find these regulations in the *Various Rules and Regulations Surrounding Gin Production* chapter at the end of this book if you'd like to pore through them, but right now I think it's necessary to point out one aspect of these mandated guidelines that threw a spanner in the works when it comes to that beautiful style of gin that we've lovingly known as London Dry Gin for over a century. London Dry Gin, as a category, probably needed some tightening up, since it used to refer to any distilled gin that was made "in the style of" London Dry—a pretty vague definition. But that's no longer true, and one of the aspects of these new regulations has made it necessary for some gins to take the word "London" off their labels. Since these new regulations went into effect, you see, in order to use the phrase "London Dry," the gin must be made by having all its botanicals distilled into it in one fell swoop—and that's not easy. Let me explain.

The temperature at which gin distillers run their stills makes a massive difference to the end product, mainly because, in lay-terms, some botanicals release their flavors better at different temperatures than others. It might be desirable, therefore, to distill the botanicals separately, each one at the appropriate temperature, and then marry the resultant distillates to make gin. Or perhaps the botanicals can be distilled in, say, three different batches, each at a different temperature, before the three "flavored vodkas" are united in a gin bottle.

This sort of stuff can make quite a huge difference to the finished product, and this is the reason that, in my humble opinion, the people who make London Dry Gin are bloody geniuses. Why? Because they can combine all their ingredients at a certain ratio, distill them out at one very specific temperature, and achieve a perfect balance in their gins. That's one very hard job to do. Very hard. I can't stress this enough.

The people who make distilled dry gins that can no longer be called "London" are bloody geniuses, too. Many of these guys have been making gin using their own methodology, and employing more than one distillation—something that's not uncommon in the gin industry—for many years, and until recently they have legally been able to use the term "London Dry" on their labels. If they change their methods now, their gin won't taste the same. Knowing how to distill different botanicals at different temperatures is one of the mind-boggling nuances of the master distiller's craft. Knowing how to distill a bunch of botanicals in one fell swoop is another.

The other major shift on the gin scene that's come about in the first decade of this century is the fact that more than a couple of producers have issued some very untraditional distilled dry gins that are nowhere near as "juniper-forward" as the mainstay bottlings such as, say, Beefeater and Tanqueray, and this has caused much discussion among bartenders and gin connoisseurs alike. I remember taking my first sip of Aviation gin a few years ago and marveling at its complexities. My second reaction to this relatively new product, though, was, "This is fabulous, but is it gin?"

I found Aviation to be very heavy on the lavender front, and although the juniper shone on through, it was nowhere near as pronounced as it was in the more traditional gins with which I was familiar. Then G'Vine gin from France happened along and I was faced with another strange bird in the gin family. The juniper was present, but the incredible floral notes in this baby put G'Vine in a whole new category for me. Again I was forced to ask, is it gin? The answer? Damned right it's gin. It's gin in the twenty-first century. And luckily for us, the new gin producers haven't been the only ones to bring us fabulous new styles of gin. You'll know what I'm talking about if you've ever sipped Beefeater 24 or Tanqueray Rangpur, for instance.

I'm determined not to be one of those old farts who despises change, though, so instead I'll be one of those old farts who embraces it. These new twenty-first century gins have brought incredibly diverse canvases on which cocktailian bartenders can paint veritable masterpieces, and I applaud the entrepreneurs and the master distillers who have brought them our way. Thanks to these guys we now have a fabulous array of gins on our backbars, and playtime at gin school has been much fun of late.

Ryan Magarian, along with his partners in Portland, Oregon, produces the aforementioned Aviation gin, and Ryan has been responsible, in large part, for helping us see gin in a new light. I've gone back and forth with this guy on the subject of what I was calling "New-Age" gins for a few years, and we've batted stuff around by email, over the phone, and briefly face to face when we've bumped into each other at various boozy events. Ryan came up with his own name for these gins, so I'm giving him space here to define his New Western Dry Gins. (That's my way for saying I'm letting him, Hugh Williams, and various other people write huge chunks of this book for me . . .)

New Western Dry Gin
by Ryan Magarian, April, 2009

> This designation seems to have evolved over the past nine years, as a result of efforts from both large brand houses and regional distillers in Europe and in the United States. In taking a good hard look at today's rather loose definition of dry gin, these distillers realized a greater opportunity for artistic "flavor" freedom in this great spirit and are creating gins with a shift away from the usually overabundant focus on juniper, to the supporting botanicals, allowing them to almost share center stage. And while the juniper must remain dominant in all dry gins these gins are most certainly defined, not by the juniper itself, but by the careful inclusion and balance of the supporting flavors, creating, what many experts believe to be, an entirely new designation of dry gin that deserves individual recognition

Thanks Ryan. Now we'll let Hugh Williams take over for a while.

A Look at Dry Gin Distillation through the Eyes of a Distiller, Paying Careful Attention to the Botanicals

What you are about to read was written by Hugh Williams, Master Distiller Emeritus for United Distillers (now part of Diageo), and the man who made Gordon's (European bottling), Tanqueray, and Booth's gins for over twenty years until he retired, circa 2000. Hugh's knowledge is vast, and I am so very grateful to this man for sharing this information with me so I could pass it on to you, dear reader. I'm also grateful to Hugh for the memory of that fabulous afternoon we spent together in the late nineties, going through samples of his botanicals as he explained each and every one of them to me, and eventually quaffing a few excellent G & Ts together. Thanks, mate.

Mother Nature, Bring it On!
by Hugh Williams

The one thing that sets a gin distiller apart and showcases his expertise in the business is the distillation of herbs and spices, called botanicals, that gives his brand its unmistakable flavour.

Gin, an English corruption and abbreviation of the Dutch word *genever*, meaning "juniper," was bought to England in the seventeenth century. At that time it consisted entirely of juniper roughly distilled in a rye-wheat mash. But over the next 100 years it underwent changes in its formulation. London had become a spice capital and was a source of many botanicals from countries in its far-flung Empire, so "London Dry Gin" became a style of manufacturing that many other cities in England copied. Distillers at that time stayed true to the roots of gin, and juniper predominated in their recipes. Today, the European Commission have passed rules insisting that, by definition, juniper must still be the predominant flavour in "London Dry Gin" and that it must be "made in a traditional still by re-distilling ethyl alcohol in the presence of all natural flavourings used."

The art of distilling all botanicals lies in knowing how to extract some or all of the volatile oils present, and this is down to the knowledge built up by experimentation over many years. We know that many botanicals have lots of different volatile oils. Some are not pleasant, but many are essential to give the proper flavour characteristics. As an example, juniper has at least 140 known compounds that make up its profile. The volatilities vary, so during distillation some may come over, but others stay behind. A distillation of botanicals is dependent upon the running speed of a still, so the distiller controls how quickly the gin runs off the still. Too fast, and you bring over some of the unwanted characters of the botanical. Too slow, and you don't bring over the ones you need. Sounds crude, but that's the way it works. Part of a brand's recipe, which is usually a well-guarded secret, is the running speed of the still, and also where the 'heart' (the product), is separated from the 'heads' (first runnings or 'foreshots') and the 'tails'(remainder or 'feints'). Both 'heads' and 'tails' contain unwanted spirit and flavour compounds. Usually, the 'heart' amounts to around 75 percent of the total spirit charged into a still.

Finally, the question has to be asked about the acquisition of botanicals and their quality. Distillers know what they want. That's acquired through experience. But they can't afford the luxury of travelling around the globe selecting when harvests are at different times of the year. The solution is to buy from spice houses, companies that specialize in importing botanicals for food producers, etc. Working together, these spice houses soon build a picture of what is required by you, and many samples are forwarded on during the harvest season. What they are unaware of is your needs. Climatic conditions, soil, regional irregularities all contribute to 'mother nature' affecting the end result. Distillation methods are straightforward, but variations in your raw materials are a greater challenge. Selecting the quality that goes into your brand is of the utmost importance. Customers insist on it. Some years you're spoilt for choice in selecting. Others are a problem. Distillers have many ways of decidingwhat is appropriate. In my experience, the best way was to make mini-distillations of each sample and to organoleptically assess it for its potential. In other words, smell it! Now, let's look at some of the main botanicals that seem to be used today to flavour many of the gin brands on the market.

Here's a selection of botanicals used to make Beefeater gin.

Botanicals

Almonds (*Prunus dulcis*)

The almond is a species of *Prunus* that belongs to the subfamily *Prunoideae* of the family *Rosaceae*. Like the walnut it belongs to the subgenus *Amygdalus*. Botanically, the almond is not a nut, but a fruit. The tree is native to the Middle East. It is small, deciduous, and grows to between 12 to 30 feet in height. The trunk can be a foot thick. The fruit matures in the autumn 7 to 8 months after flowering. In its wild form, still grown in parts of Levant, it contains glycoside amygdalin which after crushing transforms into toxic prussic acid (hydrogen cyanide). Almonds were domesticated prior to 3000 B.C. The genetic mutation caused an absence of the toxin. Almonds are now grown throughout Europe, but the major supplier is the U.S.A., accounting for about 41 percent of global production. California is the major state producer, 70 percent of the harvest being exported.

In culinary use, the many varieties, from different temperate areas, are used in confectionery, baking, and also many national dishes. Distillers have made full use of this diversity by adapting types of almonds to their specific needs. Whether sweet, savoury, nutty or roasted to their requirements, they have made full use of their potential in their brands.

Angelica (*Angelica archangelica*)

Garden Angelica, sometimes referred to as Wild Celery, is a biennial plant of the family *Apiaceae*. It grows in moist soil usually near rivers or large water deposits. Its first year is devoted to producing leaf. The second season brings forth its long fluted stem, and its blossom in July, resulting in pale yellow oblong fruits. These seeds can be, and often are, used by distillers. It takes a further year for the tuberous root system to fully develop for use, again, for distillation purposes. In its wild form, it is seen throughout Scandinavia, Greenland, Iceland, and the Faroe Islands. It prefers the colder climes of those countries so it is more common to the northern areas. Commercially, it is cultivated in Belgium, France, and Germany. The Franconian (Belgium, France) angelica is much lighter in character than the Saxonian (Germany) type, being richer and darker in composition.

From a culinary perspective, just about all of the plant has uses. For hundreds of years, it has been used to flavour liqueurs (Benedictine, Chartreuse, aquavits, and aromatized wines such as Dubonnet and vermouths. Both root and seeds were used in absinthe. Both leaves and stem were candied and cut into shapes to decorate cakes and confectionery, giving that green-looking, perfumed, sweet flavour. Many dishes, from rice in Persia to trout, jam, and omelettes in France, have used its unique flavour.

Angelica seed is rarely used by distillers these days. Pharmaceutical use of its oil for toothpaste in Europe, along with other fragrances, has limited its availability. The root is used however, in many premium brands. When removed from the ground, washed, and the taproot split, it is hung to dry. It exhibits a wonderful, dark 'chocolate-y' aroma, that sadly soon disappears. This, most likely, is the essential oil, beta-terebangelene. When dry, it is ground to a coarse mixture. Its flavour is woody, earthy and slightly sweet. However, Angelica root in a gin recipe has a unique function. It 'marries' the other botanicals together into an interwoven blend of flavours. [Note from Gary: Hugh goes on to describe the function of Angelica as having a "rainbow effect" for the other flavours in the gin, meaning that the angelica brings all the other flavours together in harmony, much like bitters brings together the whiskey and the vermouth in a Manhattan.]

Angelica Root
A sweet flavour whilst adding dryness

Calamus (*Acorus calamus*)

Sometimes called the Common Sweet Flag, it belongs to the *Acoraceae* family. A tall wetland perennial with scented leaves and rhizomes, it's been used medicinally for a wide variety of ailments, as well as a perfume addition. The plant has a single prominent mid-vein and on either side slightly raised outer veins. Although originally indigenous to India, it is now found across Europe, Central Asia, northern U.S.A., and southern Canada. The sweet, perfumed calamus is becoming a rather exotic addition to a distiller's choice of botanicals.

Caraway or Persian cumin (*Carum carvi*)

This biennial plant of the *Apiaceae* family, is native to Europe and western Asia. The plant has a similar appearance to the carrot with fine feathery leaves. The fruits (called seeds) are used in many culinary ways. Its anise-like flavour and aroma are due to its essential oils of carvone and limonene, and it is used in breads, mostly rye breads that are denser because of the yeast-killing properties of limonene. Scandinavian and central European foods are fond of using the botanical. Cheeses, casseroles, and liquors, especially aquavit and the liqueur Kummel, lean heavily on caraway for their flavour. It's not by chance that this is a botanical used purely for flavour. Medicinally, it has the property of being a digestive and is ideal in relieving "trapped wind" after consumption of food. I certainly remember as a child being given a teaspoonful of Dinneford's Gripe Water to make me burp!

Cardamom (*Elettaria cardamomum*)

Although part of the ginger family, the green form is the true cardamom. There is another variety, amomum, that is larger and dark brown in appearance. Both varieties are seedpods shaped like an American football, with a thin papery outer skin and containing black seeds. Elettaria is widely found from India to Malaysia. Amomum is found throughout Asia and Australasia. Both varieties are used in many ways. Flavouring tea and coffee in the Middle East, as medicine in the Far East, and more widely as an addition to sweet dishes. Its flavour is unique. Strong and pungent, it has to be experienced. It is used in some gin brands, but in moderation due to its overpowering nature.

Cardamom Pods
An aromatic highlight

Cinnamon (*Cinnamomum zeylanicum*)

Cinnamon is a small evergreen tree native to Sri Lanka and Southern India. Highly prized by ancient civilizations, it was part of the "cinnamon route" by Arab traders to Egypt and then on to Venice for distribution to Europe. The tree is grown for two years and then coppicing (cutting) is carried out. The next year a dozen or so shoots form from the roots. They are stripped of their bark and left to dry. Only the inner bark is peeled into very thin sheets, about a meter long, that dry in the sun and slowly curl. The air causes the rolls (quills) to darken to a red-brown colour. They are then cut into 2- to 4-inch pieces for sale.

Cassia Bark (*Cinnamomum aromaticum*)

Cassia is grown in the Far East. Often known as Chinese cinnamon, apart from its similarities in cultivation, it looks different when compared with true cinnamon. As quillings, it is darker in colour and the appearance of the rolled sheet is thicker. The differences in taste and smell are even more apparent. Cinnamon has a sweet, pungent, spicy but mild flavour. Cassia has a strong, harsh flavour without that hint of sweetness. Its use in gins is to impart that attractive spicy note to a brand. Remember Tanqueray Malacca gin?

German Chamomile (*Matricaria recutita*)

An annual plant of the sunflower family, wild chamomile grows all over Europe, Asia, America and Australia in temperate climates. The flowers have a strong, apple-like smell that is highly aromatic. Medicinally used for many ailments, it is also used by the cosmetic industry in hair conditioners. Due to its apple-like note, the addition to a gin recipe would be very pleasant.

Citrus Peels-Various

Most people are aware that citrus fruits are made up of the flesh containing the juice, the white pith containing bitter oils, and the coloured rind containing the highly aromatic oils or zest. Now look at it from a distillers point of view and "Houston, we have a problem!" Distill the juice and we get those sugars in the fruit caramelizing, resulting in a jam-like substance! We wouldn't consider distilling the pith, who needs bitter oils? The food industry does but in small amounts. So we come to the rind, or the zest that everyone smells and instantly recognizes as that fruit. The zest is very volatile and will fill a room with the aroma when peeled or torn—that's something a distiller can use. However, those volatile oils are powerful and should be used sparingly. Not only that, but there are residual sugars present that could change the character of a gin. How can you have a London Dry Gin that is sweet? I have no problem with adding a garnish to a gin that will change its character. That's the personal choice of the consumer. My bete noire is that some distillers overdo the use of peels, especially orange peel. Even more annoying, they use it as a cheap substitute for coriander. But it does not have the subtlety of coriander.

Lemon Peel

Creates a light, sharp, bright note

Orange Peel

Creates a light, sharp, bright note

Coriander Seed (*Coriandrum sativum*)

The fruit, improperly called seed, is a native of southern Europe, North Africa, and Asia Minor. The annual plants, about 12 inches high, grow wild, but are cultivated extensively in Russia, Poland, Romania, Bulgaria, and Morocco. In August, after the seeds ripen, the harvesting into swathes for drying begins. The dried swathes are then passed through threshing machines to separate the seed. Further drying then commences before the final bagging. Good quality coriander has an intense lemony-orangey character. It should not display a musty-dirty odour. Its use varies from food flavouring to medicine, and is a main constituent in various liqueurs. In a gin recipe, it invariably is the second most important botanical to juniper. It has the job of being the lighter top-note to the rich, robust fullness of juniper.

Tip of the day No. 1: Clothes moths hate being near coriander. Guard that favourite suit today!

Coriander Seeds

Adds depth of character with a peppery, orange note

Cubeb Berries (*Piper cubeba*)

Grown mostly in Java and Sumatra, it is sometimes called Java pepper. The unripe fruits are picked and dried, similar to most other pepper types. The taste is similar to most peppers, being pungent slightly bitter and persistent. Some say it is like a cross between allspice and black pepper.

Used as a seasoning for food in Indonesia and Africa, it has its uses for flavouring cigarettes and some gins in the west. Medicinally it has been used for everything from halitosis to gonorrhea!

Fennel (*Foeniculum vulgare*)

A hardy perennial, it grows wild in temperate Europe, but is regarded as abundant around the Mediterranean. It is highly aromatic and is similar to anise and star anise but milder. Used for its culinary and medicinal properties, it is a principal herb in absinthe. The bulb of the plant can be used as any root vegetable in cooking and the seeds are widely used in Italian cuisine as flavourings for sausages and meatballs. The leaves are also mixed into salads in Germany and Italy to give that mild, anise-like flavour to the dish. Medicinally, it has been used, as has caraway, to correct the flatulence of infants, mixed with sodium bicarbonate and syrup.

Tip of the day No. 2: Domestic pets don't like fleas, fleas don't like fennel!

Ginger (*Zingiber officinale*)

This perennial plant, original to China, has spread to India, Southeast Asia, West Africa, and the Caribbean. The root is really a rhizome (or underground stem), the only edible part. The fragrance and aroma is well known and is a familiar flavour in Chinese cuisine. Young rhizomes are juicy with a mild taste. Older rhizomes tend to be strong in flavour and are ground to a powder that is often used in seafood and mutton dishes. All around the world ginger is used in different ways, but in the west in is generally used only in sweet foods, cookies, candy and cakes, not forgetting ale and ginger beer. Medicinally it has been found useful for the treatment of dyspepsia, colic, nausea, and diarrhea. I'm not aware of any gin having ginger in its flavour profile, due to its sweet and powerful character. But with a little prudence and care it would make a pleasant addition to a recipe.

Grains of Paradise (*Aframomum melegueta*)

A West African spice with a pungent, peppery flavour, this herbaceous perennial is a member of the ginger family. It grows in the swampy areas of the West African coast. The reddish-brown seeds are contained in pods in the trumpet-shaped flowers. More commonly used in the culinary cuisines of West and North Africa, its use outside those areas are limited to some beers, a few gin brands, and aquavit.

Juniper Berries (*Juniperus communis*)

There are about 25 varieties of juniper that grow at considerable elevations throughout northern Europe down to the Mediterranean, central and northern Asia, and North America. *Juniperus communis* (common juniper) is an evergreen bushy shrub, slow-growing at about 2 to 3 inches a year, that produces green unripe fruits (berries) during October, depending on climatic conditions. The following year, these berries ripen, turning a deep purple colour. At the same time the bush produces more unripe green berries that will be the following year's ripe fruit. The berries are quite sparse on the branches making harvesting difficult, yielding anywhere between 2 and 8 berries from a branch. Luckily, the green berries adhere quite firmly to the branch, and the ripe berries fall with a firm shake.

As you are no doubt aware by now, juniper is the main botanical used in gin, not only from an historical perspective, but because of its flavour. Many people smelling the crushed berries for the first time say, "it's the smell of gin!" It has a rich, robust, oily, and resinous character that some say is the smell of freshly-sawn pine timber, and I can relate to that. Most distillers in making their selection of juniper for their brands consider the Italian berries from Tuscany and Umbria to be the best. Harvested from the western slopes of the Apennines, they ripen perfectly in the hot late sun of autumn. However, Mother Nature is occasionally fickle, and the harvest is not of the consistent quality that prestigious brands need. We do not sell vintage gin. We need to search for equally good alternatives for our needs. The Apennines continue around the Adriatic Sea and down into what was Yugoslavia. These areas are also a great source of fine juniper.

So how are the berries harvested? In Italy, local families from these remote villages, once their farm work has finished for the season, go up into the mountains armed with sacks and a stick. They find the shrubs and spread some sacks beneath it. They then tap the branches with the stick and collect the berries. The Italian government, some years ago, made the juniper bushes a protected plant. To damage, deface, or burn is an offence carrying a fine and/or imprisonment. It's regarded as a cash crop important to the economy. But the picking of berries was not an offence. Pickers have only one rule that they must remember. Do not mix berries from different hillsides together. Soil, micro-climates, water drainage will all have an effect on the quality of the berries. I learnt two things from the experiences of those charming villagers. If the wine vintage in Tuscany is good then so will the juniper season. The other one was that every five years, the bushes rest, as if they were exhausted. Then the following year was high yielding. Both of those observations were so true in my experience of non-intensive viticultural methods.

When the berries arrive back at the village, usually the village hall would be put to good use. A machine would be set up to separate the berries from the stalks and chaff, and then the berries would be spread out on the floor in corrals to dry, as their moisture content would be 30 percent or more. Remember, they are a fruit, and could start to ferment, which would ruin them. After a week or so, they would be bagged into open-weave bags similar to sacks used for coffee beans. They would then move onto a processing wholesaler who would grade the berries into sizes, again keeping those collections separate and allowing them to lose moisture slowly in cool, stable temperature conditions. Samples of these batches would then be sent to distillers for them to select during the buying season (November through to February).

Juniper is a diuretic, and has been used for this purpose by the pharmaceutical industry for centuries. Italian monks in the twelfth century made *aqua juniperi* by a crude distillation of berries and wine, to cure what they called "the old man's disease," or prostate problems. They even believed it would alleviate the symptoms of bubonic plague. Personally, I feel that the patient died happier from taking the medicine! Many other claims for its use have been made down through the centuries, and this can explain its migration through to northern Europe where it came to be seen as a general tonic and pick-me-up. So we get to Holland and a star is born.

Juniper also has its uses in the culinary world. Juniper-laden sauces served with game such as venison are wonderful and give that rustic charm to the dish. In northern Italy and the German border region, hams and cheeses are smoked with juniper. The French made a kind of beer called Genervrette from juniper in some of the rural areas, and in Hungary and the Czech Republic they make Borovicka, a juniper-flavored spirit that's similar to German Steinhager.

Juniper Berries
The heart of Plymouth Gin - distinctive but not overpowering

Liquorice (*Glycyrrhiza glabra*) The thickened juice of the leguminous root of the liquorice plant is condensed by grinding the root to a pulp, boiling with water, and then filtering and allowing to set to the concentration required. This stick liquorice is widely known as a candy throughout Europe. Cultivation is throughout the warmer parts of Europe, especially the Mediterranean area, and Central Asia and China. A herbaceous perennial, it grows to about 3 feet in height. Grown in deep, fertile soils the plant is harvested 2 to 3 years after planting.

Apart from its uses in candy, liquorice is fifty times sweeter than sucrose, so it also has culinary and medicinal purposes. The Chinese use it as a spice in its natural form in savoury foods such as broths and as an accompaniment to soy sauce in simmered dishes. Medicinally it is an effective expectorant, and its inclusion in a cough mixture widespread. Mouth and peptic ulcers has been shown to improve with this botanical. It is a gentle laxative.

Ground, in its natural form, it is a welcome addition to a gin recipe without showing any sweetness, as the volatile oils are captured during distillation.

Lovage (*Levisticum officinale*)
Cultivated in southern Europe, the seeds and leaves are part of the region's cuisine. Lovage is a tall (3 to 9 feet) perennial plant that resembles celery both in appearance and taste. Rarely used in gin these days as its cousin celery seed is more available, but it imparts, like celery, that fresh taste to a recipe.

Orris (*Iris . . .*)
Orris root is the rhizome of three species of iris, *Iris germanica*, *Iris florentina*, and *Iris pallida*, grown principally in northern Italy and to a lesser extent in Morocco. Around the neighbourhood of Florence, extensive cultivation of the iris is made. The rhizomes form 3- to 4-inch "fingers" underground, from which rootlets appear. After the fifth year the fingers start to decay and this is when they are harvested, the rootlets are trimmed, and the brown bark of the fingers are removed. The clusters of joined fingers are stacked in a warehouse to dry and mature. In its fresh state the odour is acrid and earthy, like toes. After two years the odour matures into the fragrance of violets, and as it continues to dry the odour becomes more intense. It is at its best for gin distillation at three years

Medicinally, it has anti-inflammatory properties and as such it has been used to treat sore throats and colds. It is also mildly diuretic. Perfumers use it in all high-quality perfume products. It has that property of "fixing" a product, thus giving it length so that it does not disappear from the wearer. My understanding is that they prefer two year old orris.

A few gin brands use orris in their recipe, and it is that perfumed flavour that is at the end of the taste sensation. What is the difference between the orris from the different regions? Moroccan fingers of orris are fat and almost round in shape. In Verona, the fingers are strung for drying, hence they are holed. Florentine is the real deal, especially three year old!

In Conclusion

There are well over 160 roots, herbs, or spices that could be used to flavour a gin recipe, so you have been spared, dear reader! I have touched on those that seem to be popular now, as well as historically. If you imagine the variations in the choice of botanicals you could use, as well as the variations in quantities of each, the permutations are staggering. Distilling your product is an art that, with experience, becomes a well-trodden path. The true art of the distiller is consistently selecting those botanicals you need, that are of the highest quality. You cannot keep samples from year to year to compare to what this season will be like. They change, just like that orris root. You learn by experience and keep a mental database of smells and flavours. Mother Nature bring it on!

Dry Gin Flashbacks

I'm pretty sure that gin was the first distilled spirit I ever tasted. I was about twelve years old at the time, living with my parents, Vi and Bernard Regan, and my maternal grandmother, Mary Elizabeth Armstrong—Nan to most folk—in the seaside town of Thornton Cleveleys on the northwest coast of England, just north of Blackpool, a very popular resort that's even tackier than Vegas. It's a fabulous place if you're looking for a party, though. Promise.

Shortly after my first sip of gin, my family got back into the pub game, but at this point we'd been out of the booze biz for about a decade, and we lived in a modern three-bedroom house just a stone's throw from the seafront. I have no idea what my mother drank at the time—she was never a big drinker—but Dad was a gin drinker, of that I'm sure. And although he was by no means a heavy drinker at that point, when he let his hair down, it hung down way low. Bernard and Vi would go out of a Saturday night, usually to a pub called the Durban, a joint on the seafront that was about a two-minute walk from our house, where they'd meet up with a bunch of friends, and it wasn't unusual for them all to come back to our house after the pub closed for a little late-night drinkie or two. They would play records by The Beatles and Gerry and the Pacemakers, Billy J. Kramer and the Dakotas, and Cliff Richards and, well, you get the picture. They'd drink and they'd dance and they'd get into the sort of philosophical discussions that people with a couple of extra drinks inside them tend toward. "Walter always said that he wanted to come back as a bird, and whenever I see the seagulls at the beach I wonder if he's one of them. I wouldn't put it past him to come back to keep his eye on us . . ." That sort of thing.

It was at one of these Saturday night get-togethers that someone or other handed me a Gin Gimlet. They didn't know it was a Gin Gimlet at the time. This was England, circa 1963, and I'm pretty sure that my parents and their friends had never heard of such a thing. To them, it was a gin and lime (Rose's lime juice cordial, no doubt). There was no ice in the glass. Lancashire folk seldom put ice in their drinks back then. I loved that gin and lime. I don't remember too much more about that night, but I remember loving that gin and lime, and I remember dancing the twist with my mother later on. Don't laugh—I won a twist competition when I was about 10. True story. I don't think I tasted liquor for a couple of years after that party, but I consciously committed to memory the fact that gin was the very first distilled spirit I ever tasted. I knew it would come in handy one day.

The gin, I think, would have been Gordon's, and I say that only because I know that Dad was a hog for Gordon's gin, and that was his brand until his dying day, back in 1977. Other brands were too fruity for Dad, or so he used to tell me, though I doubt that he sampled a huge variety of bottlings. If he was around today I bet I could show him quite a few other gins that would suit him down to the ground, but I'm happy to know that the no-nonsense European Gordon's gin was Bernard's benchmark when it came to gin, simply because that's the style of gin—slap-you-around-the-face-with-juniper-and-perfume—that I enjoy most, too. When I'm drinking Martinis, that is. And G & Ts.

Here I am at the age of 12, around the time of my first Gin Gimlet.
I look almost respectable, right?

Kathleen Hearty, Vi Regan, Bernard Regan, Jack Hearty, Rob Wright, and Marjory Wright. This picture might have been taken a little earlier than the year of the party at which I had my first sip of gin, but not too much earlier, and the people here with my parents were frequent partiers at our house.

Gin and Tonic was my highball of choice for most of the 1970s. I was a B-man for the most part: Beefeater or Boodles. I'd take a healthy measure of gin with just a splash of tonic, and a squeeze of lime. I spent most of that decade behind various bars in New York, making all sorts of psychedelic-colored drinkies for the swinging singles who crawled from bar to bar on the streets of the Big Apple, taking a few tokes from a joint as they roamed—quite acceptable on the streets of the Upper East Side at the time—and just looking for a damned good time. My generation, after all, was the one that touted peace and civil rights; we wore droopy moustaches and bell-bottom jeans, and I think I'm right in saying that we were the ones who invented sex. Well, it seemed like that at the time.

My favorite gin flashback from this period took place in1974 when I was tending bar at Drake's Drum, the joint where I was given my first job behind the stick in New York. I couldn't have asked for a better place to work. The owners, Jim Duke and Frank Casa, were easy to work for, and the customers were diverse and wonderful—actors, bankers, rugby players, lots of members of staff from the British and Australian consulates, as well as people who worked as secretaries and the like at the U.N. in order to get a diplomatic visa and hang in New York for a while.

There was sawdust on the floor at the Drum, the food was edible and cheap, regulars would order "whatever's in the Dewar's bottle, please," pretty frequently, and we served both red and white wine by the carafe: $4.75 for Beaujolais Superieur Piat Pere et Fils, or $4.25 for Liebfraumilch Franz Weber. The jukebox was one of the best in the neighborhood, and the atmosphere was one that's created only when the owners and the staff truly care about the people who frequent the joint. Drake's Drum was a classic neighborhood gin mill.

Kevin Noone and Dave Ridings—two of my mentors at Drake's Drum.
This picture was probably taken in around 1974.

For a while I worked the Sunday brunch shift at the Drum. It was real hard work, and most of my time was spent dispensing pitchers of Bloody Marys and Sangria to the servers—the floor was so busy that I didn't have much time to hang with my bar customers until later in the afternoon, but after the brunch rush died down a little I had a few hours left to take care of business and schmooze with my Sunday afternoon cronies. On one such Sunday afternoon a British guy by the name of John R. left me a hash brownie as a tip. "Sorry, Gaz, I'm broke," he explained. I'd never eaten a hash brownie before—I was 22 years old, and although I occasionally smoked a little grass, I wasn't much into drugs at all. John told me that his brownie would take about an hour to take effect. My shift ended at eight. I ate the sucker at six. I don't recommend that you try this.

Come seven o'clock that evening I was high as a kite. I had a stupid grin on my face, and I was sort of floating from customer to customer, doing my best to make it through to the end of my shift. A guy ordered a Gin and Tonic. I filled the glass with ice, and started to pour the gin—we didn't use jiggers at the Drum, we free-poured all our drinks. As I was pouring, the light caught the stream of gin in such a way that I saw a beautiful blue glow coming from the spirit as it cascaded from the bottle, and the light-show grabbed my attention. It was fabulous. The crystal-clear gin ran down the middle of an aquamarine haze, shimmering as it fell, and occasionally sparkling as though diamonds were flowing from the bottle. Suddenly I became aware of the guy who had ordered the drink, and when I focused on him on the other side of the mahogany I saw a look of horror on his face. I looked down at the glass. It was full of gin. It had been full of gin for a little while, I think. Gin was overflowing from the glass and flooding the well on my side of the bar. Don't try eating hash brownies while you're working. It's not a great idea.

Chapter 4

Dry Gin by the Bottle

Here's the chapter that brings you the nitty gritty on all your favorite brands of dry gin. It's gonna tell you how they are made, what botanicals they use, and it will go into distillation idiosyncrasies, and all sorts of crazy stuff that you didn't even know pertained to gin. Unless otherwise noted, the information in this chapter has come straight from each gin company, though we've edited some of the copy a little for flow, we left a lot of stuff the way each distillery sent it to us.

Not Only, but Also: You'll find some bar stories, or flashbacks, in this chapter. They appear next to the details of certain gins. Certain gins that remind me of certain bars, people, and events. Look specifically close to the listings for Beefeater gin, Bombay gin, Hendrick's gin, and Tanqueray gin, There's lots of trivia, quotations, and other frivolities in this section, too—it's just stuff I added to hopefully keep you entertained.

Important Stuff: The gins listed here are made in different countries, and therefore they don't all fall under the same legal guidelines. We have allowed each producer to choose their own way of describing the style of their gin, and you should be aware that not all gins listed here as being "London Dry" in style would actually be able to use those words on their label, depending on the country in which they are being marketed. All gins here, though, are distilled gins. No compound gins have been accepted for inclusion in this book.

Aviation Gin, 42% abv
www.aviationgin.com

Style: New Western Dry
Country of Origin: USA
Available in: USA, UK, and Australia
Botanicals: juniper, cardamom, lavender, anise seed, coriander, Indian sarsaparilla, and dried sweet orange peel.
Distillation: Aviation is a distilled gin that is flavored during a 48 hour maceration period (the botanicals are soaked in neutral grain rye spirit), after which, the spirit is returned to a steel still for one final distillation to bond and concentrate the flavors.

Tell us why you think your gin stands apart from all the others: Aviation gin is thought to be the first true partnership between distiller and bartender in American history, which facilitated the brand's unique opportunity to gain "outside" insight on how it might work on the palate and in cocktails, from someone with an intimate understanding of the spirit outside of the distilling arena. Secondly, Aviation is one of the first of an entirely new category of dry gins currently going under the designation; New Western Dry, for which we give the following definition: This designation seems to have evolved over the past 8 years, as a result of efforts from both large brand houses and regional distillers in Europe and in the United States. In taking a good hard look at today's rather loose definition of dry gin, these distillers realized a greater opportunity for artistic "flavor" freedom in this great spirit and are creating gins with a shift away from the usually overabundant focus on Juniper, to the supporting botanicals, allowing them to, *almost* share center stage. And while the juniper must remain dominant in all dry gins to achieve definition, these gins are most certainly defined, not by the Juniper itself, but by the careful inclusion and balance of the supporting flavors, creating, what many experts believe to be, an entirely new designation of dry gin that deserves individual recognition. As a New Western Dry Gin, Aviation takes advantage of the rich, floral and savory flavor notes of alternative botanicals such as lavender, cardamom, and Indian sarsaparilla to capture the lushness, spice, creativity, and freshness of the Pacific Northwest.

Finally, the partners found great inspiration in Dutch gin or genever which, of course, predates today's popular dry gins and is rarely seen on our shores. Dutch gin is less focused on juniper than its dry counterparts, playing up the malty characteristics of the spirit itself and, is generally enjoyed neat in the same manner that one might enjoy a dram of whiskey. It is important to note, though, that Aviation is not a Dutch gin by definition, but simply a dry gin inspired by the full throttle Dutch style of old. To them, this meant creating a full bodied product with a focus not only on the juniper and citrus, but the botanical blend as a whole, allowing it to both mix seamlessly into gin cocktails and be enjoyed all by itself in its natural state.

Aviation Gin, Continued

Any other idiosyncrasies that you'd like to tell us about? Aviation shines brightest when properly mixed in classic and modern culinary cocktails. It works best in citrus accented drinks that play off its unique notes of lavender, cardamom, and Indian sasparilla. Unlike most dry gins, however, Aviation sets itself apart with it is slightly subdued juniper and citrus presence against the back drop of creamy rye spirit which makes it uniquely enjoyable all by itself, both ice cold and at room temperature.

Where does the name Aviation come from? While the gin takes its name from the Aviation Cocktail which was invented by barman Hugo Ensslin, at New York's Hotel Wallick sometime during the early 20th century, the reason behind its selection as the identity for this uniquely Northwest style of gin goes a bit deeper. After working behind the stick for five years, Aviation gin co-founder Ryan Magarian, like so many of his industry peers, found himself stuck in a rut when it came to mixing with gin, using it, almost exclusively, for Martinis and Gin and Tonics. This all changed, though, after a fateful trip to Las Vegas where, at Olives Restaurant in the Bellagio Hotel, he was first introduced to the Aviation Cocktail. He recalls this to be a pinnacle moment in the development of not only his passion for making cocktails, but understanding the true potential of one of the world's most fully flavored tipples—dry gin. The simple and unique balance of gin, maraschino liqueur, and freshly squeezed lemon juice, he says, "without a doubt, paved the way for a much deeper appreciation of the spirit and the reality that gin, in the hands of a passionate bartender, just might be the world's most mixable spirit.

When the time came to name the gin, Aviation was suggested by Ryan because to him it represented an awakening to the true mixability of the spirit. And after kicking the name around, the fellas agreed that it represented their combined desire for Aviation gin to facilitate similar experiences for drinkers around the world.

Beefeater Gin, 40% abv and 47% abv

www.beefeatergin.com

Style: London Dry Gin
Country of Origin: England
Beefeater at 40% abv available in: UK, Spain, Russia, Greece, France, Czech Republic, Japan, Bulgaria
Beefeater at 47% abv available in: USA, Japan, Travel Retail
Botanicals: Juniper, Coriander seed, Seville orange peel, Lemon Peel, Angelica root and seed, Liquorice, Bitter almond, Orris root.
Distillation: Grain Neutral spirit at 96% vol. is charged into pot stills and reduced with water to 60%. Botanicals are weighed out and added to the spirit in the still. This charge is then allowed to steep for 24 hours prior to distillation to extract the complex flavours. The distillation process takes approximately a further seven hours, with the heads and tails separated so that only the middle cut, at around 80%, is collected for the gin. De-mineralized water is added to reduce the strength for bottling.
Tell us why you think your gin stands apart from all the others: The 24-hour steeping process is key to the complex flavours to be found in Beefeater. This helps to produce a balanced gin that is ideal for mixed drinks and cocktails. The careful choice of botanicals, selected from each year's crop, is vital to the maintenance of consistent high quality.
Any other idiosyncrasies that you'd like to tell us about? Beefeater gin is the only major international London Gin brand that continues to be distilled in London.
History: Beefeater was founded by James Burrough, who had trained as a pharmacist. Burrough bought a gin distillery in Chelsea, London, and soon developed his recipe for a new gin which he named Beefeater, after the guards at the Tower of London. The recipe remains unchanged to this day. Production of Beefeater remained in the Burrough family until 1988. Beefeater gin is now owned by Pernod Ricard and is all distilled at the London distillery at Kennington, London, by Master Distiller, Desmond Payne.

Tasting Notes for Beefeater Gin

F. Paul Pacult—*Kindred Spirits*: "Clear, ideal in its purity; one of the classiest, lushest, roundest gin bouquets in existence—spicy (coriander) and fruity—amazingly focused, the laser-beam-like aroma of juniper berry is immensely appealing, fat and marvellous; delicious multiple layers of flavor develop on the palate; at entry, a stone-dry, minerally flavor opens up, ultimately giving way to a midpalate taste of defined juniper berry; the medium-long aftertaste takes you home in a savoury, off-dry manner; doubtless this is one of the most stylish, downright succulent gins in the marketplace; slinky, sexy, and a joy to quaff; purchase in mass quantities. **** Highly recommended."

Internet Wines and Spirits: "A very stylish, hedonistic gin." SCORE : **92**

F. Sot Fitzgerald—*alcoholreviews.com*: "Beefeater Gin requires no introduction. Any bar you go to, no matter if it is a pricey club in Manhattan or a dumpy cowboy bar in Texas, will likely carry it. There is good reason for this. Beefeater is an inexpensive and very good gin."

Wine and Liquor Courier: "This is the worlds leading brand of Premium Gin. Beefeater's difference is defined by the complex recipe using high quality, exotic botanicals from throughout the world, a skilful distilling process and the quality and consistency of production that makes up this unique taste."

Geraldine Coates—*Classic Gin*: "Beefeater is the only London dry gin actually made in London. It's a dry, complex gin whose citric notes are balanced with hints of caramel. Beefeater steeps the botanicals in a pot still with the base spirit for 24 hours before distilling. This means the stills can be run only once every two days but the company's Desmond Payne believes that this slower process allows for a gentler extraction of flavour from the botanicals before distillation and makes for a more complex drink. Desmond Payne is the ultimate gin guru—he knows everything there is to know about gin. Just as importantly he has the ability to communicate his knowledge and vast experience in a delightfully down to earth manner. Like Beefeater itself Desmond is a classy Londoner who is made from top quality traditional ingredients. He's also dry, sophisticated, engaging and a crucial component of any mix."

Awards: Beefeater is the most authoritative gin brand in the world and has picked up the prestigious IWSC (International Wine and Spirits Competition) trophy for Best Gin more times (6) than any other gin brand in the last 10 years (1999, 2002, 2003, 2004, 2007, 2008). **San Francisco World Spirits Competition:** Beefeater 24—Bronze, 2009; Beefeater Dry (47%)—Gold, 2008; Beefeater Dry—Double Gold. **International Wine & Spirits Competition:** Beefeater Dry 40%: Silver, 2008; Beefeater Crown Jewel: Silver Best in Class, 2008; Beefeater Dry (47%): Gold Best in Class and Best Gin Trophy, 2007; Beefeater Crown Jewel: Trophy, 2007; Beefeater Dry 47%: Silver, 2007; Beefeater Dry 40%: Silver. **International Spirits Challenge:** Beefeater Dry 47%: Gold, 2008; Beefeater Crown Jewel: Silver, 2008; Beefeater Dry 40%: Bronze, 2008; Beefeater 24: Commended, 2007; Beefeater Crown Jewel: Gold, 2007; Beefeater Dry 47%—Silver, 2007; Beefeater Dry 40%: Bronze. **Gin Masters:** Beefeater Gin: Design & Packaging Gold, 2008; Beefeater Gin: Gold. **The Gin Challenge:** Beefeater Gin: Gold, 2008; Beefeater Gin: Design & Packaging, Silver. **Drinks International Cocktail Challenge:** Entente Cordiale by Beefeater Gin—Trophy, 2008.

Here I am with Dave Ridings (he's on your right) outside Drake's Drum, circa 1974.

The *Extra Dry* Martini, and My Part in its Downfall: A Beefeater Flashback

The very first extra-dry Gin Martini I ever made was a Beefeater Martini, so whenever I see a bottle of Beefeater my mind races back to Drake's Drum, the joint on the Upper East Side where I lost my New York bartender cherry back in 1973. We sold lots of Beefeater at the Drum, mainly in G & Ts, but we sold quite a few Beefeater Martinis, too, and the memory of the evening when one of my bosses—a guy by the name of Frank Casa—said, "Gary, make me an extra-dry Beefeater Martini, please. Straight up with a twist," always brings a bit of a grin to my face. My cocktailian skills left much to be desired back then, as Frank Casa discovered . . .

The Martini incident took place on my second or third shift at the Drum, just a month or so after I arrived in New York, and although I'd worked behind the bar in two of my parents' pubs in England, I didn't know a thing about cocktails—in northern England back then, serving a Gin and Tonic was about as close as you ever got to the craft of mixology—so before I could get a job behind the stick in the Big Apple I had to learn how to make Singapore Slings and Rusty Nails and Grasshoppers and Brandy Alexanders and Manhattans and Martinis, among myriad other Technicolor potions that were popular back then.

"Sit by the service area of the bar every night, listen to the drink orders coming in from the waitstaff, and watch the bartenders in action. You'll soon pick it up," said Dave Ridings, one of my very best friends. Dave was a regular at my parents' pub in Bolton, Lancashire, and after he moved to the States—chasing a woman—in 1968, he and I had kept in touch. By the time I arrived on his doorstep some five years later, he was a bartender/manager at Drake's Drum, and he vowed to help me get a job behind the stick before my money ran out—I'd brought enough scratch to last me for about a month, and when that ran out, if I didn't have a job, I was going to have to high-tail it back to England.

Ridings was right. Sitting by the service area worked real well for me, and it wasn't long before I'd figured out how to make the majority of drinks that were crossing the mahogany. I sat there night after night making mental notes of the drink names, the ingredients, the proportions, what kind of glass to use, and what garnish went into each cocktail. Best of all, I was drinking for free, too. I was on scholarship at the Drum.

It wasn't long before Frank Casa and Jim Duke, the guys who owned the Drum, gave me a break and awarded me one shift a week behind the bar. Dave Ridings and an Irishman by the name of Kevin Noone became my mentors, and it wasn't long before I started to feel at home at that fabulous neighborhood bar.

I made a few mistakes during my first shifts, of course. I was making Whiskey Sours with scotch, for instance, until a waitress noticed, and it's pretty amusing to note that no customer ever sent one back. I could handle the majority of cocktails pretty easily, though, and Manhattans and Martinis were easy enough, of course.

I'd seen both Ridings and Noone making Martinis, and I'd watched them put just a splash of dry vermouth into the mixing glass, adding lots and lots of gin, and stirring the drink lovingly for a good long time before straining it out into a chilled cocktail glass. When Frank Casa ordered his extra-dry Beefeater Martini, then, I was pretty confident that I could make him a good drink.

Frank was never much of a drinker, so I was surprised when he ordered a Martini at around eight-thirty on a Saturday night. But on reflection, I think he was probably testing me—this went down on my second or third shift behind the bar at the Drum. I was eager, of course, to make a good impression on Frank, and I wondered why he stressed that his Martini be "extra dry," but I didn't want to show my ignorance by asking, so I tried to logic it out. It didn't take long before I realized that if a Beefeater Martini was Beefeater and a splash of *dry* vermouth, then an extra-dry version must call for extra vermouth.

This is Frank (blonde) and Jimmy (mop-top), circa 1974. I'm still in touch with Jimmy pretty regularly, and Frank and I still exchange the occasional email. Last time I saw him I reminded him of this incident, but he didn't remember any of it. C'est la vie.

I must have poured almost as much vermouth as I did Beefeater into the mixing glass that night. I was trying to impress the boss, after all. I stirred the drink until it was as cold as can be, strained it into the cocktail glass that I'd filled with ice and water before I started to assemble the cocktail so it would be well chilled by the time the drink was ready, and after releasing the oils from the lemon twist over the top of the drink, I gently rubbed the zest around the rim of the glass so as to point up that lovely citrus aroma.

"There you go, Frank," I said as I placed the drink in front of him, and as I prepared a glass of ice water for my boss—we always gave ice water on the side of high-octane cocktails at the Drum—I watched Frank take a sip of his drink. He looked at me, his eyes wide in what, for a second, I took to be admiration. "Gary, do you think I could have a word with you at the end of the bar?" he asked . . .

The Moon and the Iced Night-Breezes

"I don't know if the moon and the iced night-breezes had got into my head . . . It couldn't have been that one very small pink gin I'd had with Slim . . . But as I strode quickly along towards Oxford Circus I felt that I was for the moment as unlike my daylight self as the London streets." *Sweethearts Unmet* by Berta Ruck, 1919.

Beefeater 24 Gin, 45% abv

www.beefeater24.com

Style: London Dry Gin
Country of Origin: England
Available in: USA, Canada, UK, Spain, Russia, France, Czech Republic, Japan.
Botanicals: juniper, coriander seed, Seville orange peel, lemon peel, grapefruit peel, angelica root and seed, liquorice, bitter almond, orris root. Chinese green tea, Japanese sencha tea.
Distillation: Grain Neutral spirit at 96% vol. is charged into pot stills and reduced with water to 60%. Botanicals are weighed out and added to the spirit in the still. This charge is then allowed to steep for 24 hours prior to distillation to extract the complex flavours. The distillation process takes approximately a further seven hours, with the heads and tails separated so that only the middle cut, at around 80%, is collected for the gin. This cut is considerably shorter than in most gins resulting in a very specific selection of botanical flavours. De-mineralized water is added to reduce the strength to 45% for bottling.
Tell us why you think your gin stands apart from all the others: The 24 hour steeping process is key to the complex flavours to be found in Beefeater gins [and this] helps to produce a balanced gin that is ideal for mixed drinks and cocktails. The introduction of teas and grapefruit peel as botanicals gives a fragrance and softness to Beefeater 24. The careful choice of botanicals, selected from each year's crop, is vital to the maintenance of consistent high quality.
Any other idiosyncrasies that you'd like to tell us about? Beefeater gin is the only major international London Gin brand that continues to be distilled in London.

Beefeater 24, Continued

History of Beefeater 24

Beefeater 24 was developed in 2008 by Beefeater gin's master distiller Desmond Payne. The introduction of tea as a botanical creates a modern gin style ideal for today's new innovative cocktail culture, but retains the traditional distillation methods of a classic London Gin. Beefeater's unique 24-hour steeping process prior to distillation gives the inspiration for the name.

Tasting Notes

Geraldine Coates—*The Spectator*—11 November 2008: "Each [botanical] contribute[s] to a clean, delightfully aromatic, exceptionally smooth gin de luxe."
Alastair Gray—*Lusso Magazine*—December 2008: "The aroma is complex and multi-layered with citrus notes from the grapefruit, tannin aromas from the Sencha tea, coupled with the characteristic bite of the juniper that develops into the spicy character brought through by the presence of angelica and coriander. On the palate you are immediately aware of the citrus notes but at no point do they overpower the complex layers of flavour ranging from the tang of juniper through to the liquorice finish. Overall a spectacularly delicious offering, and like nothing else on the market."
Robyn Lewis—*The Grocer*—November/December 2008: "finely balanced . . . . made an excellent G&T."
Awards: Beefeater is the most authoritative gin brand in the world has picked up the prestigious **International Wine & Spirits Competition** trophy for **Best Gin** more times (6) than any other gin brand in the last 10 years (1999, 2002, 2003, 2004, 2007, 2008). **San Francisco World Spirits Competition, 2009:** Beefeater 24, Bronze Medal. **International Spirits Challenge, 2008:** Beefeater 24, Commended.

Bloom Gin, 40% abv
www.bloomgin.com

Style: London Dry Gin
Country of Origin: United Kingdom
Available in: UK, Germany, USA (as of August, 2009), Denmark, Greece, Sweden, Spain (3rd quarter, 2009)
Botanicals: The botanicals that impart a distinct flavor to Bloom gin are chamomile, honeysuckle, and pomelo. Of course, juniper is at the heart of Bloom, along with an additional range of various gin botanicals to round the gin and keep it in the style of a traditional London Dry Gin.
Distillation: Bloom Gin is batch-produced using traditional methods in copper pot stills. Only the middle section (the heart) is used for the Bloom gin, as this contains the best part of the aromas suitable for Bloom. Bloom Gin is triple-distilled using demineralised fresh spring water and all natural botanicals for flavor. These botanicals complete the gin to create a smooth and soft experience rounded by subtle notes of honey and orange, perfect neat or in a naturally sweetened cocktail.
Tell us why you think your gin stands apart from all the others: Bloom Gin is inspired by nature—it is a delicate gin made in the traditional London Dry method. Our notes of chamomile, honeysuckle, and pomelo are unique and offer a delicious floral gin experience for gin and vodka lovers alike.
Any other idiosyncrasies that you'd like to tell us about? No one on the market is currently using such a collection of flowers to create a truly inspiring refined London Dry Premium Gin. The flowers used in Bloom are also edible flowers and so provide a great addition for garnishing a Bloom cocktail.
History: Created during the summer of 2007, Master Distiller Joanne Simcock was asked to create a premium gin of her choice. She was given full creative license and so, through the development of her "Gin Aroma Wheel," she set out to experiment with the aromas of many typical English Country Garden flowers. Whilst remaining true to the traditional London Dry style, Bloom gin is all about complimenting the Juniper notes not smothering them. Starting with chamomile, Joanne then incorporated honeysuckle into Bloom to provide natural sweetness and offer a warm compliment to the chamomile. Finally, she added pomelo to provide a smooth, sun-drenched citrus note. Ultimately the botanicals work in harmony to create soft, floral balance and bloom—into Bloom Gin.
Tasting Notes from the Bloom Gin Company: A light floral gin with a subtle blend of honey and orange notes, the honeysuckle provides the sweetness which is like candied fruit. The orange notes from the pomelo help round this off and its all held together by the calming influence of the chamomile which imparts a feather-like softness of floral notes.

The Dreaded Uncle Ezekiel

"How he dreaded to see Uncle Ezekiel come to help with the haying! for he carried a gin bottle in his pocket, and after resorting to it a few times, mowed stones as readily as grass." *John Burroughs: Boy and Man* by Clara Barrus, 1922.

Bluecoat American Dry Gin, 47% abv
www.bluecoatgin.com

Style: American Dry Gin
Country of Origin: U.S.A.
Available in: U.S.A. & France
Botanicals Used: Juniper berries, sweet orange peels, lemon peels, and a proprietary blend of other organic citrus peels. All the botanicals are organic.
Distillation: Our unique procedure calls for an extremely slow heating of the pot. A ten-hour process allows our Master Distiller to most efficiently separate the impure alcohols from those he desires to bottle as the finished spirit. Only a small selection of our distillate meets our purity requirement and matches the desired botanical flavors to be collected for bottling. The remainder of the distillate is discarded as impure. What has been collected for bottling is then blended with triple filtered water to 47% alcohol by volume, or 94 proof, then passed through a spirit filter and tasted. Once the Master Distiller approves the batch, it is bottled, corked, and packed for shipment.
Tell us why you think your gin stands apart from all the others: The primary difference from other dry gins is the use of organic American citrus peels, sweet orange and lemon peel. Bluecoat utilizes organic juniper berries which, in comparison to the typical berries used in most gins, transmit spicy, earthy notes as opposed to pungent evergreen ones.
History: Bluecoat American Dry Gin celebrates the American Spirit of Independence and Rebellion born in Philadelphia over two centuries ago. Philadelphia Distilling, the first craft distillery in Pennsylvania since Prohibition, introduced Bluecoat American Dry Gin to a thirsty audience in May of 2006.
Tasting Notes from Simon Difford: 4 1/2 out of 5—Simon Difford, 2007. Juniper notes of pine, sap and eucalyptus jump out on the nose. The palate is peppermint fresh and wonderfully cleansing with piny, lemony, juniper flavours. The strength adds spirity notes of black pepper
Tasting Notes from *Imbibe Magazine*, 2007: 5 Stars; This staunchly American take on the classic dry gin is pleasantly earthy and herbal in aroma and taste, with a good balance of sweet fruits, nutty notes and warming citrus, with a full, soft body
Awards: International Wine & Spirit Competition 2007: Gold Medal, Best in Class; **San Francisco World Spirits Competition 2007:** Best American Gin; **San Francisco World Spirits Competition, 2009:** Double Gold & "Best Gin."

BOMBAY DRY GIN

Bombay Dry Gin, 43% abv

Style: London Dry Gin

Country of Origin: U.K.

Available in: USA and Spain

Botanicals: Angelica Root, Coriander, Cassia Bark, Almonds, Lemon Peel, Liquorice, Juniper Berries, Orris.

Distillation: Bombay Dry is produced using Carter-head stills—the spirit vapors pass through the botanicals, which are held separately in a perforated copper basket in the neck of the still. This process, known as Vapor Infusion, is unique to Bombay Dry and Bombay Sapphire and it allows the gentle absorption of each of the aromatic flavors, resulting in a wonderfully balanced, crisp yet delicate finish.

Tell us why you think your gin stands apart from all the others: Bombay Dry appeals to the traditional gin drinker because of it's classic, complex flavour profile, emphasising a more prominent juniper note.

History: Bombay Dry is based on a secret recipe first created in England in 1761. Only a select few know in what quantities the 10 botanicals are used to create the perfectly balanced taste of Bombay Dry. The picture of Queen Victoria reflects gin's British heritage and its popularity in the Victorian era during the days of the British Empire. The history of gin is inextricably linked to its popularity in the tropical regions of the British Empire, particularly served with tonic as the quinine in the tonic water helped to overcome malaria.

Tasting Notes from Bombay Dry Gin: Bombay Dry is crisp, clean and medium bodied, with layers of citrus and mineral notes combine to create a soft, delicate and beautifully balanced spirit.

r-e-m-o-r-s-e!

Those dry Martinis did the work for me;
Last night at twelve I felt immense,
Today I feel like thirty cents.
My eyes are bleared, my coppers hot,
I'll try to eat, but I cannot.
It is no time for mirth and laughter,
The cold, grey dawn of the morning after.
The Sultan of Sulu by George Ade, 1903.

It's Steak and Kidney Pie Day at The North Star Pub: A Bombay Gin Flashback

I worked at the North Star Pub in New York's South Street Seaport for almost exactly four years, starting in February, 1988. They were four of my favorite years in the business, though I seldom worked behind the bar there—I was a manager-type at the time.

The North Star was as English as a pub could be, given that it was over 3,000 miles away from the Green and Pleasant Land, and it was Deven Black, the General Manager of the joint, who had made it that way. He refused to stock American beer, he boasted a collection of almost 100 single malt scotches, and since the pub catered to Anglophiles and transplanted Brits, he stocked lots of gins, too, Bombay and Bombay Sapphire among them. And whenever I think of these gins, I'm reminded of a guy we called Frank the Bank—a Bombay gin man through and through.

The food at the North Star was also unequivocally British. We served authentic Bangers and Mash (the sausages were made by Peter Myers, a Brit in the Village who owned a grocery store called Myers of Keswick), and we also offered Shepherd's Pie and Fish and Chips and the like. Steak and Kidney Pie, though, was not on our menu—it's a hard sell in New York—but we offered it as a special from time to time, and quite a few of our regulars, lots of them were Brits who emigrated to New York to take jobs on Wall Street, ordered it every time we chalked it up on the blackboard.

Here we see a few of the regulars at the North Star on St. George's Day, 1990— we made everyone wear the newspaper hats, and gave them all pretty line drawings of St. George slaying the dragon, and crayons with which to color them.

One of the regulars, a Canadian guy who worked at The Royal Bank of Scotland, handed me his business card one day, and asked me to call him next time we served Steak and Kidney Pie. This made me ponder, and it wasn't long before I started to compile "The Steak and Kidney Pie List." Every time the chef decided to feature the dish I'd get on the phone and call around twenty people whose numbers I'd gathered after seeing them order this British specialty. Most of the people on the list were high-level bankers and the like, so it was seldom that they actually picked up the phone.

"Tell him it's Steak and Kidney Pie Day." I'd instruct whoever answered the call.

"I beg your pardon?"

"He'll know what you mean," I'd say before hanging up and dialing the next number.

The ploy worked quite well. Not everyone on the list would show up every time I called, but we'd see, perhaps, a dozen Steak and Kidney Pie fans walk through the door on the days when we featured the dish. One day, though, this brilliant marketing scheme very nearly backfired.

Frank the Bank—the Bombay gin man—was a true Brit. He was a very successful banker who had come up from being a street kid in London. Frank the Bank had a keen sense of humor, everyone loved the man, and he was a huge fan of Steak and Kidney Pie. Frank called me over to his table one day as he was scarfing his lunch, and he told me what had gone down at work that morning after I'd spoken to his assistant.

"I was in a meeting with my 'boss of all bosses,' a guy from headquarters in London. I'd told my assistant that I wasn't to be disturbed under any circumstances, but she walked into the meeting anyway, and she shoved a note into my hand. I opened it up and read the words 'It's Steak and Kidney Pie Day.' She thought it was a code for some potentially important banking thing," Frank told me.

"What did you do?" I asked.

"Well, I love my assistant, and I didn't want to get her into trouble so I looked my boss dead in the eye and told him that I had to leave immediately. I didn't explain a thing. I left him thinking that something incredibly important personal thing must have cropped up, because otherwise there was no way I would have dared to leave him like that. Then I came down here for my Steak and Kidney Pie," he grinned.

I can't remember Frank's last name, but I do remember that he drank Bombay and Tonic at lunchtime, and after work, when he popped in for a drink before heading home, he drank Bombay Sapphire Martinis. Straight up, no garnish. I never saw him drink anything else. He was a Bombay man all the way. You've got to love a guy like Frank the Bank, right?

That's Quentin Crisp, author of *The Naked Civil Servant*, on the left. He's standing with a Pearly Queen and me. Quentin was a fascinating guy, and he'd come to the North Star as a celebrity guest for all sorts of events. He was one very special chappie.

BOMBAY SAPPHIRE

Bombay Sapphire Gin, 47% abv

www.bombaysapphire.com

Style: London Dry Gin
Country of Origin: U.K.
Available: Worldwide
Botanicals: angelica root, coriander, cassia bark, cubeb berries, grains of paradise, almonds, lemon peel, liquorice, juniper berries, orris
Distillation: Bombay Sapphire is produced using Carter-head stills—the spirit vapors pass through the botanicals, which are held separately in a perforated copper basket in the neck of the still. This process, known as Vapor Infusion, is unique to Bombay Sapphire and Bombay Dry Gin and it allows the gentle absorption of each of the aromatic flavors, resulting in a wonderfully balanced, crisp yet delicate finish.
Tell us why you think your gin stands apart from all the others: Bombay Sapphire appeals to gin and non-gin drinkers because it is less "ginny" than other gins, i.e. it doesn't have an intense and overpowering juniper flavour. Instead it has a subtle yet complex flavour which is clean, crisp and perfectly balanced.
History: Bombay Sapphire is based on a secret recipe first created in England in 1761. Only a select few know in what quantities the 10 botanicals are used to create the perfectly balanced taste of Bombay Sapphire. The picture of Queen Victoria reflects gin's British heritage and its popularity in the Victorian era during the days of the British Empire. The history of gin is inextricably linked to its popularity in the tropical regions of the British Empire, particularly served with tonic as the quinine in the tonic water helped to overcome malaria.
Tasting Notes from Bombay Sapphire Gin: Bombay Sapphire has a ripe citrus aroma with rounded spice and a touch of juniper.

Where Do the Boodles Meet?

BOODLE'S CLUB.—Where the Boodles meet. Anybody of the name of Boodle visiting London is, ipso facto, a member. A Noodle has to prove his descent from a Boodle before he can be admitted. There is a fine Boodleian Library in the Club. The Boodles were originally a set of Buddhists [who] settled in England; Boodle, or, as it was spelt, 'Bhoodle,' being only another name for Bhoodla, Bhooda or Buddha. They have now given up any distinctive creed, though the members are forced to certain outward observances, such, for instance, as eating pickles with cold meat, cheese with a knife, &c. &c. Entrance to the Club is free—when no one is looking. One Hall Porter may exclude, if strong enough. The Club-house was formerly given by the King to these Bhooddist refugees, with right of sanctuary; and now, if anyone oppressed, or in difficulties wishes his case to be tried by the old Boodleian Law, he has only to rush into the Club-hall, go on his knees, and cry 'O Boodles, O mong Boodles! à moy! Boodles à mong side!' and then he may safely leave his case in the hands of the Hall Porter. This is one of the oldest privileges still existing in the West-End ; and is one of the few that has never been abused. *Punch*, 1879.

Boodles Gin, 45.2% abv

Style: London Dry
Country of Origin: UK
Available in: USA, UK, Japan
Botanicals: juniper berries, coriander seed, angelica seed and root, cassia bark, nutmeg, sage, rosemary, caraway seed
Tell us why you think your gin stands apart from all the others: Boodles Gin has no citrus components.
Tasting Notes from the Producers of Boodles Gin: Boodles sensory profile is crisp, fresh, slightly sweet, with floral and spicy notes.

BRECON

Special Reserve

— ◆ — GIN — ◆ —

Brecon Special Reserve Gin, 40% abv

www.penderyn-distillery.co.uk

Style: London Dry

Country of Origin: Wales, UK

Available in: Mainly Wales with selected specialist outlets around the UK, Spain & France.

Botanicals: juniper berries, orange peel, cassia bark, liquorice, cinnamon bark, angelica root, ground nutmeg, coriander seeds, lemon peel, orris root.

Distillation: The five-column distilled neutral alcohol is charged into the copper pot of the still and combined with water before the botanicals are added in carefully controlled measures according to our 100-year-old recipe. The alcohol is then combined with water and reduced in strength, as pure alcohol would harden the skins of the botanicals and make extraction and infusion of the oils more difficult. The charge is heated and the vaporized spirit passes through the swan neck at the top of the still to a water cooled condenser and the resulting liquid condensate spirit is collected in the spirit safe where the quality is strictly monitored. This concentrate is traditionally combined with neutral grain alcohol in a very skilful process of blending to produce high strength gin of about 94%, which is in turn reduced in strength prior to bottling.

Tell us why you think your gin stands apart from all the others: Brecon Special Reserve Gin is hand crafted to our 100-year-old recipe, the combination of the 10 different botanicals married with Welsh spirit and our own water and drawn from beneath the distillery gives a sophisticated and fragrant gin. It is a gin that is spicy yet subtle with incredible smoothness to taste and an indulging drink that excites the palate.

History: Brecon Gin was launched in the year 2000 then it was re-branded and re-launched into its current design and packaging in 2006.

Awards: Silver Medal at the 2007 International Wines and Spirit Competition; Silver Medal at the Drinks International Gin Challenge, 2008.

Tasting notes from Brecon Gin's Master Distiller, Dr Jim Swan: Taken neat, Brecon is a big traditional juniper gin laced with coriander and revealing hints of spicy cinnamon. Add a mixer and the citrus freshness of oranges and lemons appear with nutmeg liquorice and angelica in a supporting role. The characteristic flavours go well with tonic, ice and lemon on a warm summer's day with a refreshing juniper in the lead role but Brecon's traditional heritage is equally at home besides a roaring fire on a cold night and will bring back memories of long hot summers past.

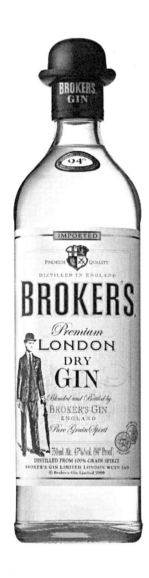

Broker's Gin, 40%abv, and 47% abv
www.brokersgin.com

Style: London Dry
Country of Origin: England
At 40% abv, Broker's is available in: UK, Canada, Denmark, Norway, Sweden, Finland, Iceland, France, Germany, Spain, Luxembourg, Greece, Gibraltar, Poland, Russia, Kazakstan, Morocco, Singapore, Malaysia, Thailand, Hong Kong, Australia, New Zealand.
At 47% abv, Broker's is available in: USA, UK, Denmark, France, Germany, Gibraltar, Russia, South Africa.
Botanicals: juniper berries, coriander seeds, cassia bark, cinnamon bark, licorice, orris, nutmeg, orange peel, lemon peel, angelica root.
Distillation: The botanicals are steeped for 24 hours in neutral grain spirit (made from 100% English wheat) in a traditional copper pot-still. The spirit is then redistilled. The "heads" and "tails" are set aside, with only the "heart" of the spirit being retained.
Tell us why you think your gin stands apart from all the others: Broker's Gin is a classic London Dry Gin with a rich aromatic nose and an intense flavor. While many new gins have opted for a more subtle character, closer to the vodka end of the flavor spectrum, Broker's Gin was created for people who really like gin.
Any other idiosyncrasies that you'd like to tell us about? The recipe is 200 years old, consequently all the botanicals used are traditional, conventional gin botanicals. There are no oddball ingredients.
History of your brand: Broker's Gin was created by brothers Martin and Andy Dawson in the late 1990s. Their goal was to present a gin with strong English imagery—the gentleman in a bowler hat, who would probably be a broker of some kind—and to use the bowler hat as a brand icon. The gin itself is hand-crafted, batch-distilled in a copper pot-still made by John Dore, the Rolls-Royce of still-makers.
Tasting Notes from the Chicago Beverage Testing Institute: "Clear. Rich, creamy, candied citrus and fruit peel aromas. Very smooth on the palate with a good balance of fresh botanicals, spicy juniper, and sweet ripe citrus fruit. Finishes with a smooth, warming peppery fade. A delicious and stylish gin for Martinis with the guts to stand up to tonic as well."
Tasting Notes from F. Paul Pacult: "In the mouth it sits well on the tongue and, thankfully, is the proper level of alcohol for gin, 94 proof. It finishes long, semi-sweet, tangy and luscious. A superbly made London Dry Gin that deserves a very close look by any admirer of that style."
Awards
London Gin Masters 2008: Masters Award. **World Beverage Competition 2007:** Platinum Award (Star of Show). *Bon Appétit Magazine* **2006:** Editor's Pick. **San Francisco World Beverage Competition 2005:** Gold Medal. **Chicago Beverage Testing Institute 2004:** Gold Medal. *Wine Enthusiast Magazine* **2003:** 95 points,; *Food & Wine Magazine 2003:* Best Gin.

As Hungry as a Hunter

"What I was then suffering from was not any longer seasickness, but starvation . . . she then prescribed a gin cocktail with a preponderance of Angostura bitters and insisted on ordering for me the right sort. I took it quiescently; indeed, I would have taken Prussic acid or any deadly thing to end my misery! The result was magical. I became forthwith as hungry as a hunter, and from that moment I got well." *Memories of a Musical Career* by Clara Kathleen Rogers, 1919.

BULLDOG London Dry Gin, 40% abv
www.BULLDOGGin.com

Style: London Dry
Country of Origin: England
Available in: USA, UK, Spain, France, Italy, Denmark, Canada, New Zealand
Botanicals: juniper, poppy, dragon eye, lotus leaves, lavender, orris root, angelica, cassia, lemon, almond, liquorice, coriander
Distillation: Small batch, hand-crafted, quadruple-distilled and triple-filtered using traditional copper pot stills and all natural ingredients from four continents, incorporating the "re-distillation" in true London Dry fashion.
Tell us why you think your gin stands apart from all the others: The first thing people notice is the striking, beautiful and radically different package and distinctively British name. We're less dry than some of the industry stalwarts and have worked to produce the finish most appropriate for mixing cocktails. BULLDOG touts itself as the world's first "sippable gin". As a result of the aforementioned, BULLDOG possesses an extremely healthy dose of sex appeal that is absent from many players in the gin category today. Also, BULLDOG employs the same recipe all around the world (unlike other brands that vary alcohol content and other things depending on geographic location). Arguably the most exotic mélange of botanicals ever used in gin.
Any other idiosyncrasies that you'd like to tell us about? One of the few gins that's actually made in London, BULLDOG dares to be bold both in terms of taste and the studded collar around the neck of the bottle
History: BULLDOG was launched in January 2007. Mr. Anshuman Vohra is founder and CEO of the brand. Our offices are in New York and we intend to sell the product globally. BULLDOG was launched because of Mr. Vohra's dissatisfaction with the other offerings in the gin category that were, in his humble opinion, too overdosed with Juniper and didn't have the right "finish". So, the quest for a new gin that would bridge the gap between sophisticated mixology and super-premium "sexiness" coveted by today's masses began. In the early phase of development, Mr. Vohra was able to use the help of an industry veteran to help launch BULLDOG quickly and efficiently.
Tasting Notes: *Wine Enthusiast Magazine*, **May 2008: Rating 90-95.** The nosing passes find classic London Dry aromas of juniper with assertive, prickly spirit and citrus. The palate entry is creamy, juniper-heavy and curiously chalky; the taste profile at midpalate is herbal, piney and citrusy. I like this gin a lot.
Patterson's *The Tasting Panel*, **May 2007, Rating 92** ("Outstanding") "The spiked dog collar bottle will appeal to younger drinkers but this is serious gin; herbal, racy and forward with aggressive flavors and great balance."
BULLDOG Gin company tasting notes: BULLDOG is aromatic, pleasant on the palate, less dry, and clean, yet distinctive on the back of the palate.

His First Gin Sling

"With his first gin sling they gave him a straw to drink through, but he soon threw it contemptuously aside, asked the waiter if he thought he was a sucking baby, and gulped the contents of his glass, and put it down with tears of indignation bursting from his eyes." *Two Sides of the Atlantic* by James Burnley, 1880.

Cadenhead's Old Raj Gin, 55% abv and 46% abv
http://www.wmcadenhead.com/

Style: Dry Gin
Country of Origin: Scotland
Available in: USA & UK
Botanicals Used & Distillation method: The gin essence is prepared by steeping the botanicals (the major one being juniper berries and including the following: coriander seed, angelica root, lemon and orange peels, orris root, cassia bark and almond powder) in an alcohol/water mixture for 36 hours and then distilling after a partial reflux in a small pot still. The flavour is obtained by making a specific cut during the distillation. The specific flavour of our Old Raj gin is obtained by the addition of saffron to the spirit.

Tell us why you think your gin stands apart from all the others: At 110 proof, it maintains a complexity and balance unlike any other gin; we also feel the flavor profile, which has obvious hints of saffron, makes Old Raj distinct and the most enjoyable gin. This delicious gin is also available in 92 proof, and the product flavor is nearly unchanged.

Tasting Notes: *Wine Enthusiast Magazine:* "This pale straw-colored gin charges up the nostrils with juniper aromas leading the way, citrus zest following, and a wonderful mélange of nuts and spices bringing up the rear. The body is big, and the ultra-dry palate is almost identical to the nose, but here, the flavors are so well integrated that subtlety seems to be the name of the game, and a softness develops in the backdrop. The finish is crisp, clean and very dry. This is an incredible bottling worthy of a crystal martini glass and very little vermouth. Old Raj also fares well neat, straight from the freezer."

Awards: 96-100 Rating "Ultimate White Spirit" *Wine Enthusiast Magazine*; Top 50 Spirits, 5 Star Rating, **Paul Pacult**.

CapRock®

ORGANIC DRY GIN

this is not your grandmother's gin™

41% ALC BY VOL   750ML

CapRock Organic Dry Gin, 41% abv

www.peakspirits.com

Style: London Dry with a balance of juniper, flower buds and citrus
Country of Origin: USA
Available in: USA
Botanicals: (We use only "whole" botanicals or juices. All USDA certified organic. No concentrates or oils.) Juniper, dried pink rose buds, dried lavender buds, dried orange peel, dried lemon peel, various seeds, spices, and fresh juices.
Distillation: The base distillate is pot distilled from organic wheat spirit and organic apple spirit fermented and distilled from organic jonathon, winesap and braeburn apple. Next the spirit is pot distilled with botanicals above in a single, final run. Some botanicals macerated, some boiled but not macerated, some steamed in the helm (above the liquid in the pot). Distillation occurs at low steam pressure in a bain-marie pot still to capture more subtleties in the botanicals. The gin distillate is then gradually cut back to 41% abv with our CapRock water, and finally the gin is filtered and bottled. **Tell us why you think your gin stands apart from all the others:** Our customers would say it appeals to both gin "purists" and to consumers that are "on the fence" about gin, so restaurants are especially interested in promoting it. Bartenders are telling us that it "changes character" when you add different things to it. It's great in a simple Martini or on the rocks. It can play active role in cocktails, but without overwhelming other ingredients. From our perspective, we think the philosophy behind our gin (and other products) is really what sets it apart (and explains its uniqueness). We really do view distilling as a culinary art and our products as agricultural products, where quality is all about farming practices. We think making a gin that is distilled from whole, organically farmed ingredients is the best way to achieve bold flavors with vibrancy and balance.
Any other idiosyncrasies that you'd like to tell us about? Peak SpiritsÒ is an estate distillery that produces artisan gin, vodka and brandies using locally grown, certified-organic stone and seed fruits (grapes, peaches, pears, apples and cherries). Our products are featured in some of the most successful, high-end venues in major markets around the country.
History: Peak Spirits was founded in 2004 by Jack Rabbit Hill Winery owners Anna and Lance Hanson. Their vision was to create an authentic distillery operation that crafted artisan spirits from the ground up-literally-with as much focus on superior farming practices as on artisan distillation techniques.
Tasting Notes from Neyah White, Nopa, San Francisco: CapRock, while definitely in the New American Gin category, bridges the West to the Old World bottlings with a big fat roundness that must be attributed to it's apple base. It relies less on herbals for complexity than the London Dry gins by pushing forward with subtle fruit notes. It's this fruit that ties the gin closer to the Plymouth style than the rest of the American gins when mixed, and provides a sturdy base for spirit driven cocktails.

Cascade Mountain Gin, 47.5% abv
http://www.bendistillery.com/

Country of Origin: USA

Style: American Style Gin

Available in: U. S. A.

Botanicals: Fresh, wild, handpicked juniper berries from the central Oregon desert.

Distillation: The spirit is distilled from grain using a continuous and an alembic pot still. Hand-picked wild juniper berries are infused into the spirit creating a gin with color similar more to a Dutch genever. The flavor profile is crisp and clean, not oily because actual juniper is used and not extracts.

Tell us why you think your gin stands apart from all the others: Cascade Mountain Gin's unique character comes from two sources—the quality of our spirit and the quality of our juniper. Both our water (pure Cascade Mountain water) and our spirit are obsessively filtered through charcoal and crushed lava rock. This gives our gin a soft, spring water-like mouth feel that, even at 95 proof, is remarkably smooth. Our juniper is handpicked and meticulously selected.

Any other idiosyncrasies that you'd like to tell us about? Each bottle of Cascade Mountain Gin is batch numbered and initialed by the person who bottled it. We feel this reinforces the small batch character of our gin. Also, since our juniper berries are picked wild we recognize that there will be subtle variation in color and flavor. Therefore batch numbering allows us to track the subtle, natural variations in each batch—much like vintages in wine.

Tasting Notes (from the producer): The flavor of Cascade Mountain Gin is complex and earthly with a hint of sage. It tastes like the high desert from which it came. While most gins seek to create flavor with multiple botanicals we trust the natural complexity of our wild juniper to give Cascade Mountain Gin a character that rich, subtle and pleasing.

Citadelle Gin, 44% abv
www.citadellegin.com

Style: French Gin made with 19 different botanicals

Country of Origin: France

Available in: UK, Spain, Italy, Germany, Japan, Malaysia, Thailand), USA, Canada.

Botanicals: juniper from France, coriander from Morocco, orange peel from Mexico, cardamom from India, liquorice from China, cubeb pepper from Java, savory from France, fennel from the Mediterranean, iris from Italy, cinnamon from Sri Lanka, violets from France, almonds from Spain, cassia from Indochina, angelica from Germany, grains of paradise from West Africa, cumin from Holland, nutmeg from India, lemon rind from Spain, star anise from France.

Distillation: Our wheat base—the finest wheat from the Beauce region of France—is distilled three times in a column still before being introduced to the 19 botanicals. To capture the botanicals freshness, the fusion is not allowed to steep—it is distilled immediately, for a fourth time.

Tell us why you think your gin stands apart from all the others: Citadelle is a classic gin in a sense that we are not looking to make a gin to please the vodka drinker. We are working for the real and uncompromising gin aficionados, the purists.

Any other idiosyncrasies that you'd like to tell us about? Citadelle's combination of juniper, cinnamon, coriander, citrus peels, herbs and violet is best against the bitter taste of quinine in tonic water.

History: In 1997, armed with the Cognac Ferrand distilling know-how we decided to do all it takes to produce the best gin possible. We did an intense research on the origins of gin and its ancient method production in order to produce THE ultimate classic gin.

Tasting Notes from the *Wine Enthusiast Magazine*: The first nosing passes find scents of fresh flowers, jasmine, honeysuckle, and cardamom; further aeration stimulates deeper, more herbal notes including anise, grains of paradise, and cinnamon. At the palate entry, the off-dry juniper presence is clearly evident; at mid-palate the taste profile turns creamy, rich, and flowery once again. Ends up off-dry, high on juniper essence, and elegant.

Awards: San Francisco World Spirits Competition (USA), 2008: Double Gold Medal. **The International Spirit Challenge, 2008 (Drinks International):** Gold medal. (More than 1000 spirits competed for best spirits in each category. Citadelle Gin was elected best Gin over all.) **Spirits Business Super Premium Gin Master, 2008:** Master. In London, the world capital of Gin, 42 different gins from around the world were blind tasted. Citadelle Gin was elected best Gin in the Super-Premium Gin category. **Concours Mondial du Vin (Brussels), 2007:** Silver Medal. **International Wine & Spirit Competition (UK), 2007:** Silver Medal. **San Francisco World Spirits Competition (USA), 2007:** Double Gold Medal. **San Francisco World Spirits Competition (USA), 2006:** Double Gold Medal. *Wine Enthusiast*, December 1st 2005: Classic (96-100), Highest Recommendation, Gin of the Year. **San Francisco World Spirits Competition, 2004:** Double Gold. **The International Wine and Spirit Competition, 2000:** Gold Medal

Citadelle Gin Reserve, 44% abv

Style: French Gin produced with 19 different botanicals, aged in Cognac casks
Country of Origin: France
Available in: UK, Spain, Italy, Germany, USA, Canada
Botanicals: juniper from France, coriander from Morocco, orange peel from Mexico, cardamom from India, liquorice from China, cubeb pepper from Java, savory from France, fennel from the Mediterranean, iris from Italy, cinnamon from Sri Lanka, violets from France, almonds from Spain, cassia from Indochina, angelica from Germany, grains of paradise from West Africa, cumin from Holland, nutmeg from India, lemon rind from Spain, star anise from France.
Distillation: Our wheat base—the finest wheat from the Beauce region of France—is distilled three times in a column still before being introduced to the 19 botanicals. To capture the botanicals freshness, the fusion is not allowed to steep—it is distilled immediately, for a fourth time.
Tell us why you think your gin stands apart from all the others: Citadelle Gin Reserve is the only Gin in the world aged for 6 months in old Cognac casks. After aging, the complexity and aromatics of Citadelle Gin are melted with a round vanilla aroma imparted from oak tannins. Most high esters are also evaporated, leaving a rounder mouth feel.
Any other idiosyncrasies that you'd like to tell us about? Citadelle Gin Reserve is released as an expression of what Gin used to taste like when it was stored in oak barrels, before plastics and other stainless steel tanks were invented.
History: We did research on how Gins were stored in the 17th century. We discovered that the only containers that were used to store the spirit before it was bottled were oak casks. We found this information fascinating as our cellar master knows very well what old Cognac casks can bring to a quality distillate that shows complexity and aromatic richness.
We decided to start the experiment about 1 year ago and age Citadelle Gin for 6 months in old Cognac casks from our cellars. The result is, needless to say, not common. However, it is absolutely delicious and we decided to release this cask selection of Citadelle Gin as an expression of an ancient style of Gin, made from the infusion of 19 botanicals and aged in Grande Champagne old Cognac casks.
Tasting Notes from the Citadelle Cellar Master: After aging, the complexity and aromatics of Citadelle Gin are finely melted with a round vanilla aroma imparted from soft oak tannins. Most high esters are also evaporated, leaving a rounder mouth feel.
Awards: Patterson's *Tasting Panel*, October 2008: 94 Points. *F. Paul Pacult's Spirit Journal:* Four Stars.

Nothing Was as Efficacious As Gin

"The Goelets had [a maid] named Jane Smith who insisted on cleaning the windows of her own room. For this purpose, she maintained, nothing was as efficacious as gin to give the proper brightness and clearness. The Goelet children were hugely entertained by seeing Jane slyly gulp down some gin and then breathe on the window. Not a drop of the precious liquor ever found its way to the glass but in this roundabout way." *In the Golden Nineties*, Henry Collins Brown, 1928.

Damrak Amsterdam Original Gin, 41.8% abv
www.damrakgin.nl

Style: A gin based on a Dutch recipe with a less pronounced juniper flavour, thus favouring more citrus flavours.

Country of Origin: Holland

Available in: USA (California, Oregon, and Washington states as of April, 2009)

Botanicals: juniper berry, coriander, lemon peel, orange peel, aniseed, cinnamon, honeysuckle (the rest is the master distiller's secret).

Distillation: Five different distillations from five different pot stills are all brought together with the botanicals, allowed to rest (marry) for over two weeks after which it is filtered and bottled.

Tell us why you think your gin stands apart from all the others: A low juniper intense, citrus dominant Gin recipe from the 1700s created by Lucas Bols, a Dutch distilling company famous for the production of genevers and liqueurs since 1575, perfect for classic and citrus-based cocktails.

Any other idiosyncrasies that you'd like to tell us about? The Master Distiller, beginning with exotic fruits, berries and spices in their natural state (never from extract), created Damrak Amsterdam Original Gin from a recipe that is quite possibly one of the oldest gin recipes in the world. With a trace of malt—attributing to its extraordinary smooth finish, Damrak Amsterdam Original Gin combines no less than 17 botanicals and is distilled five times for unparalleled clarity in a refreshing 83.6 proof spirit that is pure Dutch.

History: In 1575, a young distiller by the name of Lucas Bols began distilling spirits. Having learned the art of distillation Bols established a simple distillery in the countryside of Amsterdam. He used the exotic spices and herbs brought back to the Damrak (Amsterdam's "inner harbour") by the Dutch East India Company from Africa, Tahiti, Asia and the Caribbean to blend and distil his products. The Damrak became an important mooring place for merchant ships arriving from and departing to exotic ports of call around the world. Established as a centre of world trade, the city of Amsterdam flourished and expanded around the original distillery built by Lucas Bols.

Tasting notes from the Damrak Gin Company: Sweet candied citrus aromas with a spicy liquorice and a delicate juniper edge.

Death's Door Distilled Gin, 46% abv

www.deathsdoorspirits.com

Style: Technically London Dry, but has a sweet character like an Old Tom and a malty flavor like a Genever

Available in: United States (California, Illinois, Iowa, Indiana, Minnesota, Montana, New York, New Jersey, Wisconsin and Wyoming.)

Botanicals: A blend of wild Washington Island juniper and purchased organic juniper berries, organic coriander seed, organic fennel seed.

Distillation: Small batches (90 gallon pot still). Distilled spirits are made with Island Wheat, a special wheat grown only on Washington Island, Wisconsin. It is made into a beer mash and then distilled in at least three runs through the combination column-pot still, with botanicals extracted from a botanicals extractor between the second and third runs.

Tell us why you think your gin stands apart from all the others: Chef-created on Washington Island, WI, the Island Wheat imparts a smooth but sweet flavor that is enhanced by a beautiful nose of juniper, a spicy middle note of coriander and a delicious fennel finish. The gin mixes well in pre-prohibition cocktails, but is a good sipping gin as well. The botanical mix is very simple, so no crazy flavors or blends of twenty different flavors. Simple, smooth and exceptional.

Any other idiosyncrasies that you'd like to tell us about? We harvest the juniper berries on Washington Island, WI in the fall, and little did we know what a pain it would be. We are looking to hold a juniper harvesting weekend up on the Island the first week of November every year, so check our website for details. A once-in-a-lifetime opportunity to help harvest the botanicals for your gin!

History: Death's Door Distilled Gin has been available since June 2007. Inspired by the legendary "Death's Door" waterway between Washington Island and the Door County Peninsula, company founders began working with local farm families to restore commercial farming on Washington Island back in 2005. Wheat grown on the Island was exceptional and plentiful, so after many different products were explored, it was decided that distilled spirits would be the best way to show of the quality of the product, to tell the story of Washington Island, and to bring needed income back to farming families. Working with a small local distillery and a local chef, Death's Door Spirits developed a formulation for a gin that utilized ingredients that could be grown locally and reflected the tastes, styles and character of its origin.

KRAHN

GIN

DH Krahn Gin, 40% abv.
www.dhkrahn.com

Style: London Dry/American Dry

Country of Origin: United States

Available in: USA, Thailand, UK

Botanicals: Italian juniper berries, Moroccan coriander seed, Californian lemon peel, Californian orange peel, Californian grapefruit peel, Thai ginger.

Distillation: Distilled in a patent Stupfler alembic pot still. A multi—step maceration process extracts all of the botanical's essences and oils, imparting the flavors into the neutral spirits. Once the aromatics have been added, the spirit, loaded with flavor undergoes a single-pass distillation in order to preserve the precious essential oils and essences that were added in earlier stages. Once macerated and distilled, the batches rest in steel barrels for at least three months prior to bottling to develop the characteristic mellowness that further distinguishes DH Krahn Gin.

Tell us why you think your gin stands apart from all the others: DH Krahn Gin stands out as a gin that captures the balance between old-world, high proof, high spice London Dry gins, and new-world gins that the purist would have a hard time calling gin. This is truly a gin that the true gin drinker will appreciate yet will constantly have the non gin drinker saying "I didn't think I liked gin but I like this." As the Beverage Testing Institute so appropriately noted, DH Krahn is: "Deliciously flavorful, yet delicate."

Any other idiosyncrasies that you'd like to tell us about? Although appearance is secondary, DH Krahn Gin also distinguishes itself in the marketplace with its modern, minimalist design in a category that is filled with traditional, stodgy brands.

History: Scott Krahn, from western Canada, and David Hughes, from Long Island, started as teammates on the Cornell University hockey team, then became classmates, friends, and finally, business partners. After two years of passionate commitment to their vision, two years of meticulous research and development, two years of hard work, setbacks, and recoveries, they introduced DH Krahn Gin to the world.

Tasting Notes from the Beverage Tasting Institute: 94 points, Clear. Subtle citrus, banana custard, and mild botanical aromas. A soft, round entry leads to a super smooth, dryish light-to medium-bodied palate with delicate flavors of powdered sugar dusted lemon peels, talc, peppery spices, mild juniper, and light grassy botanicals. Finishes with a mineral, pepper, dried juniper and lemon blossom water notes. Deliciously flavorful, yet delicate.

Awards: 94 Points: Top Rated Gin of 2006: Beverage Testing Institute's International Review of Spirits.

NORTH SHORE DISTILLERY

Distiller's Gin No. 6, 45% abv

www.northshoredistillery.com/gin6.htm

Country of Origin: USA

Style: American Dry

Available: USA (Midwestern states and mail order to others)

Botanicals: Juniper, fresh lemon peel, cardamom, coriander, Ceylon cinnamon, anise seed, cubeb berries, orris root, angelica root, lavender.

Distillation: Botanicals are hand prepared, fresh for each batch. Some are macerated before distillation, while others are added at the time of distillation. Distillation is done on a 250-liter copper pot still with a specially designed head.

Tell us why you think your gin stands apart from all the others: It is smooth yet complex, and tastes like no other gin.

Awards: Gold Medal, 2008, Beverage Testing Institute, 95 points.

History of your brand: North Shore Distillery was established in 2004 by two people who are passionate about handcrafting spirits. We use a blend of old-world and modern methods to create truly original and delightful spirits. Everything is done in small batches, and much of the process is done by hand.

Tasting Notes from North Shore Distillery: Smooth, fresh juniper paired with a complex balance of citrus, spice and floral notes.

Tasting Notes from Beverage Testing Institute, 2008: "95 • North Shore Distillery Distiller's Gin No. 6 $27.99. Clear with a platinum cast. Vibrant aromas of fresh herbs and spices, piney juniper, and twisted lemon peels jump from the glass. A silky entry leads to a fruity-yet-dry medium-full body of bold cracked juniper berry, pink peppercorns, lemon curd, clove, and pastry frosting flavors. Finishes with a long interplay of resiny juniper, sweet citrus and brown spices. A superb gin that virtually bristles with fresh, 3-D flavors. Very impressive!"

The Name is not Martini

"There is a point at which the marriage of gin and vermouth is consummated. It varies little with the constituents, but for a gin with 94.4 proof and a harmonious vermouth it may be generalized at about 3.7 to one. And that is not the proper proportion, but the critical one; if you use less gin it is a marriage in name only and the name is not martini." *The Hour*, Bernard DeVoto, 1948.

Distiller's Gin No. 11, 45% abv
www.northshoredistillery.com/gin11.htm

Style: London Dry

Available in: USA (Midwestern states and mail order to others)

Botanicals: juniper, cardamom, coriander, cinnamon, cubeb berries, orris root, angelica root, anise seed.

Distillation: Botanicals are hand prepared, fresh for each batch. Some are macerated before distillation, while others are added at the time of distillation. Distillation is done on a 250-liter copper pot still with a specially designed head.

Tell us why you think your gin stands apart from all the others: It is rich, smooth and crisp, with rich juniper and spice notes.

Any other idiosyncrasies that you'd like to tell us about? We made this gin in response to feedback on our Distiller's Gin No. 6 from old-school gin drinkers who did not like the floral and citrus notes, and preferred a drier, crisper finish.

History: North Shore Distillery was established in 2005 by two people who are passionate about handcrafting spirits. We use a blend of old-world and modern methods to create truly original and delightful spirits. Everything is done in small batches, and much of the process is done by hand.

Tasting Notes from North Shore Distillery: "Rich and smooth, with abundant fresh juniper and spice undertones. A more traditional gin, with a dry, crisp finish."

Tasting Notes from Beverage Tasting Institute, 2008: "94 • North Shore Distillery Distiller's Gin No. 11 $32.99. Clear. Dense, compacted aromas of honeycomb, lime soufflé, peppery juniper, and sweet spices. A soft, silky entry leads to a fruity medium-full of citrus custard pasty, pink peppercorns, fresh herbs, and honeyed juniper berries. Finishes with an long interplay of flavor with a touch of eucalyptus and minerals. A lovely, deeply flavorful, and elegantly styled gin that will be sensational in vintage cocktails."

Awards: Gold Medal, 2008, Beverage Testing Institute, 94 points.

Dry Fly Washington Dry Gin, 40% abv
www.dryflydistilling.com

Style: Washington State Gin

Country of Origin: USA

Available in: Dry Fly Washington Dry Gin is available widely throughout the US and Western Canada.

Botanicals: juniper (Oregon), Fuji apple (Washington), coriander (Washington), hops (Washington), lavender (Washington), mint (Washington). All of our botanicals are organic.

Distillation: Distilled from a wheat base made within the distillery. No purchased neutral grain spirit used in any of our production. The gin is distilled once through the complete botanical deck.

Tell us why you think your gin stands apart from all the others: We use unique botanicals, and we are one of a very few producers who make their own spirit base.

Any other idiosyncrasies that you'd like to tell us about? The product changes as it gets colder—different botanicals come to the front. It's a softer, kinder, gentler gin. It would have been easy to make a gin like most others, but the guys at Dry Fly had their own plan. They wanted to do it differently. They wanted to appeal to gin lovers and non gin lovers alike—people looking for something special.

History: First distilled in September 2007. Currently (early 2007) 100% of production is sold.

The Female in the Faded Feathers

The two old washerwomen, who are seated on the little bench to the left of the bar, are rather overcome by the head-dresses and haughty demeanour of the young ladies who officiate. They receive their half-quartern of gin and peppermint, with considerable deference, prefacing a request for 'one of them soft biscuits,' with a 'Jist be good enough, ma'am.' They are quite astonished at the impudent air of the young fellow in a brown coat and bright buttons, who, ushering in his two companions, and walking up to the bar in as careless a manner as if he had been used to green and gold ornaments all his life, winks at one of the young ladies with singular coolness, and calls for a 'kervorten and a three-out-glass,' just as if the place were his own. 'Gin for you, sir?' says the young lady when she has drawn it: carefully looking every way but the right one, to show that the wink had no effect upon her. 'For me, Mary, my dear,' replies the gentleman in brown. 'My name an't Mary as it happens,' says the young girl, rather relaxing as she delivers the change. 'Well, if it an't, it ought to be,' responds the irresistible one; 'all the Marys as ever I see, was handsome gals.' Here the young lady, not precisely remembering how blushes are managed in such cases, abruptly ends the flirtation by addressing the female in the faded feathers . . ." *Sketches by Boz* by Charles Dickens, 1836.

Gordon's Original London Dry Gin, 37.5% abv, and 40% abv
www.gordons-gin.co.uk

Style: London Dry

Country of Origin @ 37.5% abv: Great Britain

Country of Origin @ 40% abv for USA market: USA

Note: Gordon's gin is produced at several locations following the GB production method, at both 37.5 and 40% abv.

Available in: Gordon's gin is available in many countries throughout the world, and the packaging, and sometimes the proof, differs from country to country.

Botanicals Used: Juniper, Coriander & Angelica Root. The rest are top secret.

Distillation: Confidential information

Tell us why you think your gin stands apart from all the others: Gordon's Gin is the definitive gin and has been the most popular international gin for many years. Due to its high juniper quality and content, it produces an unrivalled G&T, which is how over 90% of gin is drunk.

Any other idiosyncrasies that you'd like to tell us about? When it was first exported Australians paid for it in gold dust. The green bottle was introduced in 1903 as it was the only sort that could be produced to the necessary quantity. Gordon's is ready when, and only when, the Master Distiller says so—something he still decides by nosing the liquid personally. In GB alone Gordon's has 15 million regular consumers. It is the most popular international gin in the world.

History: Alexander Gordon was one of the first to pioneer the distillation of fine quality gin. In 1769 he founded his distilling business in the Southwark area of London and began perfecting his own brand using only the finest natural botanical ingredients to create the flavour that he desired.

Gordon's success continued in to the twentieth century and in 1903 the distinctive square faced, green bottle for the home market was introduced. In 1925 Gordon's Gin was awarded its first Royal Warrant by King George V. The years 1941 and 1952 saw Gordon's receive two more Royal Warrants from HM King George VI and HM Queen Elizabeth II respectively. Gordon's continues to be the world's most popular international gin.

Awards: We have also won multiple awards for our flavour including a Bronze in the 1996 International Wine & Spirit Awards and a Gold at the same event in 1995. The brand has also won Gold, Grand Gold and Gold (Trophy) at the Monde Selection.

A Very Vivacious Woman

"Every night in the bar we met this very vivacious woman who drank pink gin. When she got drunk all she would ever say was 'who are you, won't you give us a glimmer?' I just loved the way she said it so we became the glimmer twins." Keith Richards. *Keith Richards: The Biography* by Victor Bockris, 2003.

Greenall's Original London Dry Gin, 40% abv
www.gjgreenall.co.uk

Style: London Dry Gin

Country of Origin: United Kingdom

Available in: UK and also extensive distribution in Europe, Asia, and is currently (April, 2009) spreading into the Americas.

Botanicals: Juniper is at the heart of Greenall's Gin, which is enhanced and enlivened by seven additional quality botanicals.

Distillation: The production of Greenall's is virtually the same today as over 200 years ago, using a neutral spirit, pure local water, and copper pot stills to create a classic standard.

Tell us why you think your gin stands apart from all the others: Greenall's is a traditional in its style, and it makes a great Gin & Tonic. It's a no-nonsense gin and doesn't try to be anything more than a good traditional London Dry Gin, which is the highest classification for this drinks category.

History: G & J Greenall has been distilling superior quality gin since 1761, and is considered to be one of the oldest English Gin distilleries. Located in the lush rolling hills of the North West Country, Cheshire countryside, in the heart of the small town of Warrington, G & J Greenall's distillery has been crafting exceptional spirits, starting when Thomas Dakin began producing quality London Dry Gin in 1761. In 1786, Thomas Greenall and his sons partnered with Dakin to expand their family's spirit and beer business from St. Helens Brewery. Now, for over 247 years, the family has overseen the meticulous production of spirits for customers worldwide alongside their well-regarded Greenall's London Dry Gin. Disaster struck on October 15, 2005 when a massive fire destroyed the distillery almost entirely, but like a phoenix rising from the ashes, Greenall's Distillery was operational only six days later. Our brand new distillery features the beautifully engineered original copper stills (saved from the fire) coupled with modern technology to enhance all production.

Tasting Notes from the Good Folk at Greenall's Gin: Greenall's Gin has a silky smooth opening develops into dry rounded juniper notes and exhibits fresh yet mature citrus flavours. Greenall's Gin finishes with woody, earthy tones and warm spices, and a medium to long length—perfect for a classic Gin & Tonic.

Notes of a Recent Ramble

"The gin palaces of London are mentioned as objects of painful curiosity. I was more eager to see them than I was to gaze upon the stately walls of old Buckingham, or wander through the halls of Windsor Castle." *Europa; or, Notes of a Recent Ramble through England, France, Italy and Switzerland* by Daniel Clarke Eddy, 1852.

G'Vine Floraison Gin, 40% abv
www.g-vine.com

Style: Distilled Gin

Country of Origin: France

Note: G'Vine gins embody the vine's life cycle and illustrate the evolution of the grape through its various stages. G'Vine Floraison (*floraison* is French for "blossoming") captures the spirit of the blooming vine flower and the warmth of the summer arrival. G'Vine Floraison is smooth, vibrantly floral, warmly spicy.

Available in: US, France, England, Scotland, Ireland, Germany, Spain, Portugal, Italy, Greece, Cyprus, Denmark, Finland, Norway, Sweden, Iceland, Switzerland, Belgium, Luxemburg, Netherlands, Czech Republic, Slovakia, Japan, Puerto Rico.

Botanicals: 10 fresh whole-fruit botanicals : juniper berries, nutmeg, cubeb berries, liquorice, ginger roots, cassia bark, coriander, lime, green cardamom, as well as the unique and rare vine flowers.

Distillation: Unlike the traditional grain spirit associated with Gin production, G'Vine is made from grape spirit, much smoother and more suave with a heady body and a feeling new to the palate. The Ugni Blanc grape is turned into wine and distilled four times in a column still producing a neutral grape spirit over 96.4% abv—192.8-proof. It is the canvas on which [our distiller] prints the colors that make G'vine unique. The rare green grape flower, which blossoms only for a few days in June before maturing into a grape berry, is immediately handpicked to preserve its spellbinding fragrance. The flower is carefully macerated in the neutral grape spirit during several days to obtain the best floral essence and then distilled in a small Florentine pot still. The other nine botanicals are macerated in the neutral grape spirit over a two to five days process by family and then distilled in small copper liquor stills to insure the best quintessence. Finally, the vine flowers infusion, the botanicals distillates and more neutral grape spirit are blended together in perfect proportion and distilled in a bespoke copper pot still one last time for an absolute marriage. [Her name is Lily Fleur, and you can see her on the following page.]

Please meet Lily Fleur, the uniquely engraved exclusive
pot still dedicated to G'Vine's delicate final step.

G'Vine Floraison gin, continued

Tell us why you think your gin stands apart from all the others: Redefining and taking further the frontiers of the gin segment, G'Vine Floraison erases the preconceived ideas and changes the perception of this centuries-old spirit: it marries the ancestral grape distillation know-how and infusions practices with the groundbreaking introduction of the rare vine flower, offering a unique experience to gin afficionados and opening up the gin category to non gin drinkers.

Any other idiosyncrasies that you'd like to tell us about? The name G'Vine is the perfect visual and phonetic illustration of its origin and inspiration : one can read gin, *vigne* in French (meaning vineyard) and vine in English.

History: G'Vine is crafted by Jean Sébastien Robicquet, lead oenologist and master distiller based in the Cognac region of France by marrying local centuries-old best distillation and innovative infusion practices with the introduction of the rare grape flower.

Inspired by his wine roots, Jean Sébastien Robicquet created a unique gin that breaks away from the traditional juniper-based London dry and initiates a new "GIN-ERATION," based on the gin making traditions, dating back in 1269, when Gin was made with grape spirits.

Tasting notes from G'Vine Gin: Nose : delicate, sweet and floral, with a spicy warmth; Palate : smooth, subtle, round, grassy with flowers and spice. Floral taste of the vine flower very upfront, with juniper, cardamom and ginger following along; Finish : brings back the floral taste again, and is very long, dry and clean.

The subtle, aromatic vine flower together with the grape spirit soften the traditional juniper taste and make it a well balanced, full bodied and soft gin, appreciated by gin connoisseurs as well as non gin-drinkers.

Tasting notes from Gary Regan, *San Francisco Chronicle***:** "If you want to taste a very unusual, highly recommendable gin, look for G'Vine . . . it's the green grape flowers that give it its exceedingly intriguing, incredible seductive, floral notes. Was that gushy enough ? I like this gin"

Awards: International Review of Spirits, Beverage Tasting Institute, 2007 & 2008: Gold medal, 94 pts, "Exceptional." *F. Paul Pacult's Spirit Journal:* **** [four stars] Highly Recommended. *Wine Enthusiast:* Superb (90-95) Highly Recommended. **Drinks International Gin Challenge, 2008:** Silver medal, Best distilled gin. **San Francisco World Spirits Competition:** Silver Medal.

G'Vine Nouaison Gin, 43.9% abv

www.g-vine.com

Style: Distilled Gin

Country of Origin: France

Note: G'Vine gins embody the vine's life cycle and illustrate the evolution of the grape through its various stages : after the blossoming period in June comes the setting (*nouaison* in French), i.e. the birth of the berry. The fecundated vine flower forms a tiny green berry that fixes itself onto the stem. G'Vine Nouaison illustrates the vibrant concentration of energy, intensity and spiciness created during this period. G'Vine Nouaison is silky, intensely spicy, subtly floral.

Available in: Germany, France, UK and US.

Botanicals: Ten fresh whole-fruit botanicals : juniper berries, nutmeg, cubeb berries, liquorice, ginger roots, cassia bark, coriander, lime, green cardamom, as well as the unique and rare vine flowers.

Distillation: Unlike the traditional grain spirit associated with Gin production, G'Vine is made from grape spirit, much smoother and more suave with a heady body and a feeling new to the palate. The Ugni Blanc grape is turned into wine and distilled four times in a column still producing a neutral grape spirit over 96.4% abv—192.8-proof. It is the canvas on which [our distiller] prints the colors that make G'vine unique. The rare green grape flower, which blossoms only for a few days in June before maturing into a grape berry, is immediately handpicked to preserve its spellbinding fragrance. The flower is carefully macerated in the neutral grape spirit during several days to obtain the best floral essence and then distilled in a small Florentine pot still. The other nine botanicals are macerated in the neutral grape spirit over a two to five day process by family and then distilled in small copper liquor stills to insure the best quintessence. Finally, the vine flowers infusion, the botanicals distillates and more neutral grape spirit are blended together in perfect proportion and distilled in a bespoken copper pot still one last time for an absolute marriage.

G'Vine Nouaison Gin, Continued

Tell us why you think your gin stands apart from all the others: While most gins are made from starches like wheat, G'Vine Nouaison marries the ancestral grape distillation know-how and infusions practices with the groundbreaking introduction of the rare vine flower, offering an absolute alternative to the classic London Dry gin.

Any other idiosyncrasies that you'd like to tell us about? Each G'Vine bottle (either Floraison or Nouaison) is individually coded. A typical code looks like this: [07 A 105] 07 refers to the year of the vine flower's harvest; A is the Blending Batch, and 105 is the number of the bottle.

History: After the success of the groundbreaking Floraison, revealing a new "generation" of spirits and creating real enthusiasm for it within hedonistic consumers who were non-gin drinkers, we wanted to create a more traditional gin by elevating the alcohol level, toning down the flower expression and increasing the juniper and spices in order to satisfy the demand for a more masculine and powerful gin. Following the life cycle of the vine we created a new expression of G'vine stronger and spicier, just like the green grape setting itself onto the stem and full of energy before entering the maturation stage.

Tasting notes from G'Vine Gin: Nose : Round and warm, acutely botanical, viny, woodsy, juniper and cassia bark; Palate : Fruity and rich. Intense and complex aromas of cinnamon bark, baked citrus, floral juniper follow through on a round, silky, zesty and robust entry. Very sharp and with a solid character.; Finish : powerful interplay of juniper, herb, wood and flowery notes, fruity ripe, citrusy. G'Vine Nouaison amplifies the aromas of the spices, yet retains the sensual and silky grape base as well as the subtle floral note.

Tasting notes from Paul Pacult, *F. Paul Pacult's Spirits Journal* : "An evolving gem in the new, less juniper driven style of gin. Many gin traditionalists despise anything but London Dry, but I urge that you try this intriguing new entry. If I bestowed half stars, I'd rate Nouaison 4 1/2. It's very good and different. A gin to keep an eye on and, more importantly, buy."

Awards: 2008 International Review of Spirits, Beverage Tasting Institute: Platinum medal, 96 pts, "Superlative." *F. Paul Pacult's Spirit Journal*: **** [four stars] Highly Recommended. **Drinks International Gin Challenge, 2008:** Trophy Winner, Gold medal, Best distilled gin.

Hamptons Gin, 47.5% abv
www.hamptonsvodka.com

Style: London Dry
Country of Origin: USA
Available in: USA and Canada
Botanicals: juniper berries, orange peel, lemon peel, coriander
Distillation: Hamptons Gin is yellow corn based, it is a four-columns distillation process with a final bath of charcoal and ash.
Tell us why you think your gin stands apart from all the others: Hamptons Gin has a very smooth citrusy, fresh sweet flavor and a low juniper taste. There is no harsh aftertaste as the smoothness of the alcohol and the sweetness of the yellow corn lingers on the palate.
Any other idiosyncrasies that you'd like to tell us about? No, it's just a great gin.
History: We introduced Hamptons Gin in 2001 as a companion to our Double Gold Medal Winner, Hamptons Vodka,. It has been very well received by gin enthusiasts and industry connoisseurs, and it has garnered many industry awards and ratings.
Tasting Notes from Anthony Dias Blue: "A soft texture and smooth understated flavor"; **Tasting Notes from *The Wine Enthusiast:*** "The nose is light and fruity, with juniper nodes lurking in the backdrop, the body is big and the palate follows the nose . . . the finish is long and very warm"; **Tasting Notes *from Richard Carleton-Hacker,* Playboy:** "The corn combined with a hint of orange and lemons, gives this quadrupled distilled gin a fresh sweet flavor that's ideal on the rocks"
Awards: San Francisco World Spirits Competition, 2006: Bronze Medal. **American Taste Award of Excellence:** Twice winner (2001 and 2002). *The Wine Enthusiast Magazine:* Rated 90

Hayman's Gin, 40% abv
www.haymansgin.com

Style: London Dry
Country of Origin: England
Available in: UK and across the rest of Europe
Botanicals: Ten botanicals including juniper, citrus, coriander and angelica
Distillation: The botanicals are steeped for 24 hours before being distilled in a traditional pot still
Tell us why you think your gin stands apart from all the others: Although the recipe consists of 10 botanicals it is Christopher Hayman's belief that the careful and consistent balance of juniper, coriander, orange and lemon peel are vital in crafting a classic style of London Dry Gin to make the perfect Gin and Tonic and Gin Martini.
Any other idiosyncrasies that you'd like to tell us about? The Hayman family are the longest serving gin distillers in the UK.
History: Hayman's gin marks Christopher Hayman's 40 years involvement in the distillation of gin. Having joined James Burrough, Ltd., his family business, in 1969 he was responsible for the distillation and production of Beefeater Gin until the business was sold in the late 1980's. Over the last 20 years Christopher has been involved in a number of new gins and has now decided to launch his own.
Tasting Notes from Hayman Distillers: Fresh Citrus aromas on the nose along with Juniper notes and a wonderfully balanced, crisp yet delicate finish.

HENDRICK'S®

DISTILLED *and* BOTTLED IN SCOTLAND

GIN

Hendrick's Gin, 44% abv and 41.4% abv

www.hendricksgin.com

Style: Hendrick's could be described as a "New Age" gin because of its unique flavor profile, or, by default, it's a London Dry gin.

At 44% abv Hendrick's is available in: U.S.A. and Spain

At 41.4% abv Hendrick's is available in: U.K., and globally, apart from the U.S.A. and Spain

Country of Origin: Scotland

Botanicals: Juniper Berries, Cubeb berries, angelica root, orris root, lemon peel, orange peel, elderflower, chamomile, meadowsweet, rose petal, cucumber, caraway seed, coriander

Distillation: Copper pot distillation in Carter Head and Bennett stills (both are copper pot stills). The botanical basket method is used in the Carter Head still (where botanicals are hung in a basket in the neck of the still and introduced to the vapors of the spirit as they rise from the base of the still), and steeping method is employed in the Bennett still—the botanicals are steeped in the base spirit before it is re-distilled. The gin is then reduced to bottle proof with local Scottish spring water from the Penwhapple reservoir in Ayrshire.

Tell us why you think your gin stands apart from all the others: Our recipe of unusual botanicals makes Hendrick's stand apart from other gins, and our unique combination of styles of distillation, introducing the botanicals to the spirit in two ways, results in a delicate, fragrant, beautiful nose (due to the Carter Head still) and a full balanced imprint of flavor (attributed to the Bennett still). Most gins use one or the other, Hendrick's uses both to get the best of both worlds. Also, the excellence in copper pot distillation by William Grant & Sons (world class distillers since 1886) gives Hendrick's a significantly smooth finish, great structure and silky mouth feel. We also use unusual marketing techniques and intellectual humor throughout our campaigns, and we promote an attitude that gin can be about more than just juniper. Hendrick's has a flavor profile that opens the door to gin for many "scared" people.

History: 1886: William Grant starts building the Glenfiddich distillery and founds the family company; 1960: The Carter Head and Bennett stills are purchased at Ludlow's auction house in London by Charles Gordon, Chairman of WGS and descendant of William Grant; 1999: Hendrick's Gin is first distilled; 2000: Hendrick's Gin is launched in the USA; 2003: Hendrick's Gin launched in the UK and Spain; 2003: *The Wall Street Journal* declares Hendrick's as the World's Best Gin; 2007: David Wondrich declares Hendrick's as the most influential gin in the industry over the last 25 years (*Wine and Spirits Magazine*); 2008: Hendrick's Bartender Croquet Tournament arrives in New York !

Tasting Notes from Hendrick's Gin Brand Ambassadors Jim Ryan and Charlotte Voisey: On the nose Hendrick's is delicate and floral with aromas of fresh-cut summer grass, bright candy citrus, white to green pepper and light spice. On the palate: clean, fresh cucumber notes with a wisp of juniper spice, springtime flowers, full citrus and earthy notes which finally seep away to a triumphantly smooth finish.

Awards: San Francisco Spirits Competition, 2000: Gold Medal.

The Curious Case of a Dancing Hendrick's Gin Flashback

In the States, whenever Hendrick's gin is mentioned among the cocktail geeks with whom I tend to hang, Charlotte Voisey's name is always uttered within seconds, and when Charlotte's name comes up, smiles tend to leap to every face in the room. She's a charmer, is Charlotte Voisey, and as the official mixologist for Hendrick's gin in the U.S.A., she's garnered more attention for this most unusual spirit than you can shake a stick at. It's hard to believe that the girl was raised in Essex . . .

Here's a nice shot of the Luverly Charlotte Voisey at the Hendrick's Croquet Tourney, New York, 2009, with yours truly.

I first met Charlotte at an event at All Star Lanes, a posh bowling alley and nightclub in London (how many sentences have you seen that contain the phrase "posh bowling alley "?), right before she moved to New York. It was June, 2006. I told her to look me up once she got settled in the States. Little did I know that, less than three months later, I'd be dancing with Charlotte in a shallow paddling pool in Lima, Peru. We were both on a trip to discover the delights of Peruvian Pisco brandy, and as fellow Brits, we're drawn to water, so the sight of a paddling pool in the middle of a restaurant was irresistible to us. A wet waltz was most definitely called for. I've no idea where this urge to get wet comes from, but ask anyone from the UK about it—I swear it's part of our national DNA.

Earlier that same day, about halfway through lunch, nature had tapped me on the shoulder and I'd made my way to what turned out to be the most beautiful men's room I ever did see. The urinal was truly spectacular (there's another phrase that one seldom sees). It was a long trough made of highly polished stainless steel, and beautiful pebbles had been place in the bottom of it, giving the user of the urinal an impression, of sorts, that he was peeing into a stream. Well, something like that. As I stepped back from the trough on that oh-so-memorable day, I looked around for a sink in order to comply with the sign on the wall, even though I didn't actually work at the joint. I was surprised when I couldn't find a sink in the room, but on the wall opposite the trough I spotted a row of porcelain urinals. How curious, I thought. Why do they have two kinds of urinals? But the thought didn't last long. I looked back at the stainless steel urinal and, for the first time, I noticed that it was fitted with taps. Just like a sink . . . I went back to the dining room to dance with Charlotte.

Recently, on May 12, 2009 to be exact, Ms. Voisey was indirectly responsible for another memorable dance. It was an opportunity that I couldn't pass up. Hendrick's gin, you see, holds croquet tournaments for bartenders. Don't ask why. Even the good folk at Hendrick's aren't quite sure why they do it, but do it they do, and when these events occur, I usually join in. I arrived at this particular tourney quite early, and I was delighted to be greeted by the Statue of Liberty.

There are two women in New York City who pose as the Statue of Liberty, and I knew one of them back in the early nineties when I worked at the North Star Pub in the South Street Seaport. Her name was Jennifer Stewart. She'd pose for photographs with tourists and you could hire her to be at events and the like. Jen would sometimes come into the pub before we opened for lunch, and it was pretty amusing to see her at the bar sipping a soda with her crown sitting beside her drink. Jennifer wasn't the woman at the Hendrick's event though. This Statue of Liberty, when she's not holding her torch up high, is called Penny England. And she was gracious enough to accept my offer of a dance. That's right—I danced with the Statue of Liberty.

Be aware, then, that if you're ever lucky enough to meet Ms. Voisey, there's a good chance that you'll find yourself dancing, or getting your feet wet, or both, and if neither of those things happen, I think I can guarantee that you'll at least experience some fabulous Hendrick's cocktails. Ms. Voisey is a very curious woman.

Photograph by the one and only Jack Robertiello.

A Perfect Saturnalia of Cooks and Charwomen

"All August and September there is a perfect saturnalia of cooks and charwomen and their friends aping their mistresses—rather a loud imitation—playing croquet, giving tea and gin parties, dancing, screaming, shouting, laughing . . ." *London Characters: Illustrations of the Humour, Pathos, and Peculiarities of London Life* by Henry Mayhew, 1881.

TEN ABSOLUTES OF
CROQUET *ETIQUETTE*
How Not to Behave Like a Barbarian on the Lawn

THE SUMMER IS UPON US ONCE AGAIN, and with it another thrilling season of tension-filled croquet competition. As the sport's biggest players return from spring training, it seems a better time than any to review the rules of etiquette which gracefully govern proceedings on the lawn.

Croquet players are required to wear all white apparel unless otherwise approved by the tournament director. Polka-dots are simply out of the question.

Practicing is absolutely prohibited prior to a match lest players become accustomed to the lay of the lawn. Warm up swings are allowed in the bar area.

At no point may a player receive advice from anyone, be they partner, spectator or referee. Aluminium mallets are banned. All mallets must be hewn from wood.

No matter how hotly contested a point may be, players are prohibited from bashing each other with their mallets, unless of course they were struck first.

A player must stand off the court when the adversary is playing.

Golf carts are simply not allowed on the croquet lawn. For that matter, there are no mallet caddies as well.

Players must play with expediency. However, cocktail delays are acceptable.

In order to summon a referee, the mallet is held head up above the player's head. In order to call an 'umpire,' or assistant referee, the mallet is held horizontally above the head.

The winner offers to buy a round of Hendrick's cocktails upon the completion of the game.

Lifting a Gin Rickey

"They can say what they like about the Hawaiian Islands . . . in spite of the pleasing winds and the beautiful clear weather, things are a bit too balmy for continued physical exertion. Lifting a gin rickey is good enough exercise, and if you lift them often enough, out at Sans Souci, for instance, you can imagine anything you like about the Islands." *Under Sail* by Felix Riesenberg, 1918.

Jackelope Gin, 40% abv

www.peachstreetdistillers.com

Style: Colorado Dry

Country of Origin: USA

Available: Throughout Colorado with growing distribution in other markets. As of April 2009 we have limited distribution in New Hampshire (we ship direct to the customer), California, Kansas, and by special request in Oregon.

Botanicals: Colorado juniper berries, coriander seed, licorice root, cassia bark, angelica root, orris root, lemon peel, lime peel

Distillation: We first grind all of the botanicals by hand then we macerate them in neutral spirit then distill in a pot still creating a concentrated gin. Then the gin is blended with a small amount of neutral spirit and proofed until the right balance is achieved.

Tell us why you think your gin stands apart from all the others: The fresh flavor of the botanicals stands out. The ratio of our botanicals gives our gin a balanced, unique flavor profile not typical with other gins.

History: Rarely seen and often misspelled, the Jackelope isn't Colorado's answer to the minotaur, nor is it some bogus animal like the snipe or the antelabbit. It's a real creature. They say a flask of whiskey set out at night will work for bait when hunting Jackelope, but it doesn't (we've tried . . . many times), and why would it? It doesn't make any sense. The Jackelope live among Colorado's junipers—gin is the obvious answer. But we're not wasting this on Jackelopes, even if they do taste like lobster. It's far too fine a product; craft distilled in small batches using hand-picked Colorado juniper berries and seven other botanicals, we believe the Jackelope is the finest gin available. We think you'll agree.

Tasting Notes from Peach Street Distillers Fresh, balanced, and smooth.

The Great God Dependability

"The world became an insignificant turmoil underneath his feet, and he strolled . . . toward Madison, where at the Morrison bar they could mix the finest Tom Collins in the world . . . 'I'll drink all the Tom Collinses Jerry can mix—to the great god Dependability.'" *Everybody's Magazine*, 1922.

Juniper Green Organic London Dry Gin, 37.5% abv, 40% abv, and 43% abv

www.maisonjomere.com

Style: London Dry

At 37.5% abv, available in: UK, France, Germany, Belgium, Netherlands, Italy, Australia, New Zealand and Japan.

At 40% abv, available in: Thailand.

At 43% abv, available in: USA.

Botanicals: juniper, coriander, angelica root and savory—all certified organic.

Distillation: The organic botanicals are distilled into the organic neutral grain spirit at the Thames Distillery in London. The pot stills, known as Tom Thumb and Thumbelina, are the smallest stills in the U.K.

Tell us why you think your gin stands apart from all the others: The base of Juniper Green is bio-dynamically grown organic grain spirit that is not filtered in any way whatsoever. It is the purest spirit ever produced, making our gin the purest gin in the world. The botanicals are distilled into the spirit in two of the smallest stills in Europe with production of only 500 liters per day. The organic materials provide an incredibly fresh aroma and a zesty flavor, and the result is our Juniper Green Gin, a hand-crafted product.

History: Launched in the UK in October 1999 as the world's first Organic Gin, it is now sold in all UK national supermarket groups and widely in the independent organic health food market. In the USA, Juniper Green is available in over 20 states with fast-growing appeal. International distribution widens on a monthly basis and Juniper Green is now sold in at least 15 countries.

Awards

After Hours Magazine: 5 Stars. **Beverage Tasting Institute:** Gold Medal, Rating 91. Exceptional. **International Spirits Challenge 2003:** Gold Medal. *Food and Drink Magazine* 2004: Gold Medal. **Organic Drinks, 2004:** Gold Medal. **International Spirits Competition, 2002, 2004 & 2006:** Silver Medal (No Gold Awarded). **International Wine and Spirits Competition, 2001 & 2007:** Silver Medal (No Gold Awarded). **British Soil Association, 2002 and 2003:** Spirit of the Year. *Wine Enthusiast,* July 2003: 85-89 rating, Recommended. **Vinexpo 2003:** Gold Medal. **HRH Royal Warrant from Prince Charles: 2007.**

I Wish

"Nature has adapted me to preside over a rural Sunday-school, or a rustic temperance club, and I like not the affairs of state. I feel so stale. I wish I had a gin-cocktail." *Puck*, 1879.

Junipero Gin, 49.3% abv
http://www.anchorbrewing.com/about_us/anchordistilling.htm

Style: London Dry or Distilled Dry

Country of Origin: USA

Available in: USA (many states but not all). On a limited basis in: Canada, England, Holland, France, Spain, Germany, Switzerland, Finland, Sweden, Guam, Taiwan, Australia, New Zealand.

Botanicals: Proprietary

Distillation: All botanicals soaking "in the soup."

Tell us why you think your gin stands apart from all the others: A distinctive "backbone" of flavor and aroma good for martinis.

History: We were the first of the new gins—released on April 1, 1998.

Awards: San Francisco World Spirits Competition Double Golds for character and double Golds for packaging design.

Martin Miller's Gin, 40% abv
Martin Miller's Westbourne Strength Gin, 45.2% abv
http://www.martinmillersgin.com/

Style: London Dry Gin

At 40% abv, Martin Miller's is Available in: UK, Canada, USA, Spain, Italy, Australia

At 45.2% abv, Martin Miller's Westbourne Strength Gin is available in: UK, Canada, USA, Spain, Italy.

Botanicals: juniper, Florentine iris, cassia bark, licorice root, coriander, angelica, Seville orange peel, lemon peel, cinnamon, nutmeg, orris root

Distillation: Martin Miller's is created in the Rolls Royce of pot stills. Designed by John Dore & Company in 1903, this ancient copper pot still is named Angela. In this venerable grand dame of stills we steep our botanicals in small batches overnight before distillation. Taking only the heart of the distillate, Martin Miller's Gin is then shipped 1,500 miles to Iceland to be blended and bottled with the purest and softest water on earth. Filtered through lava, this is water that fell as rain hundreds of years ago. Extraordinarily pure, it adds the final touch of distinction to the gin, creating an unparalleled taste of freshness and smoothness without the "bite" of ordinary gins.

Tell us why you think your gin stands apart from all the others: Like a fine watchmaker, Martin has added one more 'complication' to his gin. To create a traditional gin, but with our distinctive, clear, bright citrus notes, we distil our earthy botanicals separately from the citrus peels.

Any other idiosyncrasies that you'd like to tell us about? Apart from the water? No. Martin Miller likes to say, "The only secret ingredient in my gin is our attention to detail."

History: The notion of creating an 'artisanal' gin arose over ten years ago at a dinner party in the Notting Hill hotel of English tastemaker Martin Miller. Martin, the author of the Miller's Antique Guides, and his friends, were experimenting with various gin concoctions and soon came to the opinion that none of the spirits on hand were worthy of their efforts. Thus the quest began to create a gin that matched his passion for classic indulgence; in fact, to do whatever it would take to create the quintessential gin. "This gin was really born of love, obsession, and some degree of madness," says Martin Miller. "At the time we never dreamt we would actually sell the stuff, so we spared no expense in its production. It puts us in a bit of a pickle now—though I can say, 'the only depressing thing about my gin is the price!'".

Miller's In-house Tasting Notes: Martin Miller's Gin, 40% abv: Appearance—Pure & Clear; Aroma—Sweet lemon peel and floral aromas; Flavor—A graceful entry leads to a satiny, medium to full bodied palate with intensely fruity citrus peel, mild juniper and exotic peppercorn notes; Finish—Finishes very smoothly with a long, citrus fade.

Martin Miller's Westbourne Strength Gin, 45.2% abv.; Appearance—Pure & Clear; Aroma—Sweet floral and citrus aromas with an herbaceous, juniper edge.; Flavor—Silky smooth in the mouth with a bright citrus character, spice and juniper notes.; Finish—Long, smooth, citrus fade.

Awards: San Francisco World Spirits Competition, 2006, 2007, and 2008: Martin Miller's Gin received Double Gold Medals on each of these consecutive years. **San Francisco World Spirits Competition, 2009:** Martin Miller's Westbourne Strength Gin was awarded a Gold Medal. **Beverage Testing Institute of Chicago, 2008:** Martin Miller's Westbourne Strength Gin was awarded a Platinum Medal.

Gladsome and Refreshing Qualities

The gin cocktail is known to have certain gladsome and refreshing qualities in those milder states of asthenia which follow a day's work and precede an evening meal. Dr. George T. Maxwell, of Jacksonville, Fla., however, in addition recommends the gin cocktail as closely approaching a specific in yellow fever." *American Homoeopathist*, 1890.

Nicholas Gin, 40% abv
www.nicholasgin.com

Style: American or New Western

Country of Origin: USA

Available in: USA

Botanicals: juniper, lavender, rose hips, hibiscus, coriander, fennel seed, cardamom, orange peel, lemon peel

Distillation: The botanicals are macerated in the base spirit in a proprietary manner, each for a time based on the distiller's experience and judgment as to bring forth the desired flavor in the final spirit. The spirit is then distilled in a small batch pot still.

Tell us why you think your gin stands apart from all the others: "I use nontraditional botanicals such as lavender, rose hips, and hibiscus in nontraditional concentrations. The largest concentration is the juniper berry and right behind it we add lavender. The choice of lavender was borrowed from my experience in cooking. Lavender is a bridge between the sweet or floral to the savory herbs and botanicals such as the juniper to create a balanced flavor profile. The result is a gin that tastes like no other." Nick Carbone, Proprietor/Distiller, Fat Dog Spirits.

Any other idiosyncrasies that you'd like to tell us about? "I am a micro-distiller and believe in small batch distillation which allows me to maintain more control over the spirit that is collected and therefore the flavor. I don't use dried citrus. I use fresh Florida-grown citrus which imparts a more intense flavor." Nick Carbone.

History of your brand: The first bottle of Nicholas gin was born on April 24, 2009, at 10 p.m. Not a very long history.

Tasting Notes from Nick Carbone: I taste juniper on the front followed by the very distinct lavender and then crisp coriander, cardamom and citrus.

Awards: Not yet.

No. 209 Gin, 46% abv.

www.distillery209.com

Style: We just go by Gin. We are trying to clearly differentiate ourselves from the London Dry style

Country of Origin: USA

Available in: USA, Canada, The United Kingdom, and Italy

Botanicals: Predominant botanicals include juniper berries, coriander seed, angelica root, cassia bark, cardamom and bergamot orange peel.

Distillation: No. 209 Gin is distilled in a copper pot still custom built to our specifications in Scotland. The botanicals soak overnight in a neutral spirit which is blended in the still with purified water from the Sierra Nevada mountains. The next morning, I start to heat the pot still with steam that surrounds the pot, but does not go in, thereby creating a very gentle and uniform heating process. I discard the low quality heads and tails and keep only the small heart of the distillation for No. 209 Gin. I allow the gin to rest several days before bottling, using purified Sierra Nevada water to bring the gin down to bottle strength.

Tell us why you think your gin stands apart from all the others:

Unlike London Dry gins with a big juniper note, No. 209 gin is softer on the juniper and has accentuated citrus and spice notes. The bergamot adds a zesty floral nose. These characteristics make No. 209 gin perfect for both traditional gin cocktails and the newer, more exotic creations by mixologists.

Any other idiosyncrasies that you'd like to tell us about?

Hand sorting and husking of cardamom pods. Grinding the cassia bark freshly before each distillation. Bergamot peels grown and processed to our specifications in Calabria, Italy.

History: No.209 refers to the award winning historic distillery dating from 1882 located on Edge Hill winery in St. Helena CA. It was the 209th distillery registered in the US. Mr. Leslie Rudd is the current owner of Edge Hill winery and his daughter now carries on his vision for Distillery No. 209 as the current owner and operator.

Distiller's Tasting Notes: No. 209 gin is a new style of gin that features softer juniper flavors and more pronounced citrus and spice characteristics. At full strength the nose and palate note the citrus, floral and juniper as being predominant, with an undertone of spice. When allowed to open up with air or especially water, the spirit blossoms. First notes will again be citrus highlighted with the floral notes of bergamot. As the gin passes mid-palate, the mint-like cardamom and juniper really shine through. Toward the end of your palate, the rose-like coriander predominates. The gin finishes on a welcoming cinnamon-cassia note.

A Fine Cocktail

"We can no more build a fine cocktail on a dollar gin than Whistler could paint his mother's portrait with barn paint." *The Gentleman's Companion* by Charles H. Baker, Jr. Crown Publishers, 1946.

Port of Barcelona Gin, aka Port of Dragons Gin (in Spain & UK), 44% abv.

www.barcelonagin.com

Style: Contemporary, Adventurous

Country of Origin: Spain (Distiller is a U.S. native who set up the distillery in Spain in order to have access to locally sourced top grade botanicals.)

Available in: U.S., Spain (Port of Dragons in Spain and, hopefully in the U.K. by the time this book goes to press)

Botanicals: wild juniper, iris flower root, star anise, coriander seeds, orange peels, sweet almonds, hazelnuts, lemon zest, chebub seeds, black cardamom, orris root, ginger root, nutmeg, cubeb root.

Distillation: Port of Barcelona Gin is three times distilled in alembic pot stills that are engineered specifically to capture a higher percentage of the essences of plant and botanical ingredients, creating a fuller-bodied and smoother gin. Using alembic stills, our gin is one of the first of its kind to bring the micro-distilled movement to the gin community. While standard column stills use steam heating systems and are geared toward mass production, Esmeralda's alembic stills use flame heat, require much more craftsmanship and give the distiller more control over the final product. The result is superior taste and quality over the column distillation method. The base is 100 percent malted barley, with wild juniper distilled in the head of still (very similar to the Carter-Head method but without the column) during the second distillation with 13 other botanicals distilled in the third and final distillation.

Tell us why you think your gin stands apart from all the others: The gin carries a smooth and rich body coupled with a hyper, complex flavor profile that spotlights the Juniper and coriander mixed with peppered orange and finishes long with creamy vanilla and floral notes. It is truly unique in comparison to any other gin on the market, yet it still holds on to the basic foundation of what is gin.

History: The Esmeralda Distillery, the makers of Obsello absinthe and Port of Barcelona Gin, is owned and operated by the distiller and his partners. It does not outsource its production. The Esmeralda Distillery is a fusion of modernity and antiquity, with state-of-the-art building design, quality-control measures and full scale bottling processes. Yet the hand-pounded copper alembic stills used for production revive old-world craftsmanship and skill—art forms all but forgotten in our era of mass production.

Tasting Notes from the Esmeralda Distillery, makers of Port of Barcelona: The nose opens with rich creamy fruit, and finishes with lingering floral and juniper. On the palate, it begins by touting citric orange and vacillates quickly between butter and acidic orange and lemon. It quickly transitions to a wave of perfumed juniper mid-palate before leaving with a round silk and floral finish.

Strong Likker

"Once, after a trip to America, [Ford Madox Ford, an English novelist and poet] brought back many bottles of bootleg gin and whisky to show Montparnasse the meaning of strong "likker." He arranged a long table with the bootleg at one end and French cognac, wine, and liqueurs at the other. At first each guest tried the American bathtub gin and whisky in order to turn up his nose at it. "What terrible stuff," they said. But by two in the morning the bootleg gin and whisky were all gone, while the French brandies and liqueurs had only been nibbled at." *This Must be the Place: Memoirs of Jimmie the Barman*, by Morrill Cody, 1937.

Q-Gin, 40% abv
www.qgin.com

Style: London Dry
Country of Origin: England
Available in: U.S.A. & Canada
Botanicals: lotus flower leaves, lavender, juniper
Distillation: Produced by one of England's original and most distinguished distillers, Quintessential takes the fine British tradition of gin distillation in brave new directions. Q is distilled five times to create a pure and flawless spirit. The essence of lotus leaves and lavender have been added to the traditional profile of juniper and other botanicals, giving this gin a distinctive and smooth taste matched by no other super-premium gin.
Tell us why you think your gin stands apart from all the others: Quintessential Gin is the most sophisticated super-premium gin on the market in both taste and style. Born from a unique combination of holistic lavender, leaves of the exotic lotus flower, and the refined and balanced flavor of Florentine juniper, comes Quintessential Gin. The silky flavor profile of lavender and lotus leaf combined with water from the purest springs imparts a uniquely refreshing, smooth taste.
Any other idiosyncrasies that you'd like to tell us about? At 80 proof, Q Gin is smooth enough to be taken straight up, graceful enough to be mixed in any cocktail and always deliciously unforgettable.
History: In 1761, one of the most distinguished distillers in England began producing a smooth, botanical-infused gin quite unlike the coarse imports of the times. In the bustling Navy port of Warrington, the gin was an instant hit among the wealthier classes, naval officers and exporters, bringing new life to a dying craft and a new style to England's aristocracy. Today, we proudly produce this original recipe with a unique twist for the 21st century.
Tasting Notes from *F. Paul Pacult's Spirit Journal* "Absolutely impeccable clarity and purity . . . finishes smooth . . . the right choice for drinkers . . ."
Awards: In 2005, Q Gin was awarded "The World's Smoothest Gin" Gold Award by the Beverage Testing Institute.

You Have to Eat an Olive

"You can never get drunk while drinking a Martini. It's a very social, High-Life drink, and you have to eat an olive. It's all very sophisticated." Quentin Crisp, 1996.

Rehorst Premium Milwaukee Gin, 44% abv
www.GreatLakesDistillery.com

Style: We describe our gin as not quite a London Dry and not quite a genever, thus [it's a] Milwaukee Style Gin. OK if you have to stick it into one class or the other I guess it would be a London.

Country of Origin: USA

Available in: USA

Botanicals: juniper, cardamom, coriander, Saigon cassia, lemon peel, orange peel, anise, sweet basil, Wisconsin ginseng.

Distillation: We macerate all the botanicals in our base alcohol. After maceration is complete we pour it into our pot still and commence distillation. All cuts are made according to taste—not instrumentation.

Tell us why you think your gin stands apart from all the others: Our gin is not as dry as a typical London Dry, we use a lower amount of juniper than many others and have increased the citrus. We use two botanicals that we believe have never been used in a gin before—Sweet Basil and Wisconsin Ginseng which is considered by Asian herbalists to be the highest quality Ginseng in the world.

Any other idiosyncrasies that you'd like to tell us about? Our production process is slow and expensive but we believe results in a gin of outstanding quality.

History: We are a small craft distillery—the first distillery in Wisconsin since prohibition having opened in 2006. We produce small batches of high-quality spirits, including Vodka and Gin. We are currently developing additional products including Bourbon, Malt Whisky, Grappa, Eau de vie, Absinthe, and others.

Awards: San Francisco World Spirits Competition, 2008: Double Gold Medal.

Right Gin, 40% abv
www.rightgin.com

Style: Artisanal, or "New Western Dry"
Country of Origin: Sweden
Available in: USA, UK
Botanicals: juniper (Austria), cardamom (India), coriander leaf (Russia), lime and bitter orange (West Indies), lemon and bergamot (Sicily), Sarawak black pepper (Borneo).
Distillation: We use an artisanal method whereby our grain base and each botanical are individually distilled and then blended by our master blender. This method gives us the precise control we require to ensure consistent delivery of the Right flavor profile.
Tell us why you think your gin stands apart from all the others: Right Gin addresses the polarizing taste of gin by delivering a formula for the modern palate. Right respects the classic spices but we dial down their volume while dialing up the citrus to ensure a crisp, clean finish and the absence of the heavy, oil aftertaste that is prevalent in many gins (the surprising pepper note at the end ensures one will want to "have another"). The result is a martini that is gorgeous in the nude and a highly mixable product that will bring many new consumers into the category.
Any other idiosyncrasies that you'd like to tell us about? Right's grain base is corn, which lends a faint sweetness to the taste and enhances its accessibility. We distill the corn five times. Our soft water source is from a lake near Malmo, Sweden.
History: W. L. Lyons Brown, III, created Right Gin in 2005. Brown, who spent the majority of his life pursuing his family's bourbon distilling roots, was never a huge fan of gin. "The more we studied it, the more we felt we could customize the flavor to suit today's palate in a way that brings people into the category instead of driving them out. The basic idea was to create a product that leaves a crisp, clean finish on the palate while being highly mixable. We support that with an image that aims to attract the under-30 crowd back to the category. I mean the last cool guy to drink gin was Gatsby, right?" says Brown.

Brown studied every possible element for his formula carefully as well as various distillation methods while embracing the notion that there would be no sacred cows for Right. "We chose a water source in southern Sweden for its softness; we use a corn base that respects our whisky roots and lends a fait sweetness that makes the product more inviting. We selected classic spices and citrus from the West Indies and Sicily with an unexpected pepper note that completes the finish. Right is beautifully balanced delivering a gorgeous martini and complimenting fresh ingredients in any mixed cocktail.

A Nip of Something Strong

"A top-secret source told me the other day that when the Queen Mother wants to tickle her throat with a nip of something strong, she is very partial to a gin and Dubonnet, whatever that may be exactly. Her taste for gin is, of course, well-documented (Gordon's is a loyal warrant holder). 'I couldn't get through all my engagements without a little something,' she has confided." Victoria Moore, *The New Statesman*, 19 April 1999.

Rogue Spruce Gin, 45% abv and Rogue Pink Spruce Gin, 45% abv
www.rogue.com and *www.roguespirits.com*

Note: The Rogue *Pink* Spruce Gin is the regular Rogue Spruce Gin that has been aged in Pinot Noir barrels.

Style: Leans towards London Dry

Country of Origin: United States

Available in: United States, Canada

Botanicals: spruce, cucumbers, angelica root, orange peel, coriander, lemon peel, ginger, orris root, grains of paradise, tangerine, juniper berries

Distillation: Rogue's Spruce Gin begins life as a humble grain neutral spirit, and then undergoes nothing short of a miraculous transformation in a process developed circa 800 AD by a Persian alchemist. Rogue's distillers have further refined the alembic distillation process and are currently producing their Spruce Gin in small, hand-bottled batches. Rogue's creationaries defined it something like this: the simple spirit is heated to a temperature of 176 degrees Fahrenheit in a 150 gallon Vendome copper pot still; alcohol vapors then rise up through the still column, passing through 11 botanicals on their way, trapping the botanicals' essence within the alcohol vapors. In a single pass, the copper creature does the job of what would normally be four, re-condensing the alcohol vapors and ejecting the clear liquid out at about 175 proof. The distiller then brings the Gin down to 90 proof or 45% alcohol by volume in a process known as *smithing*, whereby free-range coastal water is hand-apportioned to each small batch. Finally, the gin is hand-bottled, capped and heat-sealed in a 750ml serigraphed bottle whose artwork commemorates Oregon spruce loggers of the 1800s.

Tell us why you think your gin stands apart from all the others: Spruce. The sheer number of ingredients. The complexity of flavors. The melding of ingredients. Spruce Gin is produced in very small batches and only the best is captured.

HIstory: Since it's establishment in 2003, Rogue Spirits has developed their unique Distillates from local indgredients indigenous to the Pacific Northwest. Spruce Gin is made in smaller than normal batches and hand bottled in a 750ml serigraphed bottle, with artwork commemorating Oregon Spruce Loggers of the 1880's.

Awards for Rogue Spruce Gin: 2009 San Francisco World Spirit Competition: Double Gold. **2008 San Francisco World Spirits Competition:** Double Gold. **2008 World Beverage Competition:** Silver. **2007 World Spirits Competition:** Best American Made Gin. **2007 International Spirits Challenge:** Commended. **2007 International Review of Spirits:** Silver. **2007 International Spirits Competition:** Silver

Awards for Rogue Pink Spruce Gin: 2009 San Francisco World Spirit Competition: Silver. **2008 San Francisco World Spirits Competition:** Bronze. **2008 World Beverage Competition:** Silver.

Further Adventures of Captain Kettle

Mrs. Nilssen, of Banana, gave the pink gin cocktails a final brisk up with the swizzle-stick, poured them out with accurate division, and handed the tray to Captain Kettle and her husband. The men drank off the appetiser and put down the glasses. Kettle nodded a word of praise for the mixture and thanks to its concoctor, and Mrs. Nilssen gave a flash of white teeth, and then shuffled away off the verandah, and vanished within the bamboo walls of the pilotage. *Further Adventures of Captain Kettle* by Cutcliffe Hyne, 1899.

Seagram's Gin, 40% abv, and Seagram's Distiller's Reserve Gin, 51% abv
www.seagramsgin.com

Style: Extra Dry

Country of Origin: USA.

Available in: USA, Spain, Poland, Germany, South Africa, Australia, Finland, China, Ukraine, India and UK.

Botanicals: Juniper berries, Bitter orange, Angelica root, Coriander

Distillation: Seagram's uses a vacuum distillation process, therefore distillation occurs at a much lower temperature and more botanical flavors are retained.

Tell us why you think your gin stands apart from all the others: Seagram's Gin is the only gin which is mellowed in oak casks, creating a more mature and smoother quality spirit.

Any other idiosyncrasies that you'd like to tell us about? Seagram's is the #1 gin in the United States, and Seagram's Distiller's Reserve represents the finest samples of Seagram's classic gin, hand-selected to create a barrel-proof gin of exceptional quality.

History: Seagram's Gin was introduced to the US market in 1939 as "Seagram's Ancient Bottle Distilled Dry Gin."

Sinful Drinking

"A beleaguered Madison Avenue account executive was heard to remark during a palliative 5 P.M. Martini that his milk account would be in much better shape if he could just find some way to get people feeling as sinful drinking milk as they do drinking liquor." *The Booze Reader: A Soggy Saga of a Man In His Cups* by George Bishop, 1965.

Stirling London Dry Gin, 40% abv

www.boomsma.eu

Style: London Dry
Country of Origin: The Netherlands
Available in: Luxembourg, Belgium, Estonia, Germany
Botanicals: juniper berries, coriander, angelica
Tell us why you think your gin stands apart from all the others: Due to the perfect balance of herbs and 100% pure natural ingredients this gin has a particularly aromatic character and explicit quality.
Any other idiosyncrasies that you'd like to tell us about? Drink at room temperature or slightly chilled. Also a perfect base for a long drink!

Tanqueray® London Dry Gin, 47.3% abv
www.tanqueray.com

Style: London Dry
Country of Origin: United Kingdom
Available: Tanqueray is available worldwide. It is sold in various strengths in different markets but *all* Tanqueray is produced in Scotland and tested to ensure its quality and taste.
Botanicals: These include juniper berries, coriander seed, angelica root and others known only to the Tanqueray Master Distiller.
Distillation: Confidential information
Tell us why you think your gin stands apart from all the others: The uncompromising adherence to Charles Tanqueray's legacy of excellence ensures our master distiller continues the exacting standards of craftsmanship established in 1830; the meticulous selection of the finest and freshest botanicals guarantees an elegant and aromatic gin of substance.; The iconic stylish bottle perfectly reflects the authenticity of Tanqueray.
Any other idiosyncrasies that you'd like to tell us about? By bottling Tanqueray at a higher ABV than most other gins, Tanqueray retains its unique flavor even after dilution. The higher alcohol content sheaths the botanicals to ensure a dry, crisp, flavorful and refreshing Tanqueray and Tonic. The extra strength is also important to maintain the dryness of the juniper when making a perfectly, well-balanced and smooth dry martini cocktail.
History: At 20 years old, Charles Tanqueray established a distillery in Bloomsbury, London in 1830, setting himself the task of producing the finest London Dry Gin that would set new standards in gin production. The gin that proudly bears the Tanqueray name today took Charles Tanqueray years to perfect. He patiently experimented with different blends of the finest botanicals he could find until he produced a gin that met his requirements.
Awards: Overall Winner, Drinks International Gin Challenge Champion 2008; Double Gold Medal and Best Gin in Show, 2005 San Francisco World Spirits Competition; Double Gold Medal, 2004 San Francisco World Spirits Competition; Silver Award
—2002 International Wine and Spirits Competition; Gold Award, 2001 International Wine and Spirits Competition, Silver Award, 2000 International Wine and Spirits Competition; plus a 8 gold and silver awards, and one bronze award stretching back to 1987.

organized chaos at Painter's: A Tanqueray Flashback

In 2004, after not setting foot behind a bar for quite some time, I got back behind the stick at Painter's, my local joint in the Hudson Valley. The guys who own this place, Sal and Pete Buttiglieri, are good friends of mine, and I'd convinced them to let me open the Gallery Bar—a smallish room that's primarily used for private parties—on Wednesday nights for an event that I called *organized chaos*. I put together a cocktail menu, set down some rules such as "don't ask us to change the volume of the music, it's at exactly the right level," and I made playlists of mostly rock and roll from the 60s and 70s with some punk thrown in for good measure, and a few hokey tunes from the fifties to make sure that people were paying attention. One minute the Sex Pistols were proclaiming that "No One is Innocent," and the next thing you'd hear might be Doris Day singing "Que Sera, Sera."

here's a picture of Stan Vadrna, bartender extraordinaire from Slovakia, and a man who I'm proud to call my friend. He's behind the bar at organized chaos in this shot. He came up in 2007 to hang for a night.

organized chaos went down well with some of the locals and I managed to scare up a bit of a following on Wednesday nights. I made cocktail drinkers out of more than a few of them, too. I had construction workers from a site just down the street drinking Pisco Sours and Corpse Revivers, and a group of professional types—a photographer, a couple of I.T. people, a travel agent, and a few others—turned out on a regular basis to try something different from their usual glass of chardonnay or bottle of lite beer. One of this crowd was a guy called Bob—I never did know his last name. Bob was a vodka drinker. I was determined to put an end to that.

"Wanna try something a little different, Bob?" I asked him about three weeks into the *organized chaos* series.

"What do you suggest, Gary?"

"Oh, just leave it with me . . ."

I made him an Aviation using Tanqueray No. TEN, Luxardo maraschino liqueur, and fresh lemon juice (we had no creme de violette at the time). (Tanqueray No. TEN™, lest you don't know this, was one of, if not *the* first new gins to be launched at the end of the twentieth century that was intentionally softer, fruitier, and not as intentionally perfumed as most traditional dry gins, so it's a good bottling to serve to people who think they don't like gin.)

Bob drank three Aviations that night, and the following week he was back for more. He turned anyone who'd listen to him on to Aviations.

Here's Angus Winchester, Global Ambassador for Tanqueray Gins, and a Gin Genius if ever there was one. Angus was one of the first Brits to hop the pond to come to my Cocktails in the Country workshops, he's a compulsive sesquipedalian, and he's a darned fine chappie to boot. Like the fine range of Tanqueray gins, Angus Winchester comes at you from all angles, and he's always a welcome sight.

"Here, have a sip of this. It's the most fabulous drink I've ever had," he'd say to complete strangers at the bar. It wasn't long before Aviations were outselling every other cocktail on my list.

Bob knew that Aviations contained gin, and despite his claim that he didn't like the stuff, he conceded that he could drink it in an Aviation, just so long as the gin was Tanqueray No. TEN. He was a little taken aback then when, after frequenting my Wednesday night events for a few months, he asked for the gin bottle to show a friend what he was drinking, and I passed him the bottle of Tanqueray London Dry.

"No, Gary, this isn't it. I don't like this one. It's the one in the tall bottle," he protested.

"No, Bob. This is the gin you've been drinking for the past few weeks. I weaned you off the No. TEN™ bottling quite some time back," I told him.

I carved another notch in my belt.

Tanqueray® No. TEN™, 47.3% abv

Style: Distilled gin

Country of Origin: United Kingdom

Available in: United States, UK, and many other countries

Botanicals: white grapefruits, oranges, and limes, together with juniper berries and coriander seeds.

Distillation: Confidential information

Tell us why you think your gin stands apart from all the others: Tanqueray No. TEN is the only gin in the world distilled with handpicked, whole-fruit fresh botanicals. The Heart of Tanqueray No. TEN is produced exclusively in a special small batch still aptly dubbed "Tiny Ten," which is specifically designed to provide for the exquisite depth and character of the resulting spirit.

History: Tanqueray No. TEN was launched in the United States in 2000 to compete against the most premium white spirits in the world, it is the only gin distilled in small batches with handpicked fresh fruit and botanicals.

Awards: Gold medal in Design and Packaging category in the Drinks International Gin Challenge 2008.; Inducted into the World Spirits Hall of Fame after being voted The Best among all gins and vodkas in 2001, 2002, and 2003; 98 rating from Wine Enthusiast (2001) (Highest score ever given to a white spirit); Voted "Best New Gin" by Food & Wine (2000)

Gin Cocktails in the Andes

"Violand would seat himself at a huge table with the top a single plank of solid mahogany three inches thick and before the ingredients for a gin cocktail. At his elbow a tiny little girl, one of the daughters of the Aymara cook, took her position to trot out for anything lacking in the first array. A gin cocktail is sugar, Angostura bitters, and gin—and I have seen it served in full goblets. All the rest of the forenoon the host would busy himself compounding this. It made not the slightest difference whether anyone else in the party joined him or not, genially he would attend to it himself in little sips whose cumulative effect was prodigious. As the midday breakfast hour approached he would roar for pisco, a species of Peruvian brandy, and then, as the little Aymara maiden announced the final hour of nutrition, champagne." *Across the Andes* by Charles Johnson Post. Published by Outing Publishing Company, 1912.

Tanqueray Rangpur® Gin, 41.3% abv

Style: Distilled Gin

Country of Origin: United Kingdom

Available in: Currently available only in the United States

Botanicals: Botanicals used include rare Rangpur limes, juniper berries, coriander seed, bay leaves, ginger, angelica root, and other select botanicals.

Distillation: confidential information

Tell us why you think your gin stands apart from all the others: At the heart of Tanqueray Rangpur gin is the rare Rangpur lime, which resembles a tangerine in color, shape, and size, but imparts a mild yet juicy zest. The Rangpur limes used in distillation impart a more subtle gin taste and smooth finish. Tanqueray Rangpur gin can be enjoyed on the rocks or in cocktails made with popular mixers such as ginger ale and cranberry juice.

History: Tanqueray Rangpur gin was launched in 2007.

Tasting Notes from the Diageo Company: Beautifully balanced with classic juniper flavor delicately complemented by a juicy yet zesty hint of limes.

Awards: Double Gold, 2007 San Francisco Spirits Competition.

Six Martinis

"A woman with six Martinis can ruin a city," actor Wendell Corey in his role as Smiley Coy in *The Big Knife*, 1955.

12 Bridges Gin, 45% abv
www.Integrityspirits.com

Style: Hybrid of Genever and London Dry
Country of Origin: USA
Available in : Portland, Oregon, USA
Botanicals: Norwegian blue juniper berries, coriander seeds, dried ginger root, fresh cucumber, lemon peel, bitter orange peel, fennel seed, orris root, angelica root, grains of paradise, rose hip, and mandarin oil.
Distillation: We steep the botanicals that need a longer extraction time for 24 hours in the clean spirit, then the still is charged with the mixture, the cucumber is suspended in the vapor stream, and the rest of the botanicals are added. The spirit is then re-distilled, and the heart of the resultant distillate is our gin. The foreshots are withdrawn and used for cleaning the floor. The tails are discarded. We do not re distill either as we believe that a product is more refined by using only the hearts of the distillate.
Tell us why you think your gin stands apart from all the others: While it has more body and a large flavor profile, 12 Bridges Gin possesses a softness in the mouth feel. The flavor is complex yet more subtle than other gins. The fresh taste of cucumber is complemented by the spice of the grains of paradise and angelica. The citrus also complements the profile with refreshing brightness.
History: Integrity Spirits, the parent company of 12 Bridges Gin, intends to supplant the established institutions by artfully crafting spirits that don't just *say* that they are artisanal, but *are*, at their very essence, artisanal. Why else would we choose integrity as our name?
Our distiller, Kieran, easily acquired over nine international awards in 2006 alone and has a background in wine making and professional cooking. His friend and partner, Rich Phillips, managed the largest liquor store in Oregon for eight years, and has extensive experience in the food and beverage industry. He is as passionate about food as any of the tenets by which he lives his life.
Why the correlation between food and spirits? We believe they are synonymous. Spirits are food to the body and the soul, and when crafted with care by the hand of an artisan, they contribute to the health and enjoyment of all that taste them.
Tasting Notes from Rich Phillips, Partner in Integrity Spirits: Refreshing cucumber and citrus notes at the front with a spiciness rising from mid palate to the roof of the mouth. The Norwegian blue juniper while subtle, comes through at this point, but is sweeter and lasting through the finish.

Van Gogh® Gin

Van Gogh Gin, 47% abv
http://vangoghvodka.com/Van_Gogh_Vodka_Gin.html

Style: Distilled Gin

Country of Origin: Holland

Available in: United States, Puerto Rico, Europe, Mexico, Australia, Netherlands, Japan, Canada, Asia, Guatemala, Aruba, Bermuda.

Botanicals: angelica, coriander, grains of paradise, almonds, lemon, licorice, juniper berries, cassia bark, orris, cubeb berries

Distillation: Van Gogh Gin's 10 exotic botanicals are distilled individually in small batches. This hand-crafted process produces a gin that delivers a smooth, gentle finish while showcasing the unique essence of each flavor.

Tell us why you think your gin stands apart from all others: Under the direction of Van Gogh Founder and President, David van de Velde, Master Distiller Tim Vos, produced Van Gogh Gin to satisfy the spirit lover's refined tastes with a distinctive blend and an elegance critically acclaimed as the finest spirit in the world.

Any other idiosyncrasies that you'd like to tell us about? Van Gogh Gin, first released in 1999, was the first product produced by the Van Gogh brand. It offers a unique complement and distinction to Van Gogh Vodka brand as most flavored vodka lines do not include a quality gin.

History: Van Gogh Gin was first crafted in 1997 based on historical recipes, that date back to 1891, which were archived in the Royal Dirkzwager Distillery in Schiedam, Holland.

Awards: *F. Paul Pacult's Spirit Journal:* Five-Star rated: "Impeccable clarity." "Redefines Dutch gin in a contemporary manner that's immensely appealing"

WHITLEY NEILL

LONDON DRY GIN

INSPIRED BY AFRICA • MADE IN ENGLAND

Whitley Neill Gin, 42% abv
www.whitleyneill.com

Style: London Dry
Country of Origin: U.K.
Available in: USA, UK, Sweden, France, Germany, Denmark, Italy, Spain, Australia, Canada.
Botanicals: baobab fruit pulp, Cape gooseberries (physalis), juniper, coriander, sweet orange peel, sweet lemon peel, angelica root, orris root, cassia bark.
Distillation: The botanicals are macerated in neutral grain alcohol on the night before distillation. The spirit is then distilled in an antique copper pot still, and the resultant distillate is blended with more neutral grain alcohol to achieve consistency in flavor, then cut to bottling proof with purified, de-mineralized water.
Tell us why you think your gin stands apart from all the others: Two unique citrus African botanicals [that have] never [been] distilled in a gin before—Baobab fruit and Cape Gooseberries. A very different citrus and all-round flavour profile. A brewing and distilling heritage dating back to 1761. Less juniper in the recipe and along with the new citrus there's a little more coriander giving a more peppery nose and enlivening the unique citrus elements.
Any other idiosyncrasies that you'd like to tell us about? Five percent of Net profits from the gin are donated to Tree Aid—www.treeaid.org.uk, a charity which helps some of the poorest people in Africa secure and sustain an income from trees. $1.00 from every bottle sold at Hyatt hotels is given in addition to this.
History: Independently created and launched in September 2005 by Johnny Neill, fourth generation of the Greenall Whitley distilling family. The unique African botanicals were inspired by my South African wife.
Awards: San Francisco Spirits Competition 2007: Double Gold Medal. **Beverage Tasting Institute, Chicago, 2007:** Gold Medal—91 points rating "exceptional." **International Wine and Spirits Competition 2007:** Gold Medal, Best in Class. **Patterson's Magazine Tasting Panel, April 2008:** 95 Points, "Classic" rating. **San Francisco Spirits Competition 2009:** Double Gold Medal.

Zephyr Gin Black, 40% abv, and 44% abv
Zephyr Gin Blu, 40% abv
www.zephyrgin.com

Style (Zephyr Gin Black): London Dry Gin
Style (Zephyr Gin Blu): Dry Gin
Country of Origin: UK
Zephyr Gin Black, at 40% abv, available in: UK, France, Germany, Netherlands, New Zealand
Zephyr Gin Black, at 44% abv, available in: USA
Zephyr Gin Blu available in: UK, USA, France, Germany
Botanicals (Zephyr Gin Black): juniper berries from Macedonia, angelica root from Northern France, coriander from Bulgaria, orris root from France, lemon peel from Seville, elderflower from UK, elderberries from UK.
Botanicals (Zephyr Gin Blu): juniper berries from Macedonia, angelica root from Northern France, coriander from Bulgaria, orris root from France, lemon peel from Seville, elderflower from UK, elderberries from UK, elderberry essence, natural blue colour.
Distillation: Zephyr Gins are produced in batches in a 13,000-liter traditional copper pot still. The seven botanicals are left to steep in a mixture of alcohol and water in the pot still for 12 hours before distillation. This is known as the one-shot method. The high strength spirit is made from English wheat and lowered in strength with local water. The gin concentrate is then blended with more English wheat alcohol & neutral water (using reverse osmosis) to get the strength & flavour profile for Black Zephyr.
Tell us why you think your gin stands apart from all the others: Elderflower is our unique botanical that sets Zephyr Gin apart from other London Dry Gins
Any other idiosyncrasies that you'd like to tell us about? Zephyr Gins are produced at the family-owned Langley Distillery situated near Birmingham. They are one of the last independent gin distillers in the United Kingdom and the gins they produce are distilled using traditional copper pot stills which are over 100 years old. The distillery is sited over ancient underground water sources. The copper pot still is called Constance, Connie for short. She is named after the master distiller's mother.
History: The Zephyr Gins were created as contemporary style gins that would appeal to the traditional gin drinker as well as the younger generation who have not been introduced to gin. The concept, logo, and style were originally designed by Steve McVicar. The recipe was created by Hayman Group in the UK and enhanced by Dave Steward of Marblehead UK.
Award (Zephyr Gin Black): Chicago Beverage Institute, 2008: Gold Medal.
Award (Zephyr Gin Blu): Chicago Beverage Institute, 2008: Silver Medal.

Racy Little Spirituous Compounds

"From the time the habitual drinker in San Francisco takes his morning gin-cocktail to stimulate an appetite for breakfast, he supplies himself at intervals throughout the day with an indefinite number of racy little spirituous compounds that have the effect of keeping him always more or less primed." *Mountains and Molehills* by Frank Marryat, 1855.

Zuidam Dry Gin, 44.5% abv
www.zuidam.com

Style: Distilled Gin
Country of Origin: Holland
Available in: USA, UK, Canada, Russia, Spain, China & Holland.
Botanicals: juniper berries and iris root from Italy, coriander from Morocco, angelica root, fresh oranges and lemons from Spain, whole vanilla beans from Madagascar, licorice root from India, cardamom pods from Ceylon.
Distillation: Zuidam distills each ingredient or botanical separately. Since flavors peak at different temperatures, distilling botanicals separately, though time intensive and expensive, gives us the purest flavors possible from each ingredient. We then marry all the distillates, and allow them to mellow in stainless steel for a minimum of six weeks before bottling. This gives all of the distillates a chance to get to know each other, and to come together in harmony. The final blend is created having undergone a total of 14 distillations (five for the base spirit and nine individual distillations for each botanical.
Tell us why you think your gin stands apart from all the others: Using whole fruit to distill gives the dry gin a more citrus overtone then if using the dried peels. Separate distillations allows each botanical to show through and the whole vanilla bean binds everything together giving you a silkier feel on the palate.
History: Fred van Zuidam, formally the master distiller at De Kuyper for 30 years, and his son Patrick, are working together using traditional methods with a modern approach to gin production. Both an old-world genever gin and the new world dry gin are available side by side.

Chapter 5

Genever

Genever Defined. Sort of . . .

There are quite a few styles of genever, but it's fairly safe to say that in order to make this style of gin, a mash of grains (basically beer) is distilled into a whisky-like spirit known as malt wine. The malt wine is then married to another spirit that's essentially a dry gin, made by distilling botanicals, including juniper, into neutral grain spirits. The percentage of malt wine in any bottling of genever will drastically alter the flavor of the spirit, of course, and if genever is aged, then this, too, has an effect on the product. Author David Wondrich's formula for approximating genever by marrying 10 parts Jameson's Irish whiskey to eight parts Plymouth gin, and adding a little simple syrup (made with demerara sugar), should serve to give you an idea of the basic flavor profile of genevers.

Genever Flashbacks

Genever made a comeback in the first decade of the twenty-first century, and no one was more surprised than I was when it happened. Thirty-odd years ago, when I started tending bar at New York's Drake's Drum, there was a stone bottle of Bols genever that gathered dust on the backbar. I don't think that any of us knew what the heck it was save for "some kind of Dutch gin," so we pretty much left the stuff alone, and if you'd have told me then that genever would be so well received in this new century, I'd probably have told you that you were out of your mind. We just didn't know what we were supposed to do with this stuff.

My first real encounter with genever took place in Holland, back in 2000, when David van de Velde, the guy who brought us the Van Gogh line of gin and vodkas, took my good friend Paul Pacult, spirits writer of great renown, and me to Holland to see his gin being made. As you can see by the pictures that follow, Holland has a weird effect on folk. I can't say I was impressed by the genevers during that trip, mainly because I didn't understand them, but the coffee shops in Amsterdam were pretty cool.

Here I am firing up the stills at the Van Gogh distillery

And Paul looks very happy about something or other in this shot,
taken on the same trip to Holland.

It took that bastard David Wondrich to get me to appreciate genever. It was
his book, *Imbibe*, that pointed out that genever was the style of gin used in many
nineteenth century gin-based cocktails, so I just had to try them. Previously, like
everyone else in the past thirty years who has experimented with old cocktail
recipes, I'd made these drinks with London dry gin. Now I needed to see what
they tasted like when they were mixed up by their creators in the 1800s. Using
a bottle of genever that arrived on my doorstep one day, I fixed a few of the
cocktails that Wondrich describes in his book, and I sampled them with Chris
Gallagher, a good friend (and the guy who makes PUG! muddlers). I wish I could
say that I liked these drinks right off the bat, but I'd be lying. Genever needs to be
courted. I had to persevere a little.

It wasn't until I came up with a for a genever-based drink of my own
that I really got my head around this style of gin, but after sampling some of
the new bottling of Bols genever and a little Genevieve from San Francisco's
Anchor Distilling Company, I started to get a feel for this category of gin. And
as I experimented with it I started to understand what genever is all about. The

resultant drink—The Bold, Bright and Fearless Cocktail—was featured in the *San Francisco Chronicle* on February 15, 2009, and you'll find it in the recipe chapter of this compendium, too.

I think it's important to point out that, in order to appreciate genever, it's probably best that you don't think of it as gin at all. Our minds are programmed to think of *dry* when the gin word comes up, and genever is nothing like a dry gin at all. Thinking of gin, then, when you sip genever, is akin to thinking you have bourbon in your glass when, in fact, your host has poured you a dram of a very smoky scotch. Both are whiskies, of course, but your first sip will be jarring, to say the least. Think of genever as, well, think of it as genever. It's a product unto itself. It's a bold, bright, and fearless spirit, and it deserves to be courted and loved for its very distinctive personality. And genever changes so much from one bottling to another that although there might not be too many brands on the shelves yet, each and every one that's available to us at present, has a personality all its own.

Is It Really Gin?

Having said that it's a good idea to *think* of genever as being a spirit that's very unlike the kind of gin to which most of us are accustomed, I think it's important to note that genever is most definitely gin. It's a different style of gin from the gin with which most of us are familiar. It's the mother of dry gin.

As Wondrich tells us in *Imbibe*, many gin-based cocktails that appeared in the mid- to late-nineteenth century were made with genever. Did the recipe books of the time call for genever, though? No, they called for gin. Why? Because outside of Holland, for centuries, when people asked for gin, they expected genever-style gin, not dry gin, and until around, say, 1870, genever was the most common style of gin available in the U.S.A.

Genever is a different style of gin from any other. Vastly different. If genever is *not* gin, though—and I've heard people say exactly that—then those nineteenth-century cocktails couldn't possibly have been made with genever. Their recipes do call for gin, after all. And if genever isn't gin, then I'd be making a huge mistake in including it in *The Bartender's Gin Compendium*. Q. E. D. (I hope . . .)

This advertisement for "Holland Type" gin dates to 1900.

Now I'm turning you over to an edited version of a document that my good friend Phillip Duff sent to me in 2008. Read this and you'll get a good understanding of what genever is all about, its origins, how it's made, and all sorts of good insider information. You'll find lots of references to Bols products in the next few pages, basically because that where Phillip worked when he researched the following material.

Genever Production
by Philip Duff, edited by Gary
(*Gary's comments are in italics within the text below.*)

First, malt wine is distilled from a mash of cereals, typically rye, corn, barley, and wheat—Bols uses all but barley. The creation of the continuous still in 1831 allowed for high-quality neutral spirits to be made, which could then be used to "stretch" the malt wine (*This is much like the Scots using neutral spirits to "stretch" their single malt whiskies, resulting in blended scotches.*) into corn wine (korenwijn), old (oude) genever or young (jonge) genever. (*Young genever didn't happen until the 1950s.*)

The fermented mash of grains is distilled first in a continuous still, then it's redistilled two to three times in linked pot stills, coming off the process at between 46% and 48% abv. The first distillate that is stripped in the continuous still is called *ruwnat,* the second *enkelnat*, the third *bestnat* (which is in fact malt wine) and the optional fourth is *korenwijn.* Bols then infuses the botanicals into neutral spirits in a pot still for several hours. The still is then heated, and the infused spirits are redistilled. The botanicals are similar to the popular ones of London Dry gin—juniper, angelica, ginger, orris, coriander, liquorice. One unusual botanical used to make genever is hops. (*Apart from the hops factor, this is exactly how dry gin is made, so in effect, the Dutch make dry gin, then marry it to malt wine, the whiskey-like distillate, in order to produce genever.*)

Genever is required by law to contain juniper, but the law does not require that the spirit has to have an apparent aroma or taste of juniper (*some young genevers taste very similar to vodka, for instance*). As well as neutral spirits infused with botanicals, genever may contain "key concentrate" (a distillate of malt wine with many different botanicals) and *gebeide* malt wine, which is malt wine that has been redistilled with juniper berries.

The malt wine and botanical-infused neutral spirits will then be blended according to which type of genever is being made: a high percentage of malt wine for malt wine genever, and progressively less for corn wine, old, and young genever. If the genever is to get some aging, the malt wine and the infused neutral spirits may be aged separately, then blended and married before bottling. (*And Gary notes that, as you'll see in the upcoming definitions of various types of genever, a small amount of sugar is often added to the finished product before it's bottled.*)

The Art of Converting Whiskey Into Gin

"Having indicated the most proper means of obtaining spirits, I will now offer to the public the manner of making Gin, according to the methods used by the distillers in Holland. It may be more properly joined to the art of making whiskey, as it adds only to the price of the liquor, that of the juniper berries, the product of which will amply repay its cost . . . The Hollanders, who have long had the art of trading upon every thing, have constantly turned even their poverty to account. They have immense fabrications of gin, and scarcely any juniper trees. They only collect the berry in those countries where it is neglected as useless, as in France and Tyrol, which produce a great deal of it. The United States need have no recourse to Europe, in order to get the juniper berries: they have in abundance at home, what the Hollanders can only procure with trouble and money. They can therefore rival them with great advantage; but they must follow the same methods employed in the Holland distilleries." *The Art of Making Whiskey,* by Anthony Boucherie, 1819.

Types of Genever

Grain Genever (*Graanjenever*)

Graanjenever is a word that you might see on the label of any genever, and it merely denotes that the neutral spirits used to make that bottling was made from grain, as opposed to sugar or any other medium.

Malt Wine Genever (*Moutwijnjenever*)

Although this is a recognized term, there are no laws governing its specific manufacture. It generally refers to a genever with a high malt-wine content (above 51 percent). This category has all but died out, yet it is malt-wine genevers that Jerry Thomas was writing about, and mixing with, in the mid-1800s.

Corn-Wine Genever (*Korenwijn, Bols Corenwyn*) (*"Corenwyn" is a term that the Bols company uses on its labels, whereas "korenwijn" is the generic term for corn-wine genever*)

Corn-wine genever must contain at least 51 percent malt wine, be at least 38 percent abv and contain no more than 20 grams of sugar per liter for sweetening. Like old genever, corn-wine genever doesn't have to be aged but if it is, it has to be for a minimum of one year and in barrels of less than 700 liters. Bols Corenwyn contains 51 percent malt wine, plus a special *gebeide moutwijn* distillate—a malt wine that has been re-distilled with juniper berries. The rest is neutral grain alcohol redistilled with botanicals, principally juniper. The regular Bols Corenwyn contains just 6 grams of sugar per liter and is a blend of genever distillates that have been aged for between 2.5 to 3 years in used Limousin oak cognac barrels.

Old Genever, and Very Old Genever (*Oude* Genever, and/or *Zeer Oude* Genever)

Old genever must contain at least 15 percent malt wine, be at least 35% abv and contain no more than 20 grams of sugar per liter for sweetening. Old genever doesn't have to be aged but if it is, it has to be for a minimum of one year and in barrels of less than 700 liters. Bols Very Old Genever contains malt wine, *gebeide* malt wine, and neutral grain alcohol redistilled with botanicals. Bols Very Old Genever contains 19 percent malt wine and only 6 grams of sugar per liter. Old genever is the most common type seen outside Europe, and constitutes the bulk of sales to Argentina.

Genever aging in a warehouse at Bols.

Young Genever (Jonge Genever)

Young genever must contain a maximum of 15 percent malt wine, be at least 35% abv and contain no more than 10 grams of sugar per liter for sweetening. Bols Young Genever contains 3% malt wine and no sugar, plus extracts of apricot, clove, ginger, and liquorice, as well as "key concentrate"—a distillate of aniseed, coriander, angelica, caraway, liquorice and malt wine. Young genever is a superb mixer for long drinks [*such as Genever and Bitter Lemon*], and is excellent in gin-based cocktails as an alternative to dry gins : the malt-wine aroma and mouthfeel are still present, but the botanicals are more apparent than in more malt-wine-heavy genevers.

Aged Genever

Apart from the fact that if a label mentions aging, it must have been in a barrel of 700 liters or less for a minimum of one year, there is relatively little legislation governing genever aging. (Bokma Five Years Old is an especially successful aging for five years in Limousin oak barrels. Bols released a Six Years Old Corenwyn and a Ten Years Old Corenwyn celebrate the 400th anniversary of Rembrandt, who was a neighbour and frequent visitor to the Bols bar in central Amsterdam.)

The Celebrated Town Of Schiedam

"Farther up the river . . . is the celebrated town of Schiedam, which contained a population in 1876 of 21,532, nearly all of whom are occupied, directly or indirectly, with the manufacture and export of the celebrated Schiedam Schnapps, a gin here distilled from the juniper berry, mostly called jenever, from juniper. There are between three and four hundred distilleries in the town, and its exportation of gin is immense. There is a small port, an exchange, Hôtel de Ville, and other public edifices. As the distance from Rotterdam is only four and a half miles, those interested in gin-cocktails and such like can make an excursion from the town." *Harper's Hand-Book for Travellers in Europe* by William Pembroke Fetridge, 1879.

Genever Timeline, Courtesy of Phillip Duff, 2008 (edited slightly by Gary)

1269: First major mention of juniper-based health-related tonics and medicines in a Dutch publication, *Der Naturen Bloeme* by Jacob van Maerlant te Damme.

1552: *Constelijck Distilleer Boek* by Philippus Hermanni mentions "genever aqua vitae," referring to juniper-infused brandy.

1582: First mention of grain being used as a basis for distilling in the Netherlands: *A Guide To Distilling* by Casper Jansz. Coolhaes. Korenbrandewijn "in aroma and taste is almost the same as brandy-wine" and is "not only named brandy-wine but also drunk and paid for as brandy-wine."

1575: Bols family, then named Bulsius, arrive in Amsterdam, start distilling liqueurs, having learned distilling in Cologne before traveling to Holland.

1602: The Dutch East India Company founded. Lucas Bols becomes a preferred supplier to its inner circle, the Seventeen Gentlemen, and also got first crack at all the new herbs and spices flooding back to Europe. The sailors and officers spread genever all around the globe, and they received daily half-pint rations of genever in a specially measured pewter cup.

1646: Lucas Bols gets a licence to distill spirits in the city of Amsterdam.

1664: Lucas Bols starts the production of genever.

1672: The van Dale dictionary, Holland's "OED," notes the first published use of the word "genever."

1820: Bols reinvents Bols genever recipe, using a revolutionary new column distilling process, creating a better balance between malt wine and neutral grain alcohol and using a more subtle botanical mix. This recipe is then exported to the USA.

> (Note: Column distilling, or distilling in a continuous still, is usually performed in a device that was patented in Great Britain over a decade after Bols claims to have been using "a revolutionary new column distilling process." A spokesperson for the company told us that their records indicate that this was true, so there's a chance that they were using a still developed in France in the late 1700s that is said to have been similar to the British version that would be "invented" later. Go figure.)

1950 onward: "Jonge jenever" is introduced. It is made using less malt wine and more neutral spirits [than oude genever], typically grain-based spirits, though some less expensive ones are made with a molasses base.

2008: Genever gains protected status from the European Union in EU declaration.

Chapter 6

Genevers by the Bottle

We found a few genevers, and a genever-style gin made in San Francisco, to detail on the following pages, and we think there's a good chance that this category will continue to grow. Let's hope so.

Holland Gin.
"The brandy hath a beaming hue,
But no one knows what it is made of;
Though red itself, it makes us blue
A thing the doctors are afraid of.
Sweeter far the Holland gin,
Which looks as clear as bubbling water,
But yet turns out, when taken in,
Intoxication's subtlest daughter."
Charles G. Halpine, 1869.

A. van Wees: Zeer Oude Genever, 40% abv
De Ooievaar: Loyaal aan traditie, 42% abv
A. van Wees: Roggenaer, 15 jaar, 40% abv
www.de-ooievaar.nl

Style: Genever

Country of Origin: Netherlands

Available in (country/countries): Netherlands, UK, Japan

Botanicals for van Wees Zeer Oude Genever: juniper berries, abelmoschus (*an African plant, similar to okra*), dill, coriander, angelica, galangal (*aka blue ginger*)

Botanicals for De Ooievaar: Loyaal aan traditie: juniper berries, dill, coriander, angelica, galangal (*aka blue ginger*), liquorice wood.

Botanicals for A. van Wees: Roggenaer, 15 jaar: juniper berries, dill, coriander, angelica, liquorice wood, caraway.

Distillation: The Dutch method, Kettles build by Scheffer in the early twentieth century. Our Kettles have a unique rectification bowl, which is necessary to distill double genever (*dubbel gebeid* means distilled twice over juniper berries in one distilling process). See our web site for more details.

Tell us why you think your gin stands apart from all the others: Our products are distilled from malt wines of wheat, rye, and corn, which are distilled separately or together with different types of seeds, herbs, flowers, and sometimes fruits. Therefore we can make 17 different types of genever, each of which are clearly distinctive from each other. This is unique for Europe. Our Zeer Oude Genever rests for at least 18 months in oak casks before it's bottled.

Any other idiosyncrasies that you'd like to tell us about? Our standards are based on the traditional standards of the nineteenth century.

History: "We're a family business, and our brand, A. van Wees, dates back to 1922 when it was started by my grandfather. The brand de Ooievaar is originally from the Hague and it dates back to 1782. Some of our recipes date from the late 18th century, but most of them were developed after that time, and some of the recipes are relatively recent." Mrs. F. van Wees.

BOX: Spiders at the Heart

"I see that the firm of . . . Lucas Bols, the great Batavian strong liquor-makers, who exhibit a pile of drinkables . . . have actually had a couple of Gold Medals awarded to them . . . A tremendous quantity of liqueurs, to say nothing of absinthe and vermouth, is, to all appearance, consumed by the eminently temperate French people. They must take them, I should say, medicinally, as cordials for that complaint which Albert Smith's old-lady patient used to call 'spiders at the heart,' and for which Albert's invariable and gratefully received prescription was gin coloured pink, with cardamons." *Paris Herself Again in 1878-9* by George Augustus Sala, 1884.

Bols Genever, 42.3% abv

www.bolsgenever.com

Style: Genever

Country of Origin: Holland

Available in: Holland, Germany, U.K., France, U.S.

Botanicals: anise seeds, clove, ginger, hops, angelica roots, liquorice, and juniper berries, and several more.

Distillation: There are four different distillates used in Bols genever. The first is malt wine. Our malt wine is based on rye, wheat, and corn. In a three-step distillation (in copper stills) we reach a alcohol percentage of 47% abv. The malt wine needs a maturation period of several weeks to balance the taste component. The second is neutral grain spirit. The neutral grain spirit we use in Bols genever is base on wheat. After a three-day fermentation and a distillation process in six copper columns, the taste of this alcohol at 96% abv is very neutral. The third is a juniper berry distillate. The juniper berries are soaked in malt wine and after some time distilled in copper pot stills. The fourth is the botanical distillate. The mix of botanicals are soaked in grain neutral spirit and distilled in copper pot stills. So all four distillates are made separately and then blended together. The final blend is adjusted to 42% abv by adding very neutral tasting de-mineralized water.

Tell us why you think your gin stands apart from all the others: Genever is made with malt wine. The content of the malt wine in Bols Genever is almost 60 percent, making it unique compared to other genevers available in the U.S. Bols genever is genever as it was consumed in the high days of genever drinking in the U.S. in the nineteenth century.

Any other idiosyncrasies that you'd like to tell us about? Genever, since December 2007, is a protected category, like champagne or cognac, and can only be made in Holland, Belgium, parts of Germany (Nordrhein-Westfalen and Niedersachsen) and France Nord (59) and Pas de Calais (62).

History: See timeline on previous pages.

Tasting Notes from Master distiller Piet van Leijenhorst (Lucas Bols): Bols genever is crystal clear [with] a clean, slightly juniper berry, herbal, smooth, and malty nose. Due to the high malt-wine esters, the nose is fruity and floral. Bols genever's taste is intense, malty, sweet, and complex. It is natural, smooth, and well balanced. Bols genever's finish is long-lasting, with an enticing tingling on the tongue.

Awards: Double gold at the SF Spirits competition, 2009.

A Certain Sort Of Dignity

"The folk attempt a certain sort of dignity at the start but they cannot long stand the strain, and soon a few drinks of 'Genever' (gin) puts them at greater ease and inspires such confidence as allows them to forget themselves somewhat." *Marken and its People* by George Wharton Edwards, 1912.

Boomsma Fine Young Genever Gin, 40% abv
www.boomsma.eu

Style: Genever
Country of Origin: Netherlands
Available in: United States, Canada
Botanicals: juniper berries
Distillation: Double distilled from a blend of 100% pure grain alcohol and grain wine.
Tell us why you think your gin stands apart from all the others: Surprisingly light and elegant, pure taste due to double distillation according to old Frisian [Frisians are Dutch people of Germanic descent] recipe.
Any other idiosyncrasies that you'd like to tell us about? Best served well chilled or on the rocks.
History: Boomsma Genever is one of Boomsma's oldest products. The genever is distilled according to a secret family recipe since 1883.
Tasting Notes from Boomsma: Lightly aromatized without any artificial ingredients. Light and elegant in taste with a subtle flavor of juniper berries, coriander, and a hint of citrus.
Boomsma Real Old Geneva, 38% avb
Available in: United States
Production: Matured for at least a year in oak casks. Malt wine percentage is high, which gives the Genever its distinctive taste.
Tell us why you think your gin stands apart from all the others: The only Old Genever in the Netherlands that guarantees a maturing process of at least a year in oak casks, which results in a superb genever with an elegant, soft and silky taste.
Any other idiosyncrasies that you'd like to tell us about? Best served slightly chilled.

"Gin.—This word is a corruption of the word "genievre," or junever [sic], the French and Dutch equivalents respectively for juniper, which is the essential flavouring ingredient. It is a spirituous liquor . . . The principal varieties are the English "gin," Geneva, Hollands, and Schnapps, the difference being one of flavour, and each manufacturer has his own recipe, which is preserved as a trade secret." *The Carbohydrates and Alcohol* by Samuel Rideal, 1920.

Genevieve "Genever-Style" Gin, 47.3 abv
http://www.anchorbrewing.com/about_us/anchordistilling.htm

Style: Genever Gin or Holland's Gin or Schiedam-style Gin

Country of Origin: USA

Available in: USA (many states but not all). On a limited basis in: Canada, England, Holland, France, Spain, Germany, Switzerland, Finland, Sweden, Guam, Taiwan, Australia, New Zealand.

Botanicals: Proprietary

Distillation: Botanicals distilled in a true "pot" still of traditional genever gin shape, from a fermented and distilled mash of wheat, barley, and rye malts

Tell us why you think your gin stands apart from all the others: It's very traditional and it's the first genever-style gin made in America in modern times.

Any other idiosyncrasies that you'd like to tell us about? Genevieve uses the same botanicals as Junipero (our "martini" gin), which makes an interesting comparison between the contrasting styles.

History: Released October, 2007. Another "first" for Anchor Distilling.

The Spirits that Haunted the House

"'Your story of a haunted house turns out to be a tale of smugglers. You said you came in contact with the spirits that haunted the house in which you had spent the night?'

'And so I did, my dear young lady,' replied the old gentleman; 'and more than that, I tasted them at Captain Jeffries' house, in the form of excellent Hollands gin.'" *The London: A First-Class Magazine*, 1867.

Zuidam Genever Gin, 40% abv
www.zuidam.com

Style: Genever
Country of Origin: Holland
Available in: USA, UK, Canada, Russia, Spain, China, Holland, Belgium, Japan, Lebanon.
Botanicals: juniper berries, licorice root, whole vanilla beans, aniseed, and marjoram.
Distillation: one-third malted barley, one-third corn, one-third rye are the base grains. We distill all the grains in small pot stills three times, then we add the botanicals for a fourth and final distillation.
Tell us why you think your gin stands apart from all the others: We are the only distillery that distills our own grain for the genever, instead of purchasing the spirits on the open market.
History: Fred van Zuidam was formerly the master distiller at deKuyper for 30 years. He and his son Patrick are working together using traditional methods with a modern approach to gin production. Both an old-world genever gin and the new-world dry gin are available side by side for the first time.

Chapter 7

Old Tom

> "Old Tom, he is the best of gin.
> Drink him once, and you'll drink him agin."
> *Ernest Maltravers* by Edward Bulwer Lytton. Published by Harper & Brothers, 1838.

Old Tom Defined. Kind of . . . Old Tom gin can be a real pain in the ass. What the hell is it? It's a general term for any sweetened gin, right? Yes it is—sometimes. At other times, it seems, Old Tom is, or was, simply a brand, and the gin in the bottle bearing that brand's name might or might not have been sweetened. It's also possible—likely, in fact—that Old Tom originated as a slang term for gin. Just as some Irish folk talk about a glass of *the crayture* (or "creature") when they're referring to whiskey, there's a good chance that Londoners in the eighteenth and early nineteenth centuries would ask their serving wenches for a spot of Old Tom when they wanted a glass of any sort of gin that was available at the time. We can go around and around on this subject till kingdom come, and we'll very likely always end up in the same place.

Where did the term "Old Tom" come from? There are a few stories surrounding this one. In the history chapter of this book you'll find the story of Captain Dudley Bradstreet, the eighteenth-century government agent who tattled on underground distillers and was himself an illicit purveyor of gin in London. It was he who devised a gin-dispensing machine of sorts that hid beneath the "sign of a cat" with "a leaden pipe . . . placed under the paw." And it was from that pipe that Bradstreet dispensed his gin, but although people—myself included—have been tempted to think that the term "Old Tom" came from this enterprising chappie's tom cat, there's nothing to indicate that Bradstreet's customers called his gin "Old Tom" at all. Still, though, it's a fun story, and although Bradstreet might not be the source of the Old Tom moniker, we're pretty much sure that the tale of his illicit antics is a true one.

Who is Old Tom?

"'Who is Old Tom?' asked Mrs. Spriggins. I replied that I did not know, and asked why she asked. 'Because,' she said, 'when Mr. Spriggins and I are sitting on the piazza, every little while some of his friends come up and say that Old Tom wants to see him, and he gets up and goes off looking pleased, and comes back with his face shinier than ever and smelling of peppermint.'" *John Paul's Book: Moral And Instructive: Consisting Of Travels, Tales, Poetry, And Like Fabrications* by Charles Henry Webb. Published by Columbian Book Company, 1874.

Next up for your consideration we have a passage from *The Encyclopædia Britannica: A Dictionary of Arts, Sciences, Literature and General Information*, published by The Encyclopædia Britannica Company in 1910: "The precise origin of the term 'Old Tom,' as applied to unsweetened gin, appears to be somewhat obscure. In the English case of Boord & Son v. Huddart (1903), in which the plaintiffs established their right to the 'Cat Brand' trade-mark, it was proved before Mr. Justice Swinsen Eady that this firm had first adopted about 1849 the punning association of the picture of a Tom cat on a barrel with the name of 'Old Tom;' and it was at one time supposed that this was due to a tradition that a cat had fallen into one of the vats, the gin from which was highly esteemed. But the term 'Old Tom' had been known before that, and Messrs. Boord & Son inform us that previously 'Old Tom' had been a man, namely 'old Thomas Chamberlain of Hodge's distillery;' an old label book in their possession (1909) shows a label and bill-head with a picture of 'Old Tom' the man on it, and another label shows a picture of a sailor lad on shipboard described as 'Young Tom.'"

So the guys who compiled the *Encyclopædia Britannica* in 1910 were good enough to leave us two explanations for the birth of the term "Old Tom," and the Thomas Chamberlain yarn seems to have clinched the title *Most Likely TrueTale* (in the case of Old Tom from the Hodge's distillery, at least), but these guys also thought that Old Tom gin was *unsweetened*, and that goes against everything we've been led to believe about this style of gin until recently. We can't go back and ask them about this, though, so we'll have to let this one be a mystery.

Now let's look at an advertisement for "David McArthur & Co.'s celebrated cordial. Old Tom Gin." that I found in *Mamma's Recipes for Keeping Papa Home*, a pamphlet published in 1901 by Martin Casey & Co., a liquor dealer based in Texas. "The eminent analyst, Dr. A. Clarence Yuilles, in his analytical report upon samples furnished him states: 'David McArthur & Co.'s Old Tom possesses a very fragrant and agreeable odor and taste, characteristic of Gin of good quality . . . This spirit is of considerable strength, and *has been somewhat sweetened* [italics mine]. The flavor is particularly pleasant, due to the Juniper and other aromatic ingredients which have been used. Altogether this Gin may be said to be of very superior quality." And this, I think, pretty much tells us that most folk thought of Old Tom as being a sweetened gin, and that fact most certainly was true when it came to bottlings that were produced for the rest of the twentieth century.

One more question arises about the identity of Old Tom—was it sweetened dry gin or was it sweetened genever? David Wondrich has some thoughts on this matter, and you'll hear them before this chapter's over.

Old Tom Flashbacks

Back in 1993, during those dark years when email wasn't quite so prevalent, I wrote a snail-mail letter to United Distillers in London to ask what they could tell me about Old Tom gin. And boy, am I glad that I did. Those kind folk sent me lots of material, most of it surrounding the 1903 trademark case that's mentioned in the *Encyclopædia Britannica* cited above. The letter, accompanied by some rather fabulous copies of Old Tom labels, told me that United Distillers stopped producing Old Tom in 1987—way later than I'd suspected—and that they'd continued to sell it until 1991 when their supplies were depleted. "I attach some early Boord's gin labels which show their famous cat and barrel trademark which was introduced in 1849," wrote Philippa Davis, Assistant Brand Manager for Gordon's gin at the time.

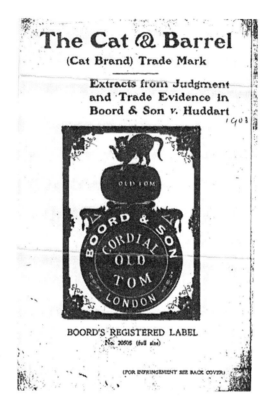

Five years went by without a word from Old Tom, but he cropped up again in 1998 after I met Hugh Williams, Master Distiller (now emeritus) for Gordon's, Tanqueray, and Booth's gins in London. Hugh was a guest on the Happy Hour radio show that I co-hosted with Paul Pacult—he of *F. Paul Pacult's Spirit Journal* fame—and Hugh and I got along famously. By this time, thank God, I was all about using email, so Hugh and I started a correspondence, and Ted "Dr. Cocktail" Haigh joined in. Looking over some of the old emails from this time period that I thankfully saved, I came across this from Hugh: "Our recipe books show [sweetened] Old Tom Gin being produced in the early 1800s. Prior to that it shows unsweetened recipes of the 1770s." So now we have an approximate starting date for sweetened Old Tom gin—the early 1800s—and 1987, at least as far as United Distillers were concerned, marked the end of production.

Hugh, God bless his little cotton socks, also sent me transcripts of both the 1903 trademark trial and of another legal investigation into the use of the term, this one heard in 1906. The later trial also involved Boord's, but this time they were going head to head with a Scottish company called Thom & Cameron.

Here's what I found in that document: "Before 1850 'Old Tom' was a name of unknown origin used by the public for gin." So, if you care to believe the transcript of that trial, we now have another tidbit of info on Old Tom. It seems likely that the moniker might have been used as an alias for gin, much like folk used to call the stuff Parliamentary Brandy and Cream of the Valley rather than utter the word *gin*. Luckily for us, this document also contained some pretty cool graphics.

Hugh and Ted and I let the Old Tom thing drop after a while, but I mentioned the Martin Casey ad that I'd found in the *Mamma's Recipes for Keeping Papa Home* pamphlet in our Ardent Spirits newsletter in late 2000, and on December 29 that year I received an email from Mark Andrews, founder of the Great Spirits company—most famous in the USA for bringing the most splendid Knappogue Castle Irish Whiskey into the country—and a mighty fine lad to boot. Here's an excerpt from the email: "On Christmas Day, while I was rummaging through the liquor closet, I happened on a bottle of OLD TOM. My father probably stored it away more than 50 years ago. I often feel that he is watching over Great Spirits, so it seems destined to be your Christmas present . . . This version of Old Tom is [made by] Booth & Co. The handsome label indicates that it was distilled and bottled by The Distillers Company, Ltd. at Linden, N. J., under the supervision of

Booth Distillers, London, England. It is 90 proof." This was going to be a treat, right?

I immediately told Hugh Williams about my good fortune. He responded thusly: "I'm very jealous of your acquisition! I've never seen a Booth's Old Tom bottle before . . . I wouldn't have the information regarding its recipe. I would have thought though that it would have been similar to the level that we used for the Gordon's version. About 0.015 kgs of sugar per litre at 88 US proof. Not enough to make the gin sweet, but enough to take the dry edge away . . . Like us, they would have dosed the sugar, made up in liquid form with demineralised water called 'capillaire,' after distillation in separate tanks from the distillation receiver. It had to be isolated because, as you know, sugar causes an obscuration to the strength when checking with a hydrometer. The sugar affects the density. This obscuration factor would be allowed for when checking with the hydrometer to get the mixture to the correct bottling strength. To ensure that the final alcoholic strength was correct, a 'burnoff' would be done. A pilot distillation of a fixed amount which would yield the correct alcohol level. Phew! Hope you were with me on that one! I thought I was going into my memoirs there!" Master distillers are such passionate souls, and I do enjoy peeking into the methods behind their madness from time to time—they carry so many jewels in those brains of theirs.

Once the bottle of Old Tom arrived safe and sound, we had to decide what to do with it, and it didn't take us long to decide to run a competition in the Ardent Spirits newsletter so we could share it with some ardent souls. We asked readers to tell us "why you need—really, really need—to taste authentic Old Tom gin." They had to abide by certain rules, too. Here's what we asked that they promise to do if they won the competition:

1. Get yourself to the tasting.
2. Supply your own accommodations, food, other drinks, clothes, etc.
3. Be neat, tidy, and well-behaved.
4. Be there on time.
5. Bring us a small present (optional).
6. Be very nice to us.
7. Come on whatever date we tell you, at whatever time we deem fit (it will probably be an afternoon affair).
8. Recite a poem for everyone at the tasting. (Okay, that one's optional, too.)
9. Wear odd socks (not optional).

The tasting took place on Wednesday, March 14, 2000. A handful of people gathered at Beekman Bar and Books, a plush cocktail lounge at First Avenue and 50th Street, to taste what we thought might be the last bottle of true Old Tom gin left on the planet. Here's what we said about it in the Ardent Spirits newsletter:

Super bartender Lou Cantres held forth from behind the stick as we tasted the Old Tom, generously donated by Mark Andrews of Great Spirits. We tasted the gin neat, then Lou made use of his considerable shaking skills to bring us some Old Tom cocktails. Conclusion? Old Tom was definitely a sweetened gin, but it certainly wasn't overly sweet. The familiar botanical flavors of London Dry gin mingled beautifully with a slight sweetness that prompted more than one guest to remark on the wonderful balance of the Old Tom bottling. And I think we all agreed that Old Tom is a perfect gin when it comes to making cocktails and mixed drinks.

Ardent Spirits would like to thank Mark Andrews for his generous donation, and many thanks are also due to Mark Grossich, owner of Manhattan's Bar and Book chain of luxury bars, for providing the venue.

The winner of the competition to attend this momentous occasion was self-confessed cocktail geek, Martin Doudoroff. Did he wear odd socks as instructed? No, he darned well didn't. He claimed it was a 'cultural thing.' We have no idea what kind of culture would strictly ban the wearing of odd socks and yet support attending a social occasion with complete disregard to the mandated dress code, but apparently Martin belongs to such a cult. We let him in anyway, and he turned out to be a grand lad!"

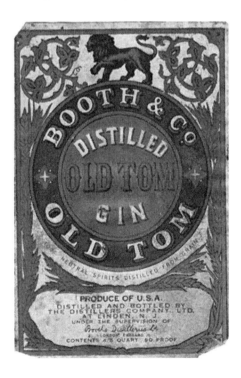

Here's the label from the bottle of Old Tom we drank that day

And Finally

Old Tom is back among the living. As far as I know, at the time of writing, there are just two bottlings on the market, Hayman's Old Tom and Ransom Old Tom. Both are sweetened gins, but they couldn't be more different from each other. David Wondrich played a hand in the formulating of Ransom. Here's what he has to say about it.

"I think gin was really a spectrum in the nineteenth century, from aromatized pot-still whiskey-style gins [e.g. genevers] to the "aromatized vodka" gins that we're familiar with now. Continuous stills didn't come into wide use until mid-century, so the Ransom is an attempt at doing the early version, sort of our look at a transitional gin. It's not as malty as a genever, but it's not neutral spirit either.

"And then there's the 'old gin' aspect, which gets mentioned a lot. A couple months in oak—call it shipping time—is an attempt at that, although some old authorities say gin should always be white. But the very fact that they had to say it suggests that it wasn't always so.".

In summation, then, taking into account all we know, all we aren't really sure of, and the wise words above from David Wondrich, I believe that the following statement is as close to the truth as we're likely to get:

> Old Tom was probably a euphemism for gin in the 1700s, and at some point in the early 1800s, when distillers started adding sugar to their gins, probably to disguise their badly made spirits, Old Tom became a term used to describe sweetened gins. These gins could have been genever, or genever-style gins that might have been aged, or could have spent time in wood when they were transported, thus getting just a little age on them. By the end of the 1800s it's more than likely that most bottlings of Old Tom gin were sweetened dry gins, and at the time of writing—summer, 2009—to the best of my knowledge Old Tom is represented by the two bottlings, Haymans, a sweetened dry gin, and Ransom., and Old Tom in the style of a slightly aged genever-style gin.

Chapter 8

Old Tom by the Bottle

As you probably just read, we found only two bottlings of Old Tom on the market at present. No doubt more will follow.

HINTS AND RULES

FOR BARTENDERS.

1. An efficient bartender's first aim should be to please his customers, paying particular attention to meet the individual wishes of those whose tastes and desires he has already watched and ascertained ; and, with those whose peculiarities he has had no opportunity of learning, he should politely inquire how they wish their beverages served, and use his best judgment in endeavoring to fulfill their desires to their entire satisfaction. In this way he will not fail to acquire popularity and success.

Bartender Jerry Thomas' first "hint or rule" for the bartender as found in his 1887 book, *The Bar-Tender's Guide or How to Mix all Kinds of Plain and Fancy Drinks*

The Fragrant Smell of Unadulterated Liquor

"I . . . have witnessed many a time the process of converting the juniper-berry into 'Old Tom.' The fragrant smell of the pure and unadulterated liquor was to me far more agreeable than the taste." *Passages from the Auto-biography of a "Man of Kent."* Edited by Reginald Fitz-Roy Stanley, 1866.

Hayman's Old Tom Gin, 40% abv
www.oldtomgin.co.uk www.alpenz.com

Style: Old Tom Gin
Country of Origin: United Kingdom
Available in: UK, Germany, Japan, USA, Australia
Botanicals: Juniper berries, Coriander seed, Angelica root, Orris powder, Orange peel, Lemon Peel, others
Distillation: Traditional column-still distillation
Tell us why you think your gin stands apart from all the others: Hayman's is the only authentic Old Tom Gin on the market, drawn from a recipe in production by the family in the late nineteenth century
History: One of the oldest distillers in the UK, the Hayman family produced this same recipe Old Tom Gin from the late 1800s into the early twentieth century. The family distillery is best known for its founder, James Burroughs, and the Beefeater brand it sold in 1987.
Tasting Notes from Hayman Distillers: Hayman's Old Tom Gin is a more botanically-intensive and lightly sweetened gin; with a more rounded and pronounced profile that lends more flavor to cocktails than its cousin, the London Dry style of gin.

MARTINI COCKTAIL.
(Use a large bar glass.)

Fill the glass up with ice;
2 or 3 dashes of gum syrup (be careful in not using too much);
2 or 3 dashes of bitters (Boker's genuine only);
1 dash of curaçao or absinthe, if required;
½ wine-glass of old Tom gin;
½ wine-glass of vermouth.

Stir up well with a spoon; strain it into a fancy cocktail glass; put in a cherry or a medium-sized olive, if required; and squeeze a piece of lemon peel on top, and serve (see illustration, plate No. 13).

MARTINE COCKTAIL.

The pics above come from the *New and Improved Illustrated Bartender's Manual* by Harry Johnson, 1900. The Martini recipe calls for Old Tom gin, and since the recipe demands "vermouth" with no descriptor, the drink would have been made with sweet vermouth, as was the style of the time. Note also that the name of the drink has been misspelled under the line drawing of the cocktail.

Ransom Old Tom Gin, 44% abv
www.Ransomspirits.com

Style: Old Tom
Country of Origin: USA
Note from Gary: *Tad Seestedt, Master Distiller of Ransom Old Tom, sent us a bit of an essay rather than sticking with the questionnaire we sent him, and we kind of admire that in a man, so read on and you'll discover all you need to know about this gin. (I added tasting notes, too.)*
Ransom Old Tom Gin: The Nitty Gritty
The Ransom Old Tom Gin recipe was developed in collaboration with author, historian and mixologist David Wondrich. After nearly two years of trials and experiments, the first batch was bottled in March of 2009. Traditional botanicals of juniper, orange, lemon, coriander, cardamom, and angelica are used for an infusion in a small percentage of high-proof corn spirits.

That small percentage is afterwards blended with a large percentage of a barley-based whisky, which is mashed and fermented in-house. All of the final distillate is passed through an alembic copper pot still. The use of a pot still helps to preserve and balance the subtle maltiness from the barley wort against the fragrance of the botanicals.

Because Ransom Old Tom Gin is barrel aged, it does exhibit an amber hue, and also picks up a hint of toast and sweetness from the oak. Only the best part of the "hearts" and a small part of the total distillate are kept for this bottling. As a result of making very precise and selective cuts at the condenser, this gin is quite aromatic and true to the botanicals, with a rich, smooth, and complex palate. It is one of the few gins today that is suitable for sipping if not used in cocktails. An additional commitment to quality is the use of only certified organically farmed ingredients.

Ransom Old Tom Gin is bottled at 44% abv, and as of April 2009 is available in the U.S. in the states of Oregon and Illinois. By late 2009 it will be available nationally within the U.S.

Ransom Spirits was first bonded in 1997 and began with production of brandy, eau de vie, and grappa. Grape—and fruit-based distillates continued until 2007, when experimentation began with gin and grain-based spirits. Currently gin, brandy, grappa, and whisky are being made on location in Sheridan, Oregon. The distillery is situated on a forty-acre farm in the coastal foothills of the Willamette Valley about 30 miles from the Pacific Ocean. Barley has been planted on the farm to make "estate" whiskies.

Tasting Notes from Gary Regan: I've never tasted anything quite like this. It's deliciously malty, wonderfully junipery, and amazingly complex. Makes the best Martinez cocktail I ever did have.

Chapter 9

Plymouth Gin

"There is a spirit called Plymouth gin, distilled in the town of Plymouth, which is very pure and wholesome, quite as much so as whiskey, and it is, I believe, a little cheaper." *The Popular Science Monthly*, 1877.

Plymouth Gin Defined

In defining Plymouth gin as a category, it's possible only to say that Plymouth is a gin that's made in Plymouth. Reason being that is that there is but the one gin made in Plymouth, so it's impossible to define characteristics that apply to "all gins" made in this English port town. That said, we can say that Plymouth gin has less juniper up front than traditional London Dry gins, and because more sweet root botanicals and fewer bitter botanicals are used in its production, Plymouth gin certainly has a style all its own. Call it a somewhat gentler gin than London Dry, but a gin with tons of character all the same. And strangely enough, because of the newly-written E.U. regulations that define styles of gin, Plymouth gin could legally be called a London Dry gin, since all the botanicals are distilled into the gin in one fell swoop. The powers that be at Coates' Plymouth Gin don't want that, though. And we don't blame them.

Plymouth Gin Flashbacks

In the mid-1990s, some of the early Internet cocktail junkies—people such as AgingWino, who turned out to be Ted "Dr. Cocktail" Haigh, for instance—started posting notices about Plymouth gin. There was a rumor that it was going to be available in the U.S.A. again soon (it had been missing from American shelves for a good long time) and people were getting excited—the brand had been bought from Allied Domecq by a gang of four entrepreneurs. Allied Domecq, a large beverage company that's no longer in existence, also owned Beefeater gin at the time, and for years they'd been plowing dollars into promoting Beefeater, while all but ignoring Plymouth. Things were about to change.

Also around this time I was lucky enough to get in touch with Sean Harrison, an ex-Royal Navy man who had been the master distiller at the distillery by the sea for two years when I interviewed him on August 9, 1996. Here's a look at some of my notes from that day.

Plymouth will probably be available in the USA prior to the end of '97.

Botanicals include juniper, coriander, angelica root, orange peel, lemon peel, orris powder and cardamom pods. No heavy, bottom end botanicals such as cinnamon are used, and this results in a drier, fruitier gin.

The original Coates' recipe [The Plymouth Gin Distillery was founded by Mr. Coates in 1703] used same botanicals as are used now . . .

Plymouth Gin Returns to the U.S.A.

Plymouth gin dates back to 1793 when the first reference to Coates & Co's Plymouth Dry Gin produced at the Black Friars Distillery—the building was built to house a Dominican order of monks known as the Black Friars—was documented, and it was a pretty big success in the States from the second it hit the market. I kept in touch with the entrepreneurs who had taken over the brand on a semi-regular basis, receiving frequent invitations to visit the distillery, and although I was eager to take them up on their kind offers, my plans to hang out with the guys in Plymouth were thwarted time and time again. No matter how hard I tried to organize a trip, something would always go wrong and I'd end up cancelling. There was a press trip to tour cocktail bars in London, with a side-trip to the Plymouth gin distillery thrown in, for instance, but I'd already booked a trip to France for the dates fixed for that one so I had to decline. My worst disappointment concerning a trip to Plymouth, though, went down in 2000 or 2001, I can't quite remember which.

I was in the north of England at the time, hanging out in Thornton Cleveleys, the town where I was raised, and Charles Rolls, one of the gang of four who had bought the Plymouth brand, called me and offered to fly up to Blackpool airport—a 30-minute drive from my mother's house—pick me up in his private plane, and fly me down to Plymouth to finally see the distillery. "Can I bring a friend?" I asked. "Sure," said Charles.

That night I saw Stan Ogden, my childhood friend—we've known each other since we were eight years old—in the Bay Horse, the pub that my parents used to run, and I invited him to come with me for a day in Plymouth. I was showing off. "Oh yes, one of the owners of the distillery will fly up here to pick us up, you know, we'll have a fabulous time . . ." I was playing at being the big shot, so something had to go wrong.

Here's my old friend, Stan Ogden—Poulton-le-Fylde's very favorite butcher.

Charles and I set a date, Stan's wife, Joanne, agreed to drive the two of us to the airport, and I set my alarm clock to give me plenty of time to get a big breakfast down me before setting off on this adventure. I awoke the following morning feeling pretty excited. Until I heard a clap of thunder, that is. I looked outside and saw a blanket of torrential rain. Small private planes don't fare too well in that sort of weather, so once again I didn't get to see Plymouth. Two days later I flew back to the States.

You'll no doubt be happy to hear that I did get to the Plymouth gin distillery eventually. In June of 2006, I was in London for the Bar Show. Jamie Terrell, bartender extraordinaire who was working with Simon Ford as an ambassador for Plymouth gin, kidnapped me and we hopped on a train to Plymouth. The day started with a couple of pints of Guinness at the train station in London, and during the train ride we kept our spirits up by quaffing a few Plymouth gin Negronis. Very tasty Negronis they were, too.

The Exhilarating Effect of Plymouth Gin

"The post-chariot that held in its musty recesses Miss Phyllida Courteen and Mr. Francis Vernon rattled on its way with all the vigour imparted by four fresh horses and the exhilarating effect of Plymouth Gin." *The Passionate Elopement* by Compton Mackenzie, 1916.

After checking into our hotel in Plymouth, Jamie and I agreed that it was probably best that we have a quiet evening since the following day we were scheduled to tour the distillery, help Sean Harrison make some gin, attend a tasting, meet various and sundry folk at the distillery, and generally be available for anything else that might crop up, so after an early dinner we just popped into a local pub for a couple of pints, paid a visit to a nearby casino, and ended up in some nightclub or other until, oh, I don't know, but unless Jamie tells me otherwise one day, I think that we got back to the hotel before dawn.

When I say that I planned to help Sean Harrison make some gin the following day, I was joking, of course, but I did make my own gin at the Plymouth distillery, and it was a pretty fascinating experience. In the distillery's laboratory Sean had set up a small still made up of flasks and beakers and the like. He had some high-proof vodka on hand and he offered me a selection of botanicals with which I could make my very own gin. How very intriguing.

I quizzed Sean endlessly about proportions and flavors and top notes and earthy tones and citrus and perfume and juniper and everything I could think of before I selected my botanicals, weighed them carefully, and allowed them to sit in the vodka for exactly 19 minutes before we started up the still. I wanted this gin to be different from all others, of course, and to my knowledge nobody else was using the 19-minute-steeping method . . .

Here's my gin being distilled.

It wasn't long before Sean and I were sipping Regan's Hand-Distilled Plymouth Gin—I think I can call it "Plymouth" since we were within the city limits, after all. Sean was pretty astounded at what I'd pulled off, and although he didn't say these words, I'm pretty sure that he was thinking something akin to "This is the worst bloody attempt at a gin that I ever tasted in my entire life." I know for sure that that's what I was thinking. I have fond memories of Plymouth.

Here's a picture taken in 2008 of Sean Harrison, Master Distiller for Plymouth Gin, with Allen Katz, Mixologist for Southern Wine & Spirits.

A Really Good Wholesome Spirit

"Who has not heard of Coates' Plymouth Gin ? One may ask why should this Plymouth Gin be so celebrated? Is there any special excellence in the water, or are we to look for the secret of its popularity in the manufacture? Possibly both, but certainly in the last. It is only natural that the traditional excellence should remain, for the Distillery is built upon the site originally occupied by the Dominicans, or Black Friars Monastery. The monks of old were always great at manufacturing brews that could tickle the appetite, and they are not wanting in that skill to-day. Have we not the delicious Chartreuse and the oily seductive liqueurs of the Benedictine to remind us of their present skill? Nothing could be more appropriate than that a Distillery should now flourish in the locality to which the Monastery gave its name. The old skill remains, and the Black Friars Distillery now launches forth on to the world a superb Gin. It has softness and aroma—special excellences. It flourishes under its own name, and is known far and wide as Coates' 'Original' Plymouth Gin. It has made its mark all over the world, and, after being established more than a century, still maintains its original superiority. There have been many competitors, but no rivals. Under various titles, such as . . . Hollands, Geneva, and Old Tom, the transparent spirit is scattered through many countries; but for real excellence, which is always the same, there is not one that can compare with the "Original" Plymouth Gin. The proprietors are naturally jealous of their reputation, and, to maintain its integrity unimpaired, they bottle, capsule, and label the whole of their produce which is intended for export on their own premises, and under their own supervision. As a consequence, the quality is always maintained and obtainable in every quarter of the globe. Those who enjoy a really good wholesome spirit on whose permanent excellence they can rely, cannot do better than test the quality of the 'Original' Plymouth Gin." Advertisement in *Royalty at Home* by Daniel Grant, 1894.

Chapter 10

Plymouth Gin by the Bottle

There's just one distillery in Plymouth, of course, but they do issue two bottlings of their wonderful gin, and a limited amount of a fabulous sloe gin. You'll find details of all three on the following pages.

Plymouth Gin, 41.2%
www.plymouthgin.com

Style: Plymouth
Country of Origin: England
Available in: Australia, Austria, Barbados, Brazil, Canada, Cyprus, Czech Republic, Denmark, Finland, France, Germany, Greece, Ireland, Italy, Japan, Latvia, Netherlands, New Zealand, Norway, Spain, Sweden, Switzerland, United Arab Emirates, United Kingdom, United States
Botanicals: Juniper Berries, Coriander, Lemon peel, Orange peel, Angelica, Orris, and Cardamom
Distillation: The botanicals are placed into a copper pot still with the base spirit. The still is heated to cook the oils out of botanicals. The distiller then picks the middle cut that is to be called Plymouth Gin.
Tell us why you think your gin stands apart from all the others: Plymouth uses lower amounts of juniper than traditional London Dry Gins and has a larger proportion of earthier botanicals as well as the sweet botanical of Angelica. This gives Plymouth a balanced and delicate palate. Plymouth also uses a water that has been softened by peat and granite that comes from the Dartmoor National Park—much the same as the water used to make single-malt Scotch.
Any other idiosyncrasies that you'd like to tell us about? Plymouth Gin is hand-crafted in England's oldest continuously operating distillery, using the same copper pot still from 1855. Plymouth Gin is one of only a small handful of gins in the world with a "Geographic Designation" similar to the *appellation controllée* designation for wine production. This means it can only be made in Plymouth, England, giving it a distinction of its own right.
History: Made in a former monastery that was built in 1432, the Black Friars Distillery has been the home to Plymouth Gin since 1793. In its past life it served as a town meeting place when the Pilgrim Fathers stayed the night before they set off from Plymouth, England to Plymouth, USA on the Mayflower. Distilling records show that the building was a mault (malt) house in 1697, distilling a number of common spirits, and in 1793 Mr. Coates founded Plymouth Gin. By 1900, Plymouth was shipping 1,000 cases a week to New York City and appeared in one of the first recorded dry martini recipes. This was printed in *Stuart's Fancy Drinks and How to Mix Them* in 1896.

Tasting Notes from the Plymouth Gin Distillery: Nose: Harmonious blend of citrus, juniper, coriander and a hint of cardamom, with deeper earthy notes of angelica and orris coming through. The coriander adds some fruitiness. The nose is clean and crisp and does not deteriorate. Taste: Very smooth and creamy on the tongue. At first the juniper and coriander dominate. Citrus flavors develop and root botanicals dry the back of the throat. The longer on the palate, the better and more balanced and taste becomes.

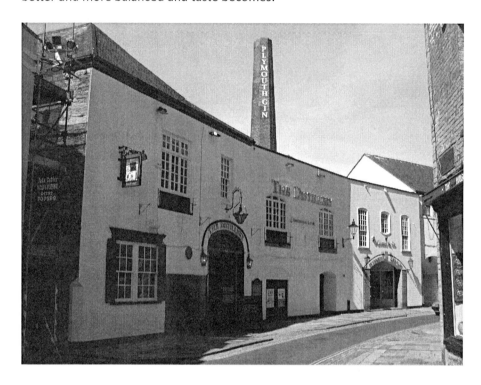

Awards: San Francisco World Spirits Competition 2008: Double Gold and Best Gin in Show. **San Francisco World Spirits Competition 2006:** Double Gold, Best Gin in Show and Best White Spirit *F Paul Pacult's Spirits Journal:* Five Stars. *New York Times,* **2007:** Best Martini Gin.

Plymouth Navy Strength Gin, 57% abv, is available in the United Kingdom, Australia and New Zealand. This is the only original Navy Strength Gin produced today.

"The extra alcohol content allows it to hold more botanical flavor yet it still retains that classic Plymouth smoothness. Plymouth Navy is a traditional strength required by the British Royal Navy, as it was a benchmark strength at which a spirit could be spilt on gun powder and it would still ignite. For almost two centuries, Her Majesty's Navy Fleet was sustained by Plymouth Gin and no ship left port without a bottle of Navy strength. At a hefty strength of 57% abv, Navy Strength offers a more intense and rich taste to the Original Strength. The fragrant and aromatic botanicals are amplified at this stronger strength, whilst retaining the smooth and soft character that Plymouth Gin is so renowned for."

The Secret Woman

"Give me a bottle of Plymouth gin an' my baccy, you can pinch me anywhere else you please." *The Secret Woman* by Eden Phillpotts, 1905.

Plymouth Sloe Gin, 26% abv, is made by steeping fresh sloe berries in high-proof Plymouth gin for four months before sugar and Dartmoor water are added to balance the liqueur before bottling. It's an entirely natural product with no added flavorings or color. The sloe berry is from the *Prunus* family and is a hard, small, purple-black fruit of the blackthorn, which traditionally grows in English hedgerows. Most of the sloes in Plymouth Sloe Gin grow wild in nearby Dartmoor National Park. Plymouth started producing Plymouth Sloe Gin in 1883 but the recipe got buried after World War II. Master Distiller Sean Harrison found the recipe and restored production of this traditional English Countryside Liqueur.

Bartenders Joaquin Simo and Alexander Day at the
New York launch of Plymouth Sloe Gin, 2008.

The Stonecutter's Wife

"He bought his wife for a stone two-gallon jar of Plymouth gin, if I was informed aright. She had belonged to a stonecutter, but as he was dissatisfied with her . . ." *In a Quiet Village* by Sabine Baring-Gould, 1900.

Chapter 11

Gin-Based Cocktails, Collinses, Highballs, Martinis, MarTEAnis, Mixed Drinks, and Other Such Formulas for Libations and Potent Potables Containing Gin in One or More of its Many Forms.

An Age of Progress

"This is an age of Progress. New ideas and new appliances follow each other in rapid succession to meet the ever increasing demand for novelties, which administer to creature comforts and gratification to fastidious tastes." *The Mixicologist* by C. F. Lawlor, 1895.

Here's the recipe chapter. The bane of a cocktail writer's existence. What to put in? What to leave out? How to style each recipe? Should I list the drinks alphabetically or by category—cocktails, highballs, slings, sours, etc. I decided on A to Z, and let everything else hang very loose indeed. On the A to Z front, I should mention, a drink such as the "1820"—a very unusual quaff, by the way—is filed alphabetically as though it was called "eighteen-twenty."

The recipes that follow have been stylized to an extent, but I haven't adhered strictly to a specific format, partially because I hate doing that, partially because I like to see the creators' personalities shine through in their recipes, and mostly because, since I'm self-publishing this book, I get to do it my way. I've had to dicker around with amounts on occasion because, despite my open letter to President Obama (*San Francisco Chronicle*, March 1, 2009), America is still on the imperial system of measurement while the rest of the world has been working on the metric system for years. I've given both measurements in each recipe here, but it isn't perfect. One fluid ounce is not exactly equal to 30 milliliters, but we pretend it is, and bartenders worldwide seem to have agreed that's how we'll translate each others' recipes. Not to worry though, I still hold that cocktail recipes are little more than guidelines, and amounts are inserted therein specifically so that we can near-as-damn-it ignore them when we make the actual drink.

You'll find lots of discussions about this drink and that drink in this chapter. Hopefully all the classic gin cocktails are here. (I discovered last minute that I'd forgotten to include the Hanky Panky, so I'm betting there's going to be one or two other drinks that I've missed. Let me know and I'll put them into a future edition.) There are lots and lots of twenty-first-century cocktailian masterpieces, too. (Not all of the bartenders credited for these drinks currently work at the bar mentioned in their recipes, but as far as I know, that's where they worked when they came up with the cocktail, or the credit reads the way each individual has requested. I hope.) Thanks to all you fabulous bartenders who contributed to this section, both for your recipes, and thanks, too, for all that you've taught me over the years.

More than Recipes

When a bartender sent me his or her thoughts on how the drink came together along with the recipe, I've sometimes included those notes here so you can get a glimpse into the mind of the cocktailian bartender. And I've also included bits of historical data and odd pieces of trivia. Sometimes the trivia pertains to the drink, sometimes you'll find odd quotes that might contain, say, the name of the cocktail or some information about one of the ingredients therein. It's just bits of bullshit to try to make the recipe chapter at least a little bit interesting.

Ingredients

Get ready to smoke some freshly-picked lavender over a bed of smoldering lapsang souchong tea if you want to make every single drink in this book. I exaggerate—but not by much. Such is the way of the twenty-first-century bartender. My generation was proud when we floated Galliano on top of a Screwdriver and called it a Harvey Wallbanger, but the same can't be said of today's bartenders. Thank God. I think it's necessary at this point in time to document exactly what the bartenders of today are up to, simply because the world has never seen this much original thinking when it comes to creativity in new cocktails. I've found the past 10 years or so to be utterly fascinating when it comes to new drinks.

Lots of the cocktail you'll find in this chapter are very simple to make, and if you see weird and wonderful ingredients, don't panic—use a decent search engine and I bet you'll find the vast majority of these items are available online.

Simple Syrup, unless otherwise noted, is made by dissolving one cup (200 g) of granulated sugar into one cup (240 ml) of water. It's good to do this over heat, but it's also wise not to let the water actually boil.

Flavored Simple Syrup, unless otherwise noted, is usually quite simple to prepare if you just apply a little common sense. Make simple syrup as above, then, when the sugar is dissolved and while the mixture is still hot, throw a bunch of basil in there and let it come to room temperature. Strain it through dampened cheesecloth and you have basil-flavored simple syrup. If you want lavender-flavored simple syrup, though, it's probably best to use lavender instead of basil . . . Get the idea? Good.

Raw Eggs are abhorrent to some, but when they're used in cocktails they can make such a fabulous difference—egg whites, when handled properly, bring a fabulous silky texture to a cocktail that just can't be otherwise attained. "But suppose I get salmonella poisoning?" you ask. Chances are you won't. I stole this from the *San Francisco Chronicle*:

So what about those salmonella risks? According to George Chang, food microbiologist and professor emeritus at UC Berkeley, "In studies of clean, intact eggs from modern egg factory facilities, less than 1 percent of the eggs contain detectable salmonella."

The risk is even smaller with egg whites. As Lawrence Pong, principal health inspector and manager of food-borne illness outbreak investigations for the Department of Public Health in San Francisco explains, "Egg whites are alkaline in nature, and salmonella colonies cannot survive there."

However, he says that colonies can grow in the yolks so there is always a slight risk if the whites are not separated properly. Nevertheless, the low risk may be another reason why people are less apprehensive about consuming raw egg whites. As Chang puts it, the risk of salmonella poisoning from eggs is "perhaps even lower than the risk of eating raw salads—definitely lower than the risk of crossing a street against a red light."

If you're the type that never crosses on red, pay close attention to your bartender as he separates the whites. Otherwise, enjoy. Excerpted from *Egg White Cocktails Going Over Easy* by Cindy Lee, Staff Writer, *San Francisco Chronicle*, June 6, 2008.

Raw Egg Stench Some folk can't stand the odor that sometimes accompanies raw eggs, and The Chief (Jon Bonné, my editor at the *San Francisco Chronicle*), advised me that a drop or two of bitters can mask this unpleasantness quite handily. At the time of writing this I believe that he was experimenting with a Margarita with raw egg white and orange bitters.

Gin You'll see more than a few recipes in this chapter that call for "gin," with no brand name or style mentioned. It's doubtful that the drink calls for genever or Old Tom gin, but any distilled gin, London Dry gin, or Plymouth gin will probably work I these cocktails, though it's good to be aware that they differ drastically from one bottling to the next.

Methodology

As is my wont, I've chosen to be minimalistic with the instructions on how to make each drink. And I've also used the creator's instructions on how to make these drinks on more than a few recipes. Sometimes their personality shines through in this sort of thing, but sometimes they use terminology that might be unfamiliar to some. For those who aren't quite sure, here's a list of commonly used terms, along with an explanation.

Build: Fill the glass with ice if called for, and add the ingredients in the order given. Add any garnish called for, stir briefly and serve.

Double-Strain: Some bartenders hate even tiny stars (shards) of ice to make their way into their cocktails, let alone the pulp from any citrus just that might be in the drink, so they hold a fine-mesh strainer over the glass and the strain the drink from the ice in the shaker or mixing glass by way of a Hawthorne (the one with the metal coil) or julep strainer.

Dry Shake: This is a relatively new method of making drinks and it pertains only to cocktails that call for raw egg whites (as far as I know). As a rule, the ingredients are added to the shaker *with no ice*, the drink is shaken for around 10 seconds in order to emulsify the egg white (make it as one with the other ingredients), and then ice is added to the shaker and the drink gets shaken again. I've heard this method called the "Mime Shake," too, and I do sort of like that since, when you see a bartender shaking a drink and there's no noise coming from the shaker, it looks as though she's miming.

Float: After making the drink, float the last ingredient on top by pouring it slowly over the back of a barspoon.

Layer: Pour the first ingredient into the glass, then slowly pour each of the other ingredients, in the order given, over the back of a barspoon so that each successive ingredient floats on top of the previous ingredient.

Muddle: Put the ingredients into an empty glass and grind them with a wooden pestle (preferably a PUG! muddler unless David Nepove reads this in which case you should use a Mister Mojito muddler) until all the juices have been extracted from any fruits and any sugar in the recipe is completely dissolved.

Rinse: Pour the ingredient called for into the glass, and by tilting the glass and rotating it at the same time, coat the entire interior of the glass.

Stir over ice and strain: Fill a mixing glass two-thirds full of ice and add the ingredients in the order given. Stir for approximately 30 seconds and strain the drink into the appropriate glass.

Shake over ice and strain: Fill a shaker two-thirds full of ice and add the ingredients in the order given. Shake for approximately 15 seconds and strain the drink into the appropriate glass.

Recipes, A to Z

> "If I was limited to just one base liquor I should unhesitatingly choose gin."
> David Embury, *The Fine Art of Mixing Drinks*, 1952.

After Hours
Adapted from a recipe by Satvik "Rick" Ahuja, Quarter Bar & Restaurant, Leicester, UK.

"I created this drink as gin is usually used in pre-dinner aperitif-style drinks, e.g., Martini, Negroni, G & T etc., or as refreshers in Fizzes, Tom Collinses, Aviations etc. I wanted to create a drink to show how gin could be used to great effect in the after-dinner category where brown spirits usually tend to dominate. Hence my use of a slightly softer yet rooty style of gin which marries well with the spice from Kummel and the nuttiness of the Maraschino also gives it the desired sweetness without making it overly cloying or heavy." Satvik "Rick" Ahuja.

45 ml (1.5 oz) Plymouth gin
10 ml (.3 oz) Luxardo maraschino liqueur
10 ml (.3 oz) Kummel
1 dash Regans' Orange Bitters No. 6
1 maraschino cherry, as garnish
Stir over ice and strain into a chilled cocktail glass. Add the garnish.

Alaska
In 1899 the state of Alaska issued the first liquor license in the U.S.A.
45 ml (1.5 oz) gin
15 ml (.5 oz) yellow Chartreuse
Stir over ice and strain into a chilled cocktail glass.

Alexander
60 ml (2 oz) gin
30 ml (1 oz) white creme de cacao
30 ml (1 oz) fresh cream
Freshly grated nutmeg, as garnish
Shake over ice and strain into a chilled cocktail glass. Add the garnish.

Six Of These Alexanders

"A rehearsal of 'Red, Hot and Blue!' was in progress. The star of the show, Jimmy Durante, sat on a shaky chair tilted against the bare bricks in the back wall of the stage. He looked as if he were trying to get as far away from other humans as possible. His face was haggard. When he took his cigar out of his big, ragged mouth his hands shook.

'I can't drink,' he said, shivering. 'Only my great sense of responsibility forced me to show up at the pickle works today. I can't drink. It's alright if I take a glass of vermoot, or some red wine. Yeh, that's all right. But last night I'm feeling thirsty, so I go to this joint across the street and I say to the bartender, 'recommend me something.' So he give me what he called an Alexander. I had about six of these Alexanders, and I get dizzy. When I go home I hit the bed and it whirls around like an electric fan. I am seasick. I'm in an awful fix. I want to die." Joseph Mitchell, *My Ears are Bent*, 2001.

Alley Cat
Adapted from a recipe by Frank Caiafa, Peacock Alley at the Waldorf=Astoria Hotel, New York City.
90 ml (3 oz) Tanqueray No. TEN
30 ml (1 oz) Benedictine
1 long orange twist (cut long to hang 'tail-like' from the glass), as garnish
Shake over ice and strain into a chilled cocktail glass. Add the garnish.

Allies Cocktail
Kummel is a liqueur flavored with caraway, fennel, and cumin, and the word "kummel" spelled in various ways but present in the Dutch, German, and Yiddish languages, can be used, in conjunction with other descriptors, to describe both caraway and cumin.
60 ml (2 oz) gin
30 ml (1 oz) dry vermouth
7.5 ml (.25 oz) kummel
Stir over ice and strain into a chilled cocktail glass.

Amalfi Coastal
Adapted from a recipe by Frank Caiafa, Peacock Alley at the Waldorf=Astoria Hotel, New York City.
45 ml (1.5 oz) Tanqueray No. TEN
30 ml (1 oz) limoncello
45 ml (1.5 oz) fresh blood orange juice
1 lemon twist, as garnish
Shake over ice and strain into a chilled cocktail glass. Add the garnish.

Amber Martini
Adapted from a recipe by Anthony DeSerio, Aspen Restaurant, Old Saybrook, CT. "In today's vodka imbibed society, gin has lost its popularity and most palates are not up to the heavy juniper taste of dry gins. However there are alternatives like Bombay Sapphire and Hendrick's that use a selection of botanicals that make the spirit more palatable. These little extra additives allow limitless possibilities in the creation of new cocktails and variations on the classics. The original Idea was simply inspired by the Amber Lounge needing a signature drink. I could have easily just gone for color and grabbed a whisky or bourbon bottle. But today's culture is not interested in that. Let's face, it the Martini is in. So how do you make Martini amber? I have two bases to work with, vodka and gin. Always a fan of the underdog let's try gin. We're going upscale so a high quality of gin is in order. Bombay Sapphire. What will mix well with it? Well the botanicals used in flavoring this product include almonds so a little amaretto will draw out that flavor. Also in Sapphire are grains of paradise which have an orange hint to them. Now along with the amaretto and a few orange bitters to play off the grains of paradise we are developing a light amber hue to the cocktail. To cut the bitterness of the gin and bitters, simple syrup or, better yet, agave nectar, finish this off creating a sweet aromatic zesty aperitif." Anthony DeSerio.
60 ml (2 oz) Bombay Sapphire gin
30 ml (1 oz) amaretto
15 ml (.5 oz) agave nectar (or simple syrup)
3 to 4 dashes Regans' Orange Bitters No. 6
Shake over ice and strain into a chilled cocktail glass with an amber swizzle stick

Anna Lovely

Adapted from a recipe by Timothy Lacey, Drawing Room at Le Passage, Chicago.
15 ml (.5 oz) green Chartreuse
60 ml (2 oz) Distiller's Gin No. 6
30 ml (1 oz) creme de peche
15 ml (.5 oz) fresh lemon juice
30 ml (1 oz) simple syrup
Rinse an old-fashioned glass with the Chartreuse. Add ice. Add the remaining ingredients and stir.

Apple Martini

"In the year 1666 [Isaac Newton] retired again from Cambridge to his mother in Lincolnshire. Whilst he was pensively meandering in a garden it came into his thought that the power of gravity (which brought an apple from a tree to the ground) was not limited to a certain distance from earth, but that this power must extend much further than was usually thought." *Conduitt's account of Newton's life at Cambridge.*

Note: In 2008 The Apple Martini was ceremonially buried in New Orleans by Simon Ford—the Plymouth Gin Man. Why? Because it wasn't a fabulous drink, that's why. Make it with gin instead of vodka, though, and despite the artificial overtones of some brands of apple schnapps, the drink becomes quite palatable. Some Bar Chefs are shaking their heads right now, but what did you expect from me? I'm the guy who likes to make drinks with Hpnotiq . . .
60 ml (2 oz) gin
30 ml (1 oz) green apple schnapps
Stir over ice and strain into a chilled cocktail glass.

Astoria Bianco

Adapted from a recipe by Jim Meehan, PDT, New York City.
60 ml (2 oz) Tanqueray gin
30 ml (1 oz) Martini & Rossi Bianco vermouth
2 dashes orange bitters (1 for Joe Fee, 1 for Gary Regan)
1 orange twist, as garnish
Stir over ice and strain into a chilled champagne coupe. Add the garnish.

Austrian Martini
Adapted from a recipe by Gary Regan, Ardent Spirits, NY, circa 1998.
The recipe used for making the Noilly Prat dry vermouth available in the U.S.A. has changed since this drink was created, and the new bottling, made the same way that NP's European version is made, is a little more floral than the one now on the shelves. You might, therefore, want to think about adding just a little less Zirbenz than is called for in this recipe to allow the new Noilly Prat to peek through the veil a little.
60 ml (2 oz) Tanqueray gin
30 ml (1 oz) Noilly Prat dry vermouth
15 ml (.5 oz) Zirbenz Stone Pine liqueur
1 lemon twist, as garnish
Stir over ice and strain into a chilled cocktail glass. Add the garnish.

Aviation
First printed mention in "Recipes for Mixed Drinks" by Hugo Ensslin, 1916. Ensslin was a bartender at the Hotel Wallick at the time, and since the recipe appeared during the First World War, when aviators were first being lauded for their heroic deeds such a dropping grenades onto enemy camps from their airplanes, the name of this drink was very timely.
45 ml (1.5 oz) gin
15 ml (.5 oz) maraschino liqueur
15 ml (.5 oz) creme de violette
15 ml (.5 oz) fresh lemon juice
Shake over ice and strain into a chilled cocktail glass.

Aviator
Adapted from a recipe by Jay Crabb, Bijou Restaurant and Bar, Hayward, CA.
In the 1930s Pan American Airways began to offer seats for 8 to 10 people on their planes carrying mainly mail, from San Francisco to Hawaii. Flight time was around 20 hours, and passengers were treated to formal meals and drinks in the cocktail lounge.
45 ml (1.5 oz) Van Gogh gin
7.5 ml (.25 oz) Luxardo maraschino liqueur
30 ml (1 oz) fresh lemon juice
15 ml (.5 oz) simple syrup
15 ml (.5 oz) Marie Brizard creme de cassis
3 dashes orange bitters
1 flamed orange twist, as garnish
Shake and strain everything except for the cassis into a chilled cocktail glass. Pour the creme de cassis down the side of the glass so that it settles at the bottom. Add the garnish.

Bar Club Press

Adapted from a recipe by Xavier Herit, Daniel, New York City.

60 ml (2 oz) Plymouth gin
22.5 ml (.75 oz) hibiscus syrup
22.5 ml (.75 oz) fresh lemon juice
1 egg white
1 lime twist, as garnish

Dry shake, then add ice and shake again. Strain into a chilled cocktail glass, and add the garnish.

Beauchamp Cocktail

Adapted from a recipe by Gary Regan and Amanda Washington at Rye, San Francisco.

Regan and Washington collaborated on this drink when Regan was selling his soul to B & B liqueur—something that he doesn't regret, by the by, cos he loves the stuff—in 2007.

2 slices peeled kiwi fruit
30 ml (1 oz) B & B
75 ml (2.5 oz) Bombay Sapphire gin
7.5 ml (.25 oz) fresh lemon juice
7.5 ml (.25 oz) simple syrup
1 lemon twist, as garnish

Muddle the kiwis with the B & B, add ice and the remaining ingredients. Shake and strain into a chilled cocktail glass. Add the garnish.

Bengali Gimlet

Adapted from a recipe by Jonny Raglin, Absinthe Brasserie & Bar, San Francisco.

1/4 fresh kaffir lime leaf
45 ml (1.5 oz) Tanqueray Rangpur gin
15 ml (.5 oz) fresh lemon juice
7.5 ml (.25 oz) fresh lime juice
20 ml (.75 oz) Curried Nectar*
1 lemon wedge, as garnish

Tear the lime leaf and drop it into a mixing glass filled with ice. Add the remaining ingredients. Shake and strain into a chilled cocktail glass. Add the garnish.

*Curried Nectar

1 1/4 cups water
1/4 cup cumin seeds
1/4 cup coriander seeds
1/4 cup allspice berries
2 tablespoons black peppercorns
2 tablespoons white peppercorns
1 teaspoon turmeric powder
2 dried Thai chilis
200 g (1 cup) sugar

Combine all the ingredients except the sugar in a heavy saucepan. Bring to a boil and boil for about 10 minutes. Slowly add the sugar, stirring constantly until it dissolves. Reduce the heat to low and simmer for about 20 minutes. Remove from the heat and let cool for about 1 hour. Strain through a cheesecloth into a glass jar. Refrigerate for up to 2 weeks.

Berry Breeze

Adapted from a recipe by Frank Caiafa, Peacock Alley at the Waldorf=Astoria Hotel, New York City.

60 ml (2 oz) raspberry, strawberry and blueberry-infused Bombay gin (steep at least three days)
15 ml (.5 oz) Cointreau
15 ml (.5 oz) simple syrup
15 ml (.5 oz) fresh lime juice
2 basil leaves
1 splash club soda

Shake everything except the club soda over ice and strain into an ice-filled highball glass. Top with club soda and stir briefly.

Big Ben

Adapted from a recipe by Philip Ward, Mayahuel, New York City.

60 ml (2 oz) Plymouth gin
15 ml (.5 oz) Grand Marnier
15 ml (.5 oz) Noilly Prat dry vermouth
1 dash Regans' Orange Bitters No. 6

Stir over ice and strain into a chilled cocktail glass.

Bijou Cocktail à la *Imbibe*

Recipe derived from David Wondrich's findings in his wonderful book, *Imbibe*. Wondrich discusses this drink, culled from Harry Johnson's 1900 book *The New and Improved Illustrated Bartender's Manual*, at length, and he also did much research on Johnson and found hardly anything to substantiate his boasts of owning fabulous saloons, winning competitions, and the like. Nevertheless, Johnson was a big shot bartender, and the Bijou is a big shot drink. Johnson's formula calls for a cherry or an olive garnish, and Wondrich wisely suggests that we go for the cherry in this case.

30 ml (1 oz) Plymouth gin
30 ml (1 oz) sweet vermouth
30 ml (1 oz) green Chartreuse
1 dash orange bitters
1 cherry, marinated in Luxardo maraschino liqueur, as garnish
1 lemon twist, as garnish

Stir over shaved ice and strain into a chilled cocktail glass.

Bitter Delight

Adapted from a recipe by David Nepove, Enrico's Sidewalk Cafe, San Francisco.

"A bitter delight, a gilded poison, a brilliant mischief, a splendid but certain misery the mercenary corrupter of his youth, the spoiler of his fortune, the ruin of his honour, and, perhaps, the destroyer of his life." *The Anatomy of Melancholy* by Robert Burton, 1824.

30 ml (1 oz) Campari
30 ml (1 oz) Citronge
15 ml (.5 oz) simple syrup
30 ml (1 oz) fresh grapefruit Juice
30 ml (1 oz) asti sparkling wine
1 spiral lemon twist, as garnish

Shake everything except the sparkling wine over ice, and strain into an ice-filled collins glass. Top with the sparkling wine and add the garnish.

Bitter End

Adapted from a recipe by Ted Kilgore, Monarch Restaurant, Maplewood, MO.

45 ml (1.5 oz) gin
15 ml (.5 oz) Campari
7.5 ml (.25 oz) green Chartreuse
7.5 ml (.25 oz) Nonino Amaro
22.5 ml (.75 oz) Martini & Rossi Bianco vermouth
22.5 ml (.75 oz) fresh orange juice
1 flamed orange twist, as garnish

Shake hard over ice for 20 seconds and strain into a chilled cocktail glass. Add the garnish. Savor the delicious bitterness!

Bitter French
Adapted from a recipe by Philip Ward, Mayahuel, New York City.
30 ml (1 oz) Plymouth gin
15 ml (.5 oz) simple syrup
15 ml (.5 oz) fresh lemon juice
7.5 ml (.25 oz) Campari
Champagne, to top
1 grapefruit twist
Shake over ice and strain into a chilled champagne flute. Top with champagne. Squeeze the twist over the drink, then discard.

Bitter Sweet Apples
Adapted from a recipe by Satvik "Rick" Ahuja, Quarter Bar & Restaurant, Leicester, UK.
"Sorry about the elaborate garnish. Hope you enjoy the drink." Satvik "Rick" Ahuja.
4 to 5 basil leaves, bruised between the palms of your hands
45 ml (1.5 oz) Beefeater gin
22.5 ml (.75 oz) fresh lime juice
10 ml (.3 oz) simple syrup
10 ml (.3 oz) Campari
90 ml (3 oz) fresh or good quality cloudy apple juice
3 apple slices soaked in Campari and coated with brown sugar, as garnish
Shake over ice and strain into a tall ice-filled glass. Add the garnish as a fan on top of the drink.

Bloodbath in the Bronx

Adapted from a recipe by Simon McGoram, Deputy Editor, Spanton Media Group, Mea Culpa Restaurant, Auckland, New Zealand.

"Hi there, I have a little submission I'd like to make from when I really was bartender—not just doing the occasional shift as I do now. The drink I'm submitting is called "Bloodbath in the Bronx" and as you may have guessed is a variation on an old Bronx cocktail/ Income Tax Cocktail. It was by created me at Mea Culpa (Latin for "I'm Guilty") a little 30 pax cocktail bar in Auckland, New Zealand in 2006. Notes: This was a very seasonal cocktail in New Zealand as we had a very short season for blood oranges which had to come form California or Australia. As such this was one for the specials list but something I enjoy when blood oranges are in season." Simon McGoram.

45 ml (1.5 oz) gin
22.5 ml (.75 oz) dry vermouth
22.5 ml (.75 oz) Spiced Sweet Vermouth*
22.5 ml (.75 oz) fresh blood orange juice
2 dashes Regans' Orange Bitters No. 6
1 blood orange wheel, as garnish.
Shake over ice and strain into a chilled cocktail glass. Add the garnish.

*Spiced Sweet Vermouth "Toast two cinnamon quills and a small handful of cardamom pods in a pan over medium-high heat. Allow to cool and infuse in vermouth (in a sealed container) for 3 days. Remove spices by straining vermouth back into a bottle for service. Useful for a variety of cocktails—particularly tasty in a rye based Manhattan." Simon McGoram.

Bloomsbury

Adapted from a recipe by Robert Hess, Drinkboy.com, Seattle.

"I set off in search of an old favorite, a Bloomsbury pub called The Lamb, which I hadn't visited in ages. Crikey, would it be a bloody boutique now or a high-end bistro serving baby vegetables to a black-clad clientele? Neither. The Lamb was just as I'd remembered it, a traditional pub at the end of snug Lamb's Conduit Street, with a wooden bar, beveled glass fixtures, nicely done prints on the wall, Young's bitter on tap and—need it be said?—too much cigarette smoke." Excerpted from London Calling, an article by David Armstrong that appeared in the *San Francisco Chronicle*, April 8, 2001.

60 ml (2 oz) Tanqueray No. TEN gin
15 ml (.5 oz) Licor 43
15 ml (.5 oz) Lillet Blanc
2 dashes Peychaud's bitters
1 lemon twist, as garnish
Stir over ice and strain into a chilled cocktail glass. Add the garnish.

Blue Gin Rizz
Adapted from a recipe by H. Joseph Ehrmann, Elixir, San Francisco.
3 kumquats
1 handful blueberries (reserve a few as garnish)
45 ml (1.5 oz) Bluecoat gin
15 ml (.5 oz) Domaine de Canton ginger liqueur
15 ml (.5 oz) simple syrup
Club soda
2 to 3 kumquat slices, as garnish
Muddle the kumquats and blueberries in a mixing glass. Add ice and the remaining ingredients, except for the soda. Shake well over ice and strain into an ice-filled highball glass. Top with the soda and add the garnishes.

Blue Ruin
Adapted from a recipe by Timothy Lacey, Drawing Room at Le Passage, Chicago.
"This recipe only works with ripe blueberries. Use only blueberries, preferably local, that are in season. The point of this drink is to showcase the blueberries. I strongly advise against making this drink in the northern hemisphere in, say, December. It will suck." Timothy Lacey.
1 handful blueberries (about 20)
10 ml (.3 oz) fresh lemon juice
22.5ml (.75 oz) simple syrup
1 pinch salt
60 ml (2 oz.) Martin Miller's gin (80 proof)
1 skewered blueberry, as garnish
Muddle the blueberries with lemon juice, simple syrup and salt in a cocktail shaker. Add ice, shake and strain into an ice-filled old-fashioned glass. Add the garnish.

Blue Train Cocktail
It's very possible that the Blue Train Cocktail was named for Agatha Christie's book, *The Mystery of the Blue Train*, a novel featuring Hercule Poirot that was published in 1928, two years prior to the drink appearing in the Savoy Cocktail Book. Rufus Van Aldin, a character in the book, stayed at the Savoy Hotel, and according to *Mystery Reader's Walking Guide: London*, the Savoy was "most definitely Christie territory."
45 ml (1.5 oz) gin
30 ml (1 oz) blue curaçao
15 ml (.5 oz) fresh lemon juice
Shake over ice and strain into a chilled cocktail glass.

Blueberry Amnesia
Adapted from a recipe by Erick Castro, Lounge ON20, Sacramento.
6 to 8 ripe blueberries
22.5 ml (.75 oz) fresh lemon juice
45 ml (1.5 oz) Plymouth gin
15 ml (.5 oz) Luxardo limoncello
15 ml (.5 oz) simple syrup
Club soda
4 sugar-coated blueberries on a cocktail sword, as garnish
Muddle the blueberries and lemon juice in a mixing glass. Add ice and the remaining ingredients except soda. Shake over ice and strain into an ice-filled collins glass. Top with soda and add the garnish.

Bold, Bright, and Fearless Cocktail
Adapted from a recipe created by Gary Regan to toast the 144th anniversary of the *San Francisco Chronicle* in 2009.
If you use Bols genever in this cocktail, you'll be sipping a kind, gentle cocktail with a goodly dose of character, and if you're not a big fan of whiskey, the Bols bottling should suit you well. If you are truly Bold, Bright, and Fearless, though, and if you like a tot of whiskey every now and again, use Anchor Distillery's Genevieve to make this cocktail. The Genevieve version is quite a doozy.
45 ml (1.5 oz) genever
15 ml (.5 oz) Cointreau
15 ml (.5 oz) pineapple juice
15 ml (.5 oz) fresh lemon juice
1 dash Angostura bitters
1 lemon twist, as garnish
Shake over ice and strain into a chilled cocktail glass. Add the garnish.

Botanical Breeze
Adapted from a recipe by Gary Regan, Ardent Spirits, NY.
The herbs, barks, and spices used to make liqueurs such as B & B or Benedictine, are referred to as the "botanicals." And the same is true of similar ingredients used in the production of gin, vermouth, bitters, and many other spirituous products. Cinnamon, cardamom, saffron, vanilla, coriander, myrrh, hyssop, and nutmeg are among the 27 botanicals used to make Benedictine and B & B.
45 ml (1.5 oz) Bombay Sapphire gin
15 ml (.5 oz) B & B
15 ml (.5 oz) St. Germain elderflower liqueur
15 ml (.5 oz) fresh lime juice
1 slice peeled kiwi fruit, as garnish
Shake over ice and strain into a chilled champagne coupe. Float the garnish.

Breakfast Martini

Adapted from a recipe by Salvatore Calabrese, Salvatore@Fifty, London.
Salvatore Calabrese, known as The Maestro, is one of London's most celebrated bartenders, and rightly so. The man runs a very stylish, somewhat exclusive cocktail lounge that's as comfortable as a neighborhood tavern and as refined as Buckingham Palace.

50 ml (1.75 oz) Bombay gin
15 ml (.5 oz) Cointreau
15 ml (.5 oz) lemon juice
1 1/2 teaspoons orange marmalade
Shredded orange peel, as garnish

Place all ingredients in the shaker with ice, shake sharply to allow the marmalade to mix, strain into a chilled cocktail glass and add the garnish.

Bronx Cocktail

The story of the creation of this drink is detailed in *The Old Waldorf-Astoria Bar Book*, and although the book claims that it was created prior to 1917, no clue exists there to give an indication of the precise year of its birth. According to the book, the bartender who first made the Bronx was a certain Johnnie Solon (or Solan), and he made the drink as a response to a challenge from a waiter by the name of Traverson. The Bronx was a variation of a popular drink of the time known as the Duplex (sweet and dry vermouth with orange bitters), and it became so popular that the bar was soon using more than a case of oranges per day. The book quotes Solon as saying: "I had been at the Bronx Zoo a day or two before, and I saw, of course, a lot of beasts I had never known. Customers used to tell me of the strange animals they saw after a lot of mixed drinks. So when Traverson said to me, as he started to take the drink in to the customer, 'What'll I tell him is the name of this drink?' I thought of those animals, and said, 'Oh, you can tell him it is a Bronx.'"

60 ml (2 oz) gin
7.5 ml (.25 oz) sweet vermouth
7.5 ml (.25 oz) dry vermouth
30 ml (1 oz) fresh orange juice
2 dashes orange bitters
1 orange twist, as garnish

Shake over ice and strain into a chilled cocktail glass. Add the garnish.

Bronx Cocktail à la *Imbibe*

Recipe derived from David Wondrich's findings in his wonderful book, *Imbibe*.
Wondrich nails the date of this one to 1900, or thereabouts . . . He found reference
to it on a menu owned by the New York Historical Society, with the words "about
1895" written in pencil. Since the Zaza cocktail is also on the menu, and since, as
Wondrich points out, that cocktail was named for an 1899 play, the menu must be
from 1900. Or thereabouts. Noting that he enjoys a fair amount of orange juice in
his Bronx, Wondrich then does us the favor of finding a recipe that calls for very
little. It was printed in *World Drinks and How to Mix Them* by William T. Boothby, a
book published in 1908, and this recipe is labeled "à la Billy Malloy, Pittsburgh, PA."
30 ml (1 oz) Plymouth gin
30 ml (1 oz) dry vermouth
30 ml (1 oz) sweet vermouth
1 teaspoon fresh orange juice
2 dashes orange bitters
Shake over cracked ice and strain into a chilled cocktail glass.

Bronx Cocktail à la Wondrich

Recipe derived from David Wondrich's wonderful book, *Imbibe*.
Wondrich gives a formula for a very strong Bronx Cocktail (see the Bronx Cocktail
à la *Imbibe* recipe above) in his groundbreaking book, then he goes on to say that
he prefers to make them in the style of Johnny Solon, the famed bartender at
the Waldorf-Astoria who has been credited, perhaps erroneously, with creating
the drink. Here, then, is Wondrich's fave recipe for the Bronx: "When the heat is
oppressive, a nice, cold Bronx prepared thus is a fine thing," he says.
45 ml (1.5 oz) gin (Plymouth, Beefeater, Tanqueray, or "any other good London
dry gin")
22.5 ml (.75 oz) fresh orange juice
1 teaspoon dry vermouth
1 teaspoon sweet vermouth
Shake over cracked ice and strain into a chilled cocktail glass.

Caprice

According to the Merriam-Webster's Online Dictionary, caprice can be defined
as "a sudden, impulsive, and seemingly unmotivated notion or action," as in, "by
sheer caprice she quit her job."
45 ml (1.5 oz) gin
15 ml (.5 oz) dry vermouth
15 ml (.5 oz) Benedictine
1 dash orange bitters
1 lemon twist, as garnish
1 maraschino cherry, as garnish
Stir over ice and strain into a chilled cocktail glass. Add the garnishes.

Caricature Cocktail

Adapted from a recipe by Gary Regan, Ardent Spirits, NY.

This drink is actually a rip-off of a drink called the Old Flame, created by Dale DeGroff. Gary Regan played around with Dale's formula a little, then named the drink in honor of Dale's wife, Jill DeGroff, a graphic artist who executes fabulous caricatures of the world's leading cocktailian bartenders.

45 ml (1.5 oz) gin
15 ml (.5 oz) sweet vermouth
20 ml (.75 oz) Cointreau
15 ml (.5 oz) Campari
15 ml (.5 oz) fresh grapefruit juice
1 orange twist, as garnish
Shake over ice and strain into chilled cocktail glass. Add the garnish.

Carousel

Adapted from a recipe by David Nepove, Enrico's Sidewalk Cafe, San Francisco.4 mint leaves
15 ml (.5 oz) fresh lemon juice
45 ml (1.5 oz) Tanqueray No. TEN gin
22.5 ml (.75 oz) Citronge
In a mixing glass, muddle the mint leaves with the lemon juice. Add ice and the remaining ingredients. Shake and strain into a chilled sugar-rimmed cocktail glass.

Casino Royale

Adapted from a recipe by Dale DeGroff, author of *The Essential Cocktail*, New York City.

Casino Royale, by Ian Fleming, 1953, features double agent Vesper Lynd, the woman for whom the Vesper cocktail is named. Bond describes the drink thusly: "Three measures of Gordon's, one of vodka, half a measure of Kina Lillet. Shake it very well until it's ice-cold, then add a large thin slice of lemon-peel."

15 ml (.5 oz) gin
30 ml (1 oz) maraschino liqueur
30 ml (1 oz) fresh orange juice
7.5 ml (.25 oz) fresh lemon juice
Champagne
1 orange peel spiral, as garnish
Shake the gin, liqueur, and juices over ice, and strain into a chilled cocktail glass. Top with the champagne and add the garnish.

Celine Fizz

Adapted from a recipe by Philip Ward, Mayahuel, New York City.
60 ml (2 oz) Plymouth gin
15 ml (.5 oz) St Germain elderflower liqueur
15 ml (.5 oz) fresh grapefruit juice
7.5 ml (.25 oz) simple syrup
7.5 ml (.25 oz) fresh lemon juice
1 dash Regans' Orange Bitters No. 6
1 egg white
Club soda, to top
1 grapefruit twist
Dry shake, then add ice and shake again. Strain into a chilled fizz glass and top with soda. Squeeze the twist over the drink, then discard.

Chamomile Cocktail

Adapted from a recipe by Jim Meehan, PDT, New York City.
45 ml (1.5 oz) Plymouth gin
30 ml (1 oz) chilled brewed chamomile tea
15 ml (.5 oz) Marolo Grappa & Chamomile liqueur
15 ml (.5 oz) honey syrup (1:1)
1 lemon twist, as garnish
Stir over ice and strain into a chilled champagne coupe. Add the garnish.

Chanticleer Cocktail

Reformulated from a recipe found in *The Old Waldorf-Astoria Bar Book*.
The word *chanticleer* is French for "rooster," and at the old Waldorf-Astoria bar, the drink was served with "a Cock's Comb, if desired."
30 ml (1 oz) gin
45 ml (1.5 oz) dry vermouth
15 ml (.5 oz) Cointreau
1 orange twist, as garnish
Stir over ice and strain into a chilled cocktail glass. Add the garnish.

Chatham Cocktail

Adapted from a recipe in *Jones' Complete Barguide*, 1977.
Rumor has it that this drink was created during WWII for Princess Juliana of the Netherlands. She was in exile at the time, and she and her family spent some of the war years at the Chatham Bars Inn in Massachusetts. We can't find anything that substantiates this claim, though.
60 ml (2 oz) gin
15 ml (.5 oz) Domain de Canton ginger liqueur
15 ml (.5 oz) fresh lemon juice
Shake over ice and strain into a chilled cocktail glass.

Ching

Adapted from a recipe submitted to us by Sarah Mitchell, Lab-Townhouse, London.
"The Ching was created at the Lab Bar by Chris Perrie, and it's named after Tim Stones, the previous Lab gin princess. Ching was a nickname of Tim's at one point. It's because of Tim that I love gin so much. Nothing to do with us sampling while we were behind the bar together or anything like that . . ."

45 ml (1.5 oz) Tanqueray or Beefeater gin
15 ml (.5 oz) John D. Taylor's Velvet Falernum
15 ml (.5 oz) fresh lime juice
1 barspoon vanilla sugar
1 splash cloudy apple juice
1 dash ginger cordial
4 mint leaves
1 mint sprig, as garnish
1 apple fan, as garnish

Build in a highball glass over crushed ice, churning to break the leaves slightly. Garnish with a mint sprig and an apple fan it you are feeling it.

Christopher Bloom!

Adapted from a recipe by Charlotte Voisey, Mixologist, Hendrick's Gin.
This was one of the drinks served at the Hendrick's Bartender's Croquet Tourney in New York, May 12, 2009. The drink was served in dainty little tea cups that were fitted with stems such as the stems we see on cocktail glasses. You probably don't have any of these curious glasses, so you might want to serve the Christopher Bloom! in a tea cup or in a cocktail glass. It's a decision you're going to have to make on your own.
"Christopher Bloom was a fabulous and very jolly contestant in our Chicago leg of the Hendrick's Bartender Limerick and Cocktail Competition back in January of this year. His enthusiasm behind the bar was infectious! So much so that I created a cocktail in his honor." Charlotte Voisey, Mixologist, Hendrick's Gin, 2009.

45 ml (1.5 oz) Hendrick's Gin
22.5 ml (.75 oz) Solerno blood orange liqueur
30 ml (1 oz) Fuji apple juice
7.5 ml (.25 oz) maraschino liqueur
7.5 ml (.25 oz) fresh lemon Juice
1 barspoon rose syrup
2 dashes Peychaud's bitters
1 edible flower, as garnish

Combine ingredients over ice, shake smartly. Puff up chest and declare the cocktail name proudly as it is served up in a tea time martini glass. Add the garnish. Wink. Serve.

Claridge Cocktail

Reformulated from a recipe found in *The Savoy Cocktail Book*, 1930.

Claridge's, the London hotel owned at the time by Richard D'Oyly Carte, was where Ada (Coley) Coleman got her start behind the stick. Coley, who went on to achieve fame behind the bar at the Savoy, was fond of telling people that although she never married, she'd been "looked after."

30 ml (1 oz) gin
30 ml (1 oz) dry vermouth
15 ml (.5 oz) Cointreau
15 ml (.5 oz) apricot brandy
Stir over ice and strain into a chilled cocktail glass.

Clover Club Cocktail

The first recipes for the Clover Club called for raspberry syrup, which has sometimes been replaced by grenadine. If you have no raspberry syrup, though, Chambord black raspberry liqueur will work, or look for a bottle of creme de framboise.

60 ml (2 oz) gin
30 ml (1 oz) fresh lemon juice
1 egg white
7.5 ml (.25 oz) raspberry syrup or Chambord
Shake over ice and strain into a chilled cocktail glass.

Cocktail des Fines Herbes

Adapted from a recipe by Gary Regan, Ardent Spirits, NY.

This is a variation on the Pompier Cocktail (which calls for cassis instead of the B & B), and in turn, the Pompier Cocktail was based on the Pompier Highball, a drink found in Charles Baker, Jr.'s *The Gentleman's Companion*, 1939. I developed this drink using the Noilly Prat Original dry vermouth, a product made available in the U.S.A. in early 2009. And since he was sucking up to the Bacardi company at the time, he specifically used Bombay Sapphire gin in this variation, and threw in a little B & B for good measure.

60 ml (2 oz) Noilly Prat Original dry vermouth
15 ml (.5 oz) Bombay Sapphire gin
7.5 ml (.25 oz) B & B
1 lemon twist, as garnish
Stir and strain into a chilled cocktail glass. Add the garnish.

Cool As a Cucumber Elixir

Adapted from a recipe by Angie Jackson, Freelance Mixologist, and Traveling Elixir Fixer from ultimate-elixirs.com, Chicago.

"Cool As a Cucumber Elixir is a light, clean and crisp cocktail utilizing the beautiful citrus and floral notes of Hendrick's gin and the delicate market fresh aromas of cucumber and dill. This ultimate home-entertaining cocktail is versatile enough to be served cocktail style in the evening paired with light appetizers, or served on the rocks with cucumber wheels layered in the ice for a nice brunch-drink alternative. I highly recommend dancing around shamelessly to Duffy's "Mercy" while consuming [this drink]. Cheers!" Angie Jackson.

60 ml (2 ounces) Hendrick's gin*
60 ml (2 ounces) Ocean Spray white cranberry juice
22.5 ml (.75 ounce) fresh lemon juice
3 thin-sliced cucumber wheels
1 fresh dill sprig, as garnish

Shake the gin, juices, and 2 of the cucumber wheels over ice, and strain into a chilled cocktail glass. Add the garnishes.

*Angie also makes this drink with the North Shore Distillery's Distiller's Gin No. 6.

Cornwall Negroni

Adapted from a recipe by Philip Ward, Mayahuel, New York City.

This drink is a fabulous variation on the regular Negroni, and it's named for the town of Cornwall, New York. Philip Ward, creator of this drink, is thought to have been banned from Cornwall . . .

60 ml (2 oz) Beefeater gin
15 ml (.5 oz) Campari
15 ml (.5 oz) Punt e Mes
15 ml (.5 oz) sweet vermouth
2 dashes orange bitters
1 orange twist, as garnish

Stir over ice and strain into a chilled cocktail glass. Add the garnish.

Corpse Reviver No. 2

Based on Harry Craddock's 1930 recipe in *The Savoy Cocktail Book*. Craddock noted that, "Four of these taken in swift succession will unrevive the corpse again."
20 ml (.75 oz) gin
20 ml (.75 oz) Cointreau
20 ml (.75 oz) Lillet Blanc
20 ml (.75 oz) fresh lemon juice
2 dashes absinthe
Shake over ice and strain into a chilled cocktail glass.

Correct Cocktail

Adapted from a recipe by Gary Regan, Ardent Spirits, NY.
"The opposite of a correct statement is a false statement. But the opposite of a profound truth may well be another profound truth." Niels Bohr, 1885-1962.
45 ml (1.5 oz) Right gin
15 ml (.5 oz) Domain de Canton ginger liqueur
15 ml (.5 oz) Cointreau
15 ml (.5 oz) fresh lemon juice
2 dashes Regans' Orange Bitters No. 6
1 lemon twist, as garnish
Shake over ice and strain into a chilled champagne flute. Add the garnish.

Country Cocktail

Adapted from a recipe by Dale DeGroff, author of *The Essential Cocktail*, New York City.
"Too bad the only people who know how to run the country are busy driving cabs and cutting hair." George Burns, 1896-1996.
45 ml (1.5 oz) Tanqueray gin
15 ml (.5 oz) John D. Taylor's Velvet Falernum
15 ml (.5 oz) simple syrup
20 ml (.75 oz) fresh lime juice
15 ml (.5 oz) Berentzen's Apfelkorn
1 wide slice English cucumber skin, as garnish
1 thin wheel of English cucumber, as garnish
Kosher salt mixed with dry thyme.
Shake over ice and strain into a chilled cocktail glass rimmed with the salt/thyme mixture. Add the garnishes.

Cranberry Cobbler
Adapted from a recipe by Jim Meehan, PDT, New York City, and Michael Madrusan.
4 cranberries, cooked in simple syrup till they almost pop
15 ml (.5 oz) cranberry simple syrup (reserved from cooking the berries)
1 orange wedge
1 lemon wedge
60 ml (2 oz) Beefeater gin
22.5 ml (.75 oz) Lustau East India sherry
1 mint sprig, as garnish
Muddle the fruit and cranberry syrup in a mixing glass. Add ice and the remaining ingredients. Shake and strain into an ice-filled highball glass. Add the garnish.

Creole Lady
Adapted from a recipe by Neyah White, Nopa, San Francisco, 2008.
The word creole can be used to describe someone of European descent who was born in the West Indies, and it also refers to people descended from the French settlers of Louisiana.
37.5 ml (1.25 oz) gin (Martin Miller's Westbourne Strength is good here)
20 ml (.75 oz) Clement Creole Shrubb
15 ml (.5 oz) fresh lemon juice
20 ml (.75 oz) egg white
Shake hard over ice and strain into a chilled cocktail glass.

Crossroads Cooler
Adapted from a recipe by Ryan Maybee, Owner/Sommelier, JP Wine Bar & Coffee House, Kansas City, MO.
45 ml (1.5 oz) dry chardonnay
45 ml (1.5 oz) cucumber-infused Beefeater gin
15 ml (.5 oz) mint syrup
15 ml (.5 oz) fresh lime juice
1 thin slice fresh cucumber, as garnish
Shake over ice and strain into a chilled tall collins glass. Add the garnish.

Cucumber-Melon
Adapted from a recipe by Nate Windham, Palapa's Surfside, Colorado Springs, CO. "I am currently the Executive Bartender for Palapa's Surfside in Colorado Springs. I also write a cocktail column for a paper here in town that is online at steppinoutmag.com. Just wanted to send a couple of my own gin cocktails for the Compendium. I could do this all day . . . . What fun!" Nate Windham.
1 mint sprig
1 large melon ball
1/2 inch cucumber slice
45 ml (1.5 oz) Beefeater gin
15 ml (.5 oz) Noilly Prat dry vermouth
15 ml (.5 oz) fresh lime juice
15 ml (.5 oz) simple syrup
1 small melon ball wrapped in cucumber, as garnish
1 small mint sprig, as garnish
Muddle the mint, melon ball, cucumber, sugar and lime juice in a mixing glass. Add ice and the remaining ingredients. Shake and strain into an ice-filled highball glass. Add the garnish.

Cynartown
Adapted from a recipe by Philip Ward, Mayahuel, New York City.
60 ml (2 oz) Beefeater gin
22.5 ml (.75 oz) Carpano Antica
15 ml (.5 oz) Cynar
1 cherry, as garnish (not a maraschino for god's sake)
Stir over ice and strain into a chilled cocktail glass. Add the garnish.

Daisy Mae
Adapted from a recipe by Philip Ward, Mayahuel, New York City.
60 ml (2 oz) Junipero gin
22.5 ml (.75 oz) green Chartruese
22.5 ml (.75 oz) simple syrup
30 ml (1 oz) fresh lime juice
1 mint sprig, as garnish
Shake over ice and strain into an ice-filled highball glass. Add the garnish.

Darling Clem

Adapted from a recipe by H. Joseph Ehrmann, Elixir, San Francisco. Created for the Monday Mixing Competition sponsored by Bluecoat gin at Rye, San Francisco, 2008. 2nd Place Prize winner.

"This cocktail plays on the sweet orange notes of the Bluecoat gin but still allows for the gin to shine as the backbone of the cocktail. Harvey's Orange Aperitif brings nice warm nutty notes from the sherry, while the clementine syrup adds a great citrus sweetness and the basil accentuates the botanicals." H. Joseph Ehrmann.

Half a pint of loose, torn organic basil
2 barspoons Clementine Syrup*
Regans' Orange Bitters No. 6
15 ml (.5 oz) Harvey's Orange Aperitif
60 ml (2 oz) Bluecoat gin
Clementine Basil Garnish**
Lightly muddle the torn basil in a mixing glass. Add ice and the remaining ingredients. Shake hard for 10 seconds and double strain into a chilled cocktail glass. Add the garnish.

*Clementine Syrup: Juice enough clementines (organic if possible) to make 1 cup of juice. Put in a pot and bring to a boil. Slowly stir in 200 g (1 cup) of organic sugar and bring back to a boil. Reduce heat and simmer for 10 minutes or until syrupy. Cool and transfer to a recycled bottle, and store in the refrigerator.

**Clementine Basil Garnish: Peel and separate a clementine. Puncture a hole in the center of the wide exterior surface of a segment with a toothpick. Pull a small basil leaf from the top of a sprig, leaving as much stem as possible. Using the toothpick, push the stem into the clementine so that the leaf sticks out. Pierce the segment across the middle of the widest surfaces until halfway and rest the garnish on the side of the cocktail glass.

Debonaire Cocktail (Miami Version)

Adapted from a recipe by Matt Goodyear, The Havana Club of Miami, Miami, FL.
"Not sure if someone already came up with this, but I ran out of sweet vermouth for a Negroni, substituted Dubonnet and added bitters—tasty." Matt Goodyear.
Note: There are two other cocktails with similar names—the "Debonair" (scotch-based) and "Debonnaire" (brandy-based).
45 ml (1.5 oz) Campari
45 ml (1.5 oz) Dubonnet Rouge
45 ml (1.5 oz) Right gin
1 orange twist, as garnish
1 dash orange bitters
Shake over ice and strain into a chilled cocktail glass. Add the garnish.

Delicious Cocktail

Adapted from a recipe by Ryan Magarian, Restaurant Zoe, Seattle.

"God has so made the mind of man that a peculiar deliciousness resides in the fruits of personal industry." Dr. Samuel Wilberforce, 1805-1873.

60 ml (2 oz) Tanqueray No. TEN gin

30 ml (1 oz) fresh lime juice

30 ml (1 oz) simple syrup

5 fresh mint sprigs, dusted with confectioners' sugar, as garnish

Shake over ice and strain into a chilled, sugar-rimmed cocktail glass. Add the garnish.

DellaPenna #2

Adapted from a recipe by Lance J. Mayhew, Beaker and Flask/50 Plates, Portland, OR.

"This recipe was developed specifically for Aviation gin's flavor profile, so if possible, I'd like to keep it Aviation." Lance J. Mayhew.

45 ml (1.5 oz) Aviation gin

15 ml (.5 oz) Damiana liqueur

1 tsp Smoked Peach Vinegar*

Tonic water

1 slice fresh peach, as garnish

Combine first three ingredients in a highball glass. Add ice and tonic to fill. Add the garnish.

*Smoked Peach Vinegar

240 ml (8 oz) peach vinegar (preferably Fauchon's)

Put in a smoker at 180 degrees F (82 degrees C) for 3 hours. Strain through a coffee filter and let come to room temperature before using.

Dirty Martini

Be very careful with the olive brine in the Dirty Martini—too much simply ruins the drink.

75 ml (2.5 oz) gin

15 ml (.5 oz) dry vermouth

1 teaspoon olive brine

1 olive, as garnish

Stir over ice and strain into a chilled cocktail glass. Add the garnish.

Doc Daneeka Royale

Adapted from a recipe by Alexander Day, Death & Company, New York City.
60 ml (2 oz) Plymouth gin
15 ml (.5 oz) lemon juice
15 ml (.5 oz) grade A maple syrup
Champagne
1 grapefruit twist, as an aromatic garnish
Shake over ice and strain into a chilled champagne flute. Top with champagne. Release the oils from the grapefruit twist onto the top of the drink, then discard the twist.

Dog's Nose

The Dog's Nose is mentioned in Dickens' Pickwick Papers, and his great grandson, Cedric Dickens, claimed in his book *Drinking with Dickens* that a certain Mr. Walker thought that tasting a Dog's Nose twice a week for 20 years had lost him the use of his right hand. Mr. Walker had since joined a temperance society. This is a strange mixture, indeed, but it works very well.
360 ml (12 oz) Guinness
2 teaspoons brown sugar
60 ml (2 oz) gin
Freshly grated nutmeg, as garnish
Pour the Guinness into a large sturdy glass and heat it in a microwave for about 1 minute. Add the brown sugar and gin and stir lightly. Add the garnish.

Douglas Fir Gimlet

Adapted from a recipe by Audrey Saunders, Pegu Club, New York City.
45 ml (1.5 oz) Beefeater 24 gin
22.5 ml (.75 oz) Clear Creek Douglas Fir eau de vie
22.5 ml (.75 oz) fresh lime juice
15 ml (.5 oz) Grapefruit Syrup*
15 ml (.5 oz) simple syrup (1:1, uncooked)
1 lime wheel or Douglas Fir tip, as garnish
Shake over ice and strain into a chilled champagne coupe. Add the garnish.

*Grapefruit Syrup: Zest the skin of 1 grapefruit into 2 cups of (1:1) simple syrup. Refrigerate for 24 hours. Strain off zest, pressing down on the solids to extract essential oils. Store in the refrigerator.

Dubonnet Cocktail

"[The Queen Mother] had a considerable capacity—champagne was her favourite drink and gin and Dubonnet—but she never regarded Dubonnet as being alcoholic. She had an unquenchable appetite for life, shall we put it that way." Nick Witchell, BBC's royal correspondent, April 11, 2002.

45 ml (1.5 oz) Dubonnet Rouge
45 ml (1.5 oz) gin
1 lemon twist, as garnish
Stir over ice and strain into a chilled cocktail glass. Add the garnish.

Earl Grey MarTEAni

Adapted from a recipe by Audrey Saunders, Pegu Club, New York City.

"I don't refer to this drink as a cocktail since it doesn't have any bitters in it. Instead, I stick with MarTEAni, a term that I came up with as an appropriate way to classify tea-based drinks. At that same moment in time, there was also a debate (on egullet or drinkboy, I believe) that everyone was having about both the overly-loose use of the term "martini" to describe all drinks in a V-shaped glass, and also the fact that "martini menus" were becoming overkill. I agreed with it being overkill, and felt that by playing with the spelling of "MarTEAni", that I was off the hook based on a technicality. It seems to have stuck since then, I've seen other folks using it too." Audrey Saunders.

52.5 ml (1.75 oz) Earl Grey-Infused Tanqueray gin*
22.5 ml (.75 oz) fresh lemon juice
30 ml (1 oz) simple syrup (1:1, uncooked)
1 egg white
1 lemon twist, as garnish
Shake over ice and strain into a chilled, sugar-rimmed champagne coupe. Add the garnish.

*Tea-Infused Gin: Measure 1 tablespoon of high-quality, loose, Earl Grey tea into 1 cup of Tanqueray gin. Let sit at room temperature for 2 hours. Strain off the solids and store in refrigerator. **Note:** Do not press down on solids when straining as this will release additional tannins into the infusion, which is undesirable.

Eclipse Cocktail Redux

Adapted from a recipe by Gary Regan, Ardent Spirits, NY.

This drink was based on the Eclipse Cocktail, detailed in *The Savoy Cocktail Book*, 1930. The original drink contained just three ingredients, Sloe gin, dry gin, and grenadine. The grenadine was poured into a cocktail glass containing a "ripe olive," and the other ingredients were mixed, then floated on the grenadine. Yuck.

1 maraschino cherry
20 ml (.75 oz) PAMA pomegranate liqueur
45 ml (1.5 oz) gin
45 ml (1.5 oz) sloe gin
1 orange twist, as garnish

Drop the cherry into a chilled cocktail glass and pour the PAMA into the glass. Stir the gin and sloe gin together over ice, and pour carefully over the PAMA, making sure that the mixture floats on the liqueur. Add the garnish.

1820

Adapted from a recipe by Misty Kalkofen, Drink, Boston.

Misty Kalkofen is one of Boston's most highly regarded mixologists. She is a graduate of the rigorous Beverage Alcohol Resource (B.A.R.) program, and has been featured in *The Wall Street Journal*, *Bon Appetit*, *Wine & Spirits*, *Imbibe*, and *Tasting Panel*, among others. She is president and founder of the Boston chapter of Ladies United for the Preservation of Endangered Cocktails (LUPEC) and her articles about cocktails, spirits, and women's history feature prominently on the group's website, lupecboston.com. This drink was devised for the Gala following the James Beard Awards, 2009.

52.5 ml (1.75 oz) Bols genever
7.5 ml (.25 oz) Gallino l'Autentico
15 ml (.5 oz) fresh lemon juice
15 ml (.5 oz) Lavender Simple Syrup*
1 barspoon Del Maguey Minero mezcal
1 dash Fee Brothers Whiskey Barrel Aged bitters

Shake over ice and strain into a chilled cocktail glass.

* **Lavender Simple Syrup:** "For the lavender syrup I have been gently heating half a cup of water (120 ml), half a cup of sugar (100 g) and 4 tablespoons of lavender gently until the sugar dissolves. Remove from heat, allow to cool, then strain through a fine strainer. I know lots of folks like no-heat syrups, but in this case I really needed the presence of lavender in order for it to be noticed next to the maltiness of the genever and a wee bit of heat was the best way to accomplish that." Misty Kalkofen.

Elder Fashion
Adapted from a recipe by Philip Ward, Mayahuel, New York City.
60 ml (2 oz) Plymouth gin
15 ml (.5 oz) St. Germain elderflower liqueur
1 dash Regans' Orange Bitters No. 6
1 grapefruit twist, as garnish
Stir over ice and strain into an ice-filled highball glass. Add the garnish.

Elephants Sometimes Forget
Adapted from a recipe by Satvik "Rick" Ahuja, Quarter Bar & Restaurant, Leicester, UK.
"Although this is not an original recipe, it is a cracking little drink found in *Bartender's Guide* by Trader Vic (1948 ed.), and probably one of the best named drinks ever." Satvik "Rick" Ahuja.
45 ml (1.5 oz) gin
15 ml (.5 oz) Cherry Heering
15 ml (.5 oz) fresh lemon juice
7.5 ml (.25 oz) dry vermouth
1 dash Regans' Orange Bitters No. 6
Shake over ice and strain into a chilled cocktail glass.

English Rose Cocktail
Adapted from a recipe in the first edition (1935) of *Old Mr. Boston*.
The English Rose is a great drink, and it's also the name of a song recorded by The Jam in 1978—look for it on the *All Mod Cons* album.
45 ml (1.5 oz) gin
20 ml (.75 oz) dry vermouth
20 ml (.75 oz) apricot brandy
7.5 ml (.25 oz) fresh lemon juice
1 to 2 dashes grenadine
Shake over ice and strain into a chilled, sugar-rimmed cocktail glass.

Entente Cordiale
Adapted from a recipe by Chris Holloway, Room, Liverpool, England.
30 ml (1 oz) Beefeater gin
22.5 ml (.75 oz) Cherry Herring
22.5 ml (.75 oz) Calvados
10 ml (.3 oz) Noilly Prat Amber vermouth
10 ml (.3 oz) Benedictine
1 orange twist, as garnish
1 marinated cherry, as garnish
Stir over ice and strain into an ice-filled old-fashioned glass. Add the garnish.

Eucalyptus Martini
Adapted from a recipe by Humberto Marques, Oloroso, Edinburgh.
45 ml (1.5 oz) Tanqueray No. TEN gin
30 ml (1 oz) Eucalyptus Syrup*
30 ml (1 oz) fresh lime juice
10 ml (.3 oz) Cointreau
1 dash egg white
1 eucalyptus leaf, as garnish
Shake over ice and double-strain into a chilled cocktail glass. Add the garnish.

*Eucalyptus Syrup
480 ml (16 oz) water
480 grams (2.5 cups) sugar
1/3 cup fresh eucalyptus leaves
Mix the sugar with water and bring to a boil. Add the eucalyptus leaves, simmer for 1 minute, the remove from the heat and allow the mixture to come to room temperature. Liquidize the syrup, strain it through a double layer of dampened cheesecloth, and store in the refrigerator.

Everest
Adapted from a recipe by Gary Regan, Ardent Spirits, NY.
Tea is one of the botanicals used in Beefeater 24 gin, and tea got Regan to thinking about India. India made him think of curry, and curry made him think of Thai curry. That's where the coconut-curry paste idea came from. The Everest was the name of an absolutely fabulous—though very much hole-in-the-wall—Indian restaurant in Blackpool, England, where Regan use to go for late night vindaloos in the early 1970s. That's where the name came from.
75 ml (2.5 oz) Beefeater 24 gin
2 to 3 barspoons Coconut-Curry Paste*
15 ml (.5 oz) fresh lemon juice
Pinch of curry powder, as garnish
Shake over ice and strain into a chilled cocktail glass. Add the garnish.

* **Coconut-Curry Paste:** Mix 1 teaspoon curry powder with 45 ml (1.5 oz) Coco Lopez to make a paste. Store in the refrigerator.

Fizz Francais

Adapted from a recipe by Ted Kilgore, Monarch Restaurant, Maplewood, MO.

6 to 8 mint leaves
15 ml (.5 oz) simple syrup
22.5 ml (.75 oz) fresh lemon juice
45 ml (1.5 oz) G-Vine gin
15 ml (.5 oz) yellow Chartreuse
Sparkling wine
1 mint leaf, as garnish

Muddle the mint, simple syrup, and lemon juice in a mixing glass. Add ice, gin and
Chartreuse. Shake and fine strain into a chilled cocktail glass. Top with sparkling
wine and add the garnish.

Flame of Love

Adapted from a recipe created for Dean Martin by Pepe Ruiz, a famous "bartender
to the stars" who worked at Chasen's Bar in West Hollywood. It's acceptable to
use vodka to make this drink if you don't mind sipping an inferior cocktail.

15 ml (.5 oz) dry sherry
2 orange twists
90 ml (3 oz) gin

Rinse a chilled cocktail glass with the sherry, and discard the excess. Flame one
of the orange twists into the glass. Stir the gin or vodka over ice, strain it into the
glass, and flame the remaining orange twist over the drink.

Flying Hemingway

Adapted from a recipe by Ryan Magarian, Portland, OR.

60 ml (2oz) Aviation gin
7.5 ml (.25 oz) Maraska maraschino liqueur
22.5 ml (.75 oz) fresh lime juice
15 ml (.5 oz) fresh grapefruit juice
7.5 to 15 ml (.25 to .5 oz) simple syrup
1 grapefruit wheel, as garnish
1 maraschino cherry, as garnish

Shake over ice and strain into a chilled cocktail glass. Add the garnish.

Fleur Verte

Adapted from a recipe by Junior Merino, Rayuela, New York City.

1/3 kiwi, peeled and sliced
2 basil leaves
10 ml (.33 oz) simple syrup
45 ml (1.5 oz) G'vine Nouaison gin
7.5 ml (.25 oz) fresh lime juice
75 ml (2.5 oz) brut champagne

Muddle the kiwi, basil, and syrup in a mixing glass. Add the lime juice, G'vine, and ice. Shake and double strain into a champagne flute. Add the champagne and stir briefly.

Fog Cutter

If you're feeling a little foggy, think of it as having your head in the clouds—that's what fog is, after all. It's a low-flying cloud.

45 ml (1.5 oz) light rum
15 ml (.5 oz) brandy
15 ml (.5 oz) gin
60 ml (2 oz) fresh orange juice
15 ml (.5 oz) fresh lemon juice
15 ml (.5 oz) orgeat syrup
7.5 ml (.25 oz) cream sherry

Shake everything except the sherry over ice and strain into an ice-filled collins glass. Float the sherry.

Follow That Black Rabbit

Adapted from a recipe by Kristian Kramp, Karriere, Denmark

"Love Fernet Branca! But it's hard to use in cocktails—especially in large quantities—because the flavour of it is so big and overpowering. This recipe actually dawned on me while I was sleeping—no, seriously! I figured it out in a dream I had. The name?: Well, it's a really long story . . . it's a mixed inspiration from Donnie Darko, Alice in Wonderland and booze . . . seeing what it is, and how it came to be, the name just seems appropriate. If you are not a big fan of Fernet Branca, then maybe using a little less Fernet and a little more gin could do the trick." Kristian Kramp

22.5 ml (.75 oz) Fernet Branca
22.5 ml (.75 oz) Beefeater gin
10 ml (.3 oz) fresh lemon juice
22.5 ml (.75 oz) fresh orange juice
22.5 ml (.75 oz) maple syrup

Shake over ice and strain into an ice-filled chilled highball glass.

French 75

According to esteemed booze historian, David Wondrich, this is one of the very few legitimate classic cocktails that was born in speakeasies during prohibition. It was named for a French 75-mm field gun that was invented in the late 1800s.

1 teaspoon simple syrup
15 ml (.5 oz) fresh lemon juice
30 ml (1 oz) gin
120 ml (4 oz) chilled champagne

Pour the ingredients into the order given in a crushed-ice filled collins glass. Stir briefly.

French Pearl

Adapted from a recipe created in 2006 by Audrey Saunders, Pegu Club, New York City.

1 sprig of fresh mint
7.5 ml (.25 oz) Pernod (not absinthe)
25 ml (.75 oz) simple syrup
25 ml (.75 oz) fresh lime juice
60 ml (2 oz) Plymouth gin

In an empty mixing glass muddle the mint with the Pernod, simple syrup, lime juice, and the gin. Add ice, shake, and double strain the drink into a chilled cocktail glass. ("The opacity of the drink is the pearl," Audrey Saunders.)

French Revolution

Adapted from a recipe by Christine D'Abrosca, Malo Restaurant, Los Angeles

60 ml (2 oz) Martin Miller's Westbourne Strength gin
22.5 ml (.75 oz) Lillet Blanc
15 ml (.5 oz) St. Germain elderflower liqueur
2 dashes Fee Brother's Orange bitters
Lucien Albrecht Cremant d'Alsace Sparkling Rose

Stir over ice all ingredients except the Lucien. Strain into a chilled cocktail glass and float a little Lucien Albrecht Cremant d'Alsace Sparking Rose.

Fuzzy Logic

60 ml (2 oz) Beefeater gin
45 ml (1.5 oz) fresh orange juice
15 ml (.5 oz) peach schnapps
2 dashes Benedictine

Shake over ice and strain into a chilled cocktail glass.

Gala Affair
Adapted from a recipe by Joshua Haig Harris, 15 Romolo, San Francisco.
3 slices Gala apple
5 to 7 fresh basil leaves
22.5 ml (.75 oz) fresh lemon juice
45 ml (1.5 oz) Right gin
30 ml (1 oz) unfiltered apple juice
30 ml (1 oz) simple syrup
15 ml (.5 oz) egg white
15 ml (.5 oz) Laird's Applejack (or Calvados)
1 thin apple wedge, as garnish
1 basil sprig, as garnish
Muddle the apple and basil with the lemon juice in a mixing glass. Add the remaining ingredients. Dry shake, then add ice and shake again. Double strain into a chilled cocktail glass. Add the garnishes.

G, G & G
Adapted from a recipe by Ago Perrone, Connaught Hotel, London
30 ml (1 oz) G'Vine Nouaison
30 ml (1 oz) Galliano L'Autentico
30 ml (1 oz) pink grapefruit juice
2 dashes Regans' Orange Bitters No. 6
1 grapefruit twist, as garnish
Stir over ice and strain into an ice-filled rocks glass. Add the garnish.

Gibson
Reportedly created in the 1930s at New York's Players Club by bartender Charlie Connolly. This version is said to have been named for famed magazine illustrator Charles Dana Gibson, who requested "something different" from Connolly. The Gibson, sans onions, existed prior to Prohibition, though, and at that time it was seemingly just another name for a Dry Gin Martini.
75 ml (2.5 oz) gin or vodka
15 ml (.5 oz) dry vermouth
1 or 3 cocktail onions, as garnish
Stir over ice and strain into a chilled cocktail glass. Add the garnish.

Gin and Tonic

I seem to have lost the recipe for this one, so I'm hoping you'll be able to figure it out for yourself. If memory serves it works well with a wedge of lime as a garnish. And don't forget to squeeze the lime into the drink for your guest, either. I hate when bartenders do that.

Oh Those Bhisti Boys

"After dismounting and imbibing a refreshing 'peg' of gin-and-tonic, a grateful beverage with which to wash the dust out of our throats, we hastily donned our bathing—drawers, whilst the bhisti gave us our evening tub. A simple arrangement this, consisting of squatting on a piece of board whilst the bhisti, from his skin mussuck, treats you to a douche." *Stray Sport* by James Moray Brown, 1893.

Gin Cocktail

This is a simple drink adapted from Jerry Thomas' 1862 book, *The Bar-Tender's Guide or How to Mix all Kinds of Plain and Fancy Drinks*, reformulated a little after consulting a few other nineteenth-century tomes. The Gin Cocktail serves as a great example of how differently our early forebears used syrups, liqueurs, and juices—they were called for in miniscule portions, and the resultant drinks were of a style almost unknown today. Choosing absinthe over curaçao, of course, drastically changes this drink, though both are viable. Originally the Gin Cocktail would have been made with genever, though some nineteenth-century formulas for this one call for Old Tom gin—which radically changes the cocktail yet again.

60 ml (2 oz) gin (dry, Old Tom, or genever)
15 ml (.5 oz) simple syrup
7.5 ml (.25 oz) curaçao or absinthe
2 dashes Angostura bitters
1 lemon twist, as garnish
Stir over ice and strain into a chilled cocktail glass. Add the garnish.

Gin Fizz

Spelled Gin Fiz in Jerry Thomas' 1876 book, *The Bar-Tender's Guide or How to Mix all Kinds of Plain and Fancy Drinks*, this drink could have been originally made with genever or Old Tom gin, and indeed, "The Only" William Schmidt allowed either style in his book, *The Flowing Bowl: When and What to Drink*, 1892. On the whole, the difference between a Tom Collins and a Gin Fizz is the fact that a Tom Collins is built over ice in a collins glass, whereas the Fizz is shaken over ice and strained into a chilled glass—a small wine goblet works well—before the club soda is added. In *Imbibe*, David Wondrich holds that the Gin Fizz was a very popular eye-opener in the late 1800s, and holds that it was, "what a sporting man [would knock back] directly upon rising."

60 ml (2 oz) gin
15 ml (.5 oz) fresh lemon juice
7.5 ml (.25 oz) simple syrup
Club soda

Shake the gin, lemon juice, and simple syrup over ice. Strain into a small wine goblet, and top with the club soda.

A Man Known as Gin Fizz

"At one end of the bar sat a man known to the Quarter as "Gin Fizz," who had fallen asleep in a large plate of tomato soup, his head right in the bowl! Next to him dsat a very wealthy Englishwoman, her feet on another stool, her furs dangling, her hat over one eye—also sound asleep. Beside her on the floor another woman rested in slumber on the bar rail. And so on around the bar. I would wake them up, one by one, and try to give them soda to get sober, but it was no use. Once awake, each would cry, 'Another drink, Jimmie! God! Give me another drink!' I gave them drinks that were mostly water, and eventually they all came to. I took Gin Fizz downstairs and washed the tomato soup out of his hair with some difficulty." *This Must be the Place: Memoirs of Jimmie the Barman*, by Morrill Cody, 1937.

Gin Gimlet

This drink is thought to be named for Sir Thomas D Gimlette, KCB, Surgeon General of the Royal Navy who retired in 1913. Gimlette is said to have introduced the drink in order to persuade sailors to drink lime juice as an anti-scorbutic. There's no hard evidence to support this theory, but the British Royal Navy perpetuates the tale on its web site. There's also a chance that the drink is named because it's a piercing potion, and a gimlet is a tool used to pierce holes in things. If you don't like either of those theories you'll have to make up you own . . .

75 ml (2.5 oz) gin
20 ml (.75 oz) lime juice cordial, such as Rose's
1 lime wedge, as garnish

Stir over ice and strain into an ice-filled old-fashioned glass. Add the garnish.

Gin Jubilee

Adapted from a recipe by H. Joseph Ehrmann, Elixir, San Francisco.

1 handful bing cherries (reserve 1 for garnish)
1 handful blueberries
60 ml (2 oz) Bluecoat gin
15 ml (.5 oz) honey

Muddle the cherries and blueberries in a mixing glass. Add ice and the remaining ingredients Shake well for 10 seconds and double fine strain into a chilled cocktail glass. Add the garnish.

Gin Rickey

This is a variation on the Joe Rickey, a whiskey-based drink created by, or for, Colonel Joe Rickey, Democratic lobbyist of the late nineteenth century who hung out at Shoemaker's, a Pennsylvania Avenue joint in Washington D.C. that was frequented by all the usual suspects—politicians and journalists, that is.

The Gin Rickey was probably first made with genever, and in 1900, famed bartender Harry Johnson suggested using genever or Old Tom, so there would have been a little sweetness in the original that played nicely with the lime juice. If you use dry gin for this drink, you might want to add just a little simple syrup.

22.5 ml (.75 oz) fresh lime juice
60 ml (2 oz) gin (your call)
120 ml (4 oz) club soda
1 lime wedge, as garnish

Pour the ingredients into an ice-filled collins glass and stir briefly. Add the garnish.

Mark Twain. Not.

"In New York, Colonel Rickey's favorite Bar and lobby had been in the Hoffman House, but he soon found the Waldorf. In the early days of the brass rail bar, his long, gray mustache and black slouch hat caused him often to be mistaken for Mark Twain." *Old Waldorf Bar Days*, by Albert Stevens Crockett, 1931.

Gin Sling à la *Imbibe*

Recipe derived from David Wondrich's findings in his wonderful book, *Imbibe*. Sort of . . . Jerry Thomas' 1862 book, *The Bar-Tender's Guide or How to Mix all Kinds of Plain and Fancy Drinks*, contains a recipe for a Gin Sling that's no more than an ounce each of water and gin (it would have been genever), a teaspoon of sugar, and a lump of ice. Stir them all together, grate a little nutmeg on top, and there you have it. Probably not really worth recreating, but for the record, this is what our nineteenth-century forebears would have been making when asked for a Gin Sling. The drink was offered hot as well as cold, and some 50 years later, in the 1912 edition of the *Hoffman House Bartender's Guide*, hot is the only way it's presented. In *Imbibe*, Wondrich offers what he calls a "composite" recipe for the drink, and although he notes that genever would have been the original choice of gin in this cocktail, he also notes that "you can get away with something like Plymouth." The formula given here is not the one detailed in *Imbibe*. It's a variation on that one. It has been tinkered with only to make it easier to be reproduced for twenty-first-century bartenders. It should taste pretty similar to the drink as it was served in the late 1800s, though your choice of gin will, of course, alter the profile significantly.

60 ml (2 oz) (genever, Old Tom, Plymouth, or dry) gin
7.5 ml (.25 oz) simple syrup (a little less if you use genever or Old Tom)
Freshly grated nutmeg, as garnish
Stir over ice and strain into a chilled cocktail glass. Add the garnish.

gin~esaisquoi

Adapted from a recipe by Jeff Grdinich, White Mountain Cider Company, Glen, NH.

1 fresh egg white
60 ml (2 oz) Hendrick's gin
45 ml (1.5 oz) Fee Brothers Falernum syrup
45 ml (1.5 oz) Lillet Blanc
2 dashes Regans' Orange Bitters No. 6
Sprinkling of ground cardamom, as garnish

Dry shake for about 10 seconds to emulsify egg white. Add a large scoop of ice and shake again. Strain into a chilled cocktail glass. Add the garnish.

Ginger Collins

Adapted from a recipe by Frank Caiafa, Peacock Alley at the Waldorf=Astoria Hotel, New York City.

75 ml (2.5 oz) ginger-and-lemongrass-infused Bombay gin (steep for one week)
37.5 ml (1.25 oz) fresh lemon juice
37.5 ml (1.25 oz) simple syrup
1 splash club soda
1 maraschino cherry, as garnish

Shake over ice and strain all but the club soda into an ice-filled highball glass. Top with club soda and stir briefly. Add the garnish

GINger Snap

Adapted from a recipe created by Gary Regan, Ardent Spirits, NY, 2008.

"Queen Victoria—how glad I am she had such a good, loving husband, to compensate her for the misery of being a queen—tried her best to abolish the custom, prevalent in England at dinner, of the gentlemen remaining to guzzle wine after the ladies left. I am aware that guzzle is an unladylike word but, as no other fits in there, I shall use it. Well—she succeeded only in shortening the guzzling period—not in abolishing it so those consistent men remained, to drink toasts to 'lovely women,' whose backs they were so delighted to see retreating through the door." *Ginger-snaps* by Fanny Fern, 1870.

45 ml (1.5 oz) Beefeater gin
15 ml (.5 oz) Domain de Canton ginger liqueur
15 ml (.5 oz) Cointreau
15 ml (.5 oz) fresh lemon juice
1 dash Angostura bitters
Club soda
1 lemon twist, as garnish

Shake everything except the club soda over ice. Strain into an ice-filled collins glass, top with club soda, stir briefly, and add the garnish.

Girl From Cadiz
Adapted from a recipe by Ryan Maybee, Owner/Sommelier, JP Wine Bar & Coffee House, Kansas City, MO.
12 dried juniper berries
45 ml (1.5 oz) Henrick's gin
45 ml (1.5 oz) Lustao fino sherry
15 ml (.5 oz) mint syrup*
15 ml (.5 oz) fresh lemon juice
Dissected strands of lemongrass, as garnish
Muddle the juniper berries and lemon juice in a cocktail shaker. Add ice, syrup, gin, and sherry. Shake and strain over ice into a tall collins glass. Add the garnish.
*Mint Syrup: See instructions for flavored simple syrup at the beginning of this chapter.

Golden Cup
Adapted from a recipe by Charles Vexenat, London.
1/8 Granny Smith apple (diced)
1 inch cucumber (diced)
45 ml (1.5 oz) Beefeater 24 gin
22.5 ml (.75 oz) orange curaçao
22.5 ml (.75 oz) amontillado sherry
Club soda
1 mint sprig, as garnish
Muddle the diced apple and cucumber with the gin in a mixing glass. Add ice and the remaining ingredients, and stir briefly. Pour everything into a large wine goblet, and add the garnish.

Goldfish Cocktail
Served at the Aquarium Speakeasy in Manhattan during Prohibition, the original recipe, detailed in *On the Town in New York*, by Michael and Ariane Batterberry, called for equal amounts of each ingredient. The proportions in this adaptation of the Goldfish result in the gin not being so overpowered by the Goldwasser, and the vermouth forms a subtle backdrop.
60 ml (2 oz) gin
30 ml (1 oz) dry vermouth
15 ml (.5 oz) Danziger Goldwasser
Stir over ice and strain into a chilled cocktail glass.

Greek Vesper
Adapted from a recipe by Ektoras Binikos, Aureole restaurant, New York City.
Vesper is the Latin word for "evening star," and was the son of the dawn goddess,
Aurora. So there.
30 ml (1 oz) gin
15 ml (.5 oz) Grand Marnier
15 ml (.5 oz) fresh lime juice
1 dash creme de cassis
1 sprig lemon thyme, as garnish.
Shake over ice and strain into a chilled cocktail glass. Add the garnish.

Green Fever
Adapted from a recipe by Joshua Haig Harris, 15 Romolo, San Francisco.
15 ml (.5 oz) Q tonic water
30 ml (1 oz) fresh lime juice
6 to 8 basil leaves
60 ml (2 oz) Right gin
15 ml (.5 oz) Basil Syrup*
1 basil sprig, as garnish
Pour the tonic into a chilled cocktail glass and set aside. Fill a mixing glass with ice.
Add the lime juice and basil leaves. Muddle vigorously (muddling this way is what
gives the drink its brilliant color). Add the remaining ingredients. Shake over ice
and double strain into the cocktail glass. Add the garnish.

Basil Syrup: Heat 1 liter (about 1 qt) water and 4 cups (800 g) sugar until the
sugar is completely dissolved. Add 1 bunch of basil, cover, let it sit for 30 minutes,
then strain out the basil.

G'time
Adapted from a recipe by Junior Merino, Rayuela, New York
3 fresh basil leaves
45 ml (1.5 oz) G'vine Floraison gin
10 ml (.3 oz) fresh lime juice
90 ml (3 oz) white grape juice
1 lemon half-moon, as garnish
Muddle the basil leaves, add ice and the other ingredients, shake gently and
strain into an ice-filled old-fashioned glass. Add the garnish.

G'vine Orchid
Adapted from a recipe by Junior Merino, Rayuela, New York City.
45 ml (1.5 oz) G'vine Floraison gin
45 ml (1.5 oz) pink grapefruit juice
15 ml (.5 oz) elderflower syrup (or simple syrup)
45 ml (1.5 oz) brut champagne
1 orchid, as garnish
Shake the gin, juice, and syrup over ice. Strain into an ice-filled highball glass, add the champagne and stir briefly. Add the garnish.

Hanky Panky Cocktail
"The late Charles Hawtrey . . . was one of the best judges of cocktails that I know. Some years ago, when he was over-working, he used to come into the bar and say 'Coley, I am tired. Give me something with a bit of punch in it.' It was for him that I spent hours experimenting until I had invented a new cocktail. The next time he came in I told him I had a new drink for him. He sipped it, and, draining the glass, he said, 'By Jove! That is the real hanky-panky!'" Ada Coleman, Head Bartender at London's Savoy Hotel from 1903 until 1926.
45 ml (1.5 oz) gin
45 ml (1.5 oz) sweet vermouth
2 dashes Fernet Branca
1 orange twist, as garnish
Stir and strain into a chilled cocktail glass. Add the garnish.

Gypsy
45 ml (1.5 oz) gin
45 ml (1.5 oz) sweet vermouth
1 maraschino cherry, as garnish
Stir over ice and strain into a chilled cocktail glass. Add the garnish.

Hawaiian Cocktail
Adapted from the recipe in 1935's *Old Mr. Boston* with the addition of bitters. Pineapples, a fruit necessary to the preparation of this drink, got their name from Europeans who, when they first saw them in the 1600s, thought that they resembled pine cones.
60 ml (2 oz) gin
15 ml (.5 oz) Cointreau
15 ml (.5 oz) pineapple juice
2 dashes Angostura bitters
Shake over ice and strain into a chilled cocktail glass.

Hayes Shift No.1
Adapted from a recipe by Alexander Day, Death & Company, New York City.
7.5 ml (.25 oz) absinthe, to rinse the glass
60 ml (2 oz) Anchor Genevieve gin
22.5 ml (.75 oz) fresh lemon juice
22.5 ml (.75 oz) simple syrup
1 egg white
3 dashes Fee's orange bitters
3 dashes Regans' Orange Bitters No. 6
Club soda
Dry shake the gin, lemon, simple syrup and egg white. Add ice. Shake and strain into a chilled, absinthe-rinsed fizz glass*. Discard ice from shaker. Add orange bitters and spray surface area of shaker with soda. Add small amount of soda to cocktail, then scoop orange bitter foam from shaker on top of drink.
*A fizz glass can be similar to a short champagne flute, or (according to CocktailDB. com) they can be in the style of the short juice glasses used at diners.

Holy Vesper
"In the presence of these spiritual truths, what are these little questions of meat and drink, of pleasure and ease—the trifling themes of popular casuistry? They fall into their proper insignificance and we press our way forward along a triumphant career, honorable in its course, and faithful to that crown which awaits all true and constant service." *Harvard Vespers: Addresses to Harvard Students by the Preachers to the University*, 1886-1888 by Harvard University,1888.
45 ml (1.5 oz) vodka
20 ml (.75 oz) Tanqueray No. TEN gin
3 dashes B & B
1 lemon twist, as garnish
Stir over ice and strain into a chilled cocktail glass. Add the garnish.

Hoskins Cocktail
Adapted from a recipe by Chuck Taggart, circa 2004.
"All Excess is ill: But Drunkenness is of the worst Sort. It spoils Health, dismounts the Mind, and unmans Men: It reveals Secrets, is Quarrelsome, Lascivious, Impudent, Dangerous and Mad. In fine, he that is drunk is not a Man: Because he is so long void of Reason, that distinguishes a Man from a Beast." William Penn, 1644-1718.
60 ml (2 oz) Plymouth gin
20 ml (.75 oz) Torani Amer
15 ml (.5 oz) maraschino liqueur
7.5 ml (.25 oz) Cointreau
1 dash orange bitters
1 flamed orange twist, as garnish
Stir over ice and strain into a chilled cocktail glass. Add the garnish.

Hot Charlotte

Adapted from a recipe by Murray Stenson, Zig Zag Café, Seattle.
Murray Stenson created this drink as a tribute to Charlotte Voisey, mixologist for
Hendrick's gin, after they met at Tales of the Cocktail in New Orleans in July, 2008.
1 teaspoon finely diced cucumber
4 to 6 dashes Tabasco sauce
50 ml (1.75 oz) Hendrick's gin
30 ml (1 oz) St. Germain elderflower liqueur
15 ml (.5oz) fresh lemon juice
Club soda
1 cucumber wheel, as garnish
Shake everything except for the soda over ice and strain into ice-filled collins
glass. Top with club soda, stir briefly, and add the garnish.

Houndstooth

Adapted from a recipe by Joshua Haig Harris, 15 Romolo, San Francisco.
We were told that this drink was created by Gregor De Gruyther, a cocktailian
maven and creator of the Nuclear Daiquiri who lives in London, but when we
contacted him he said no, Joshua Haig Harris created it at Nopa in San Francisco.
Joshua said yes, indeed, he did create it, but he works at 15 Romolo, not Nopa
(where Neyah White, creator of the Aztec's Mark, works). See what trouble we
went to in order to bring you this cocktail?
37.5 ml (1.25 oz) Right gin
15 ml (.5 oz) Baileys Irish Cream
15 ml (.5 oz) Benedictine
60 ml (2 oz) hazelnut milk
Grated nutmeg, as garnish
Ground cinnamon, as garnish
Shake over ice and strain into a small wine goblet. Dust with the grated nutmeg
and cinnamon.

Income Tax Cocktail

Although people in the U.S.A. paid income tax during the Civil War, and at a couple
of other times in the 1800s, it wasn't until 1913, when the Sixteenth Amendment
was passed, that it became a permanent part of American life.
60 ml (2 oz) gin
7.5 ml (.25 oz) sweet vermouth
7.5 ml (.25 oz) dry vermouth
30 ml (1 oz) fresh orange juice
2 dashes Angostura bitters
1 orange twist, as garnish
Shake over ice and strain into a chilled cocktail glass. Add the garnish.

Inquisition
Adapted from a recipe by Joshua Haig Harris, 15 Romolo, San Francisco.
6 bing cherries
60 ml (2 oz) Right gin
15 ml (.5 oz) Navan vanilla liqueur
15 ml (.5 oz) vanilla syrup
15 ml (.5 oz) aged balsamic vinegar
15 ml (.5 oz) egg white
2 skewered cherries (ideally, 1 bing and 1 Ranier), as garnish
Muddle the cherries in a mixing glass. Add the remaining ingredients. Dry shake, then add ice and shake again. Double strain into a chilled cocktail glass. Add the garnish.

Inscription
Adapted from a recipe by Edward Henwood, Aldea Restaurant, New York City.
"This is an amped up of version of my Expatriate (gin and pastis), created at Lucques in Los Angeles. The new products did inspire, and of course demanded, their own voice—and here 'tis. Simplicity. It's called The Inscription to give a wink at 'nothing is written in stone.' I'm glad to be back in this wicked city." Edward Henwood.
Pernod absinthe, to rinse the glass
60 ml (2 oz) Beefeater 24 gin
15 ml (.5 oz) St. Germain elderflower liqueur
1 flamed orange twist, as garnish
Rinse a chilled cocktail glass with Pernod absinthe. Stir the gin and the liqueur over ice and strain into the prepared glass. Add the garnish.

Italian Pear Fix
Adapted from a recipe by Nate Windham, Palapa's Surfside, Colorado Springs, CO
30 ml (1 oz) Plymouth gin
22.5 ml (.75 oz) Poire William
7.5 ml (.25 oz) Pernod
15 ml (.5 oz) fresh lemon juice
7.5 ml (.25 oz) simple syrup
Club soda
1 star anise pod, as garnish
Shake over ice and strain into a highball glass two-thirds filled with crushed ice. Top with soda and add the garnish.

Jockey Club

The Jockey Club, an organization that records the lineages of thoroughbred horses in North America, was started in 1894, and according to the club's traditions, "the date of birth for all thoroughbreds is deemed to be January 1 of the year of foaling." There must be massive horsie parties at stables on New Year's Day, huh?

45 ml (1.5 oz) gin
7.5 ml (.25 oz) creme de noyaux
7.5 ml (.25 oz) fresh lemon juice
1 dash Angostura bitters
1 dash orange bitters
1 lemon twist, as garnish
Shake and strain into a chilled cocktail glass. Add the garnish.

John Collins

The John Collins was named for the head waiter at Limmer's, a joint in London that Dickens was known to visit on occasion. (See Tom Collins entry for a discussion of both drinks.)

75 ml (2.5 oz) genever
30 ml (1 oz) fresh lemon juice
20 ml (.75 oz) simple syrup
Club soda
Shake everything except for the club soda, and strain into an ice-filled collins glass. Top with club soda.

The Last of Limmer's

"My name is John Collins, head waiter at Limmer's,
Corner of Conduit Street, Hanover Square,
My chief occupation is filling brimmers
For all the young gentlemen frequenters there."
"The Last of Limmer's" by John Morley, *Macmillan's Magazine*, 1904.

John Collins Gin Punch
This recipe is loosely based on bits and bats of information found in David Wondrich's wonderful book, *Imbibe*.
45 ml (1.5 oz) genever
15 ml (.5 oz) maraschino liqueur
15 ml (.5 oz) simple syrup
15 ml (.5 oz) fresh lemon juice
1 dash orange bitters
Club soda
1 lemon twist, as garnish
Shake everything except for the soda over ice and strain into an ice-filled collins glass. Top with club soda, stir briefly, and add the garnish.

Joy Division
Adapted from a recipe by Philip Ward, Mayahuel, New York City.
"I stood under a golden canopy, drunk with joy and blessed with heavenly peace. I saw these words, 'I think ever of thee,' not only in my heart, but in every flower, on every leaf, and written by the sun in the heavens, and in the stars." *Berlin and Sans-Souci, or, Frederick the Great and His Friends: An Historical Romance* by L. Mühlbach. Translated from the German by Mrs. Chapman Coleman and her Daughters, 1905.
60 ml (2 oz) Beefeater gin
30 ml (1 oz) Noilly Prat dry vermouth
15 ml (.5 oz) Cointreau
4 dashes absinthe
Stir over ice and strain into a chilled glass slipper. No garnish.

Julius Flip
Adapted from a recipe by Ted Kilgore, Monarch Restaurant, Maplewood, MO.
45 ml (1.5 oz) gin
15 ml (.5 oz) Benedictine
22.5 ml (.75 oz) fresh lemon juice
30 ml (1 oz) simple syrup
1 whole raw egg
2 dashes Regans' Orange Bitters No. 6
Dry shake all ingredients for 10 seconds. Add ice and shake hard for 45 seconds. Strain into a chilled cocktail glass. "Flippin' tasty!" Ted Kilgore.

Kismet Cocktail
Adapted from a recipe by Lance J. Mayhew, Beaker and Flask/50 Plates, Portland, OR
60 ml (2 oz) Aperol
30 ml (1 oz) John D. Taylor's Velvet Falernum
30 ml (I oz) Aviation gin
Shake over ice and strain into a chilled cocktail glass.

La Louche
Adapted from a recipe by Charlotte Voisey, Mixologist, Hendrick's Gin.
If you ask for a louche in France, chances are good that someone will hand you a ladle, but in Holland you'll have to request a *gietlepel*. Germans call it a *chöpflöffel*, Italians use a *siviera* to get their soup to the bowl, and in Spain you'll get a ladle if you ask for a *cucharón*. Providing there's one handy, that is
45 ml (1.5 oz) Hendrick's gin
15 ml (.5 oz) Lillet Rouge
7.5 ml (.25 oz) yellow Chartreuse
15 ml (.5 oz) fresh lime juice
1 lime wheel, as garnish
Shake over ice and strain into a chilled cocktail glass. Add the garnish.

Lambeth Lemonade
Adapted from a recipe by Nick Strangeway, London
45 ml (1.5 oz) Beefeater 24 gin
22.5 ml (.75 oz) Lillet Blanc
10 ml (1.3 oz) Homemade Raspberry Syrup* or creme de framboise
Fever Tree Bitter Lemon**
1 lemon wedge, as garnish
1 fresh raspberry, as garnish
Pour the gin, Lillet, and raspberry syrup into an ice-filled collins glass. Top with the soda, stir briefly, and add the garnishes.

Homemade Raspberry Syrup: Rinse and pat dry one cup of fresh raspberries, place them in a in bowl and cover with simple syrup. Leave overnight, strain through a double layer of dampened cheesecloth, and store in the refrigerator.
**If Fever Tree Bitter Lemon is unavailable, use a good brand of tonic water, such as Fever Tree, with a splash of fresh lemon juice.

Last Drop

Adapted from a recipe by Frank Caiafa, Peacock Alley, Waldorf=Astoria & Handle Bars, New York City.

75 ml (2.5 oz) Citadelle Gin Reserve (Cognac Barrel aged)
22.5 ml (.75 oz) fresh lemon juice
22.5 ml (.75 oz) simple syrup
10 drops Mathilde blackcurrant liqueur (or French cassis)

Shake the gin, lemon juice, and simple syrup over ice and strain into a chilled cocktail glass. Drip the liqueur into the center of the glass causing it to pool at bottom glass.

Last Word

This drink has been credited to Frank Fogarty, a man who, in 1912, was considered to be the most popular entertainer in vaudeville according to *The New York Morning Telegraph*. "The single thing I work to attain in any gag is brevity," said Fogarty when asked the secret of his success. "You can kill the whole point of a gag by merely [using one] unnecessary word."

20 ml (.75 oz) dry gin
20 ml (.75 oz) maraschino liqueur
20 ml (.75 oz) green Chartreuse
20 ml (.75 oz) fresh lime juice

Shake over ice and strain into a chilled cocktail glass.

Le Bateleur

Adapted from a recipe by Alexander Day, Death & Company, New York City.

60 ml (2 oz) Beefeater gin
22.5 ml (.75 oz) Punt e Mes
15 ml (.5 oz) Strega
7.5 ml (.25 oz) Cynar
1 dash Angostura bitters
1 lemon twist, as garnish

Stir over ice and strain into a chilled cocktail glass. Add the garnish.

Leo Di Janeiro

Adapted from a recipe by Leo "Prince Cocktail" DeGroff, New York City.

60 ml (2 oz) Tanqueray gin
90 ml (3 oz) pineapple juice
4 dashes Angostura bitters
1 lemon twist, as garnish

Shake over ice and strain into an ice-filled highball glass. Add the garnish.

Libation Goddess
Created by Mardee Haidin Regan and Gary Regan in 2002 in honor of Audrey "Libation Goddess" Saunders, Queen of The Pegu Club, New York City.
60 ml (2 oz) gin
20 ml (.75 oz) white creme de cacao
15 ml (.5 oz) cranberry juice
1 lime wedge, as garnish
Stir over ice and strain into a chilled cocktail glass. Add the garnish.

Light and Day
Adapted from a recipe by Alexander Day, Death & Company, New York City.
60 ml (2 oz) Plymouth gin
15 ml (.5 oz) yellow Chartreuse
7.5 ml (.25 oz) Maraska maraschino liqueur
7.5 ml (.25 oz) fresh orange juice
3 dashes Peychaud's bitters
Stir over ice and strain into a chilled cocktail glass.

London Calling (Liverpool Version)
Adapted from a recipe by Chris Holloway, Room, Liverpool, England.
"One of the best selling modern gin cocktail here at Room & Grille restaurants (Leeds, Manchester, Liverpool, Lincoln, Harrogate, Hoxton [& King's Cross] is a little drink called London Calling. The drink came about from messing around with classics in an attempt to twist them around, and this one evolved from a Singapore Sling which was originally made with Cherry Heering—hence the name (Heering/Calling). The name also refers, of course, to the fairly iconic Clash song. We've made it with almost all gins except Hendricks or Martin Miller's. Beefeater works particularly well . . . Any other details you might need, drop us a line." Paraphrased from an email from Chris Holloway.
45 ml (1.5 oz) Tanqueray gin (though any good London dry gin will suffice)
10 ml (.3 oz) Cherry Marnier
22.5 ml (.75 oz) fresh lemon juice
3 dashes Angostura orange bitters
1 splash maraschino syrup, or more to taste
1 lemon twist, as garnish
1 maraschino cherry, as garnish
Shake over ice and fine strain into a chilled cocktail glass. Add the garnish.

London Calling (Chicago Version)
Adapted from a recipe by Lynn House, Graham Elliot, Chicago
"The name came to me first. I am a huge fan of the Clash and the song kept rolling around in my head and I knew that I would eventually make a British-inspired drink. Nothing more British than the Pimm's Cup, so I deconstructed the basic elements of it—ginger, cucumber, and apple. This drink has been one of the top sellers at Graham Elliot Restaurant—Plymouth gin and Pimms No.1 Cup are two utterly English ingredients," Lynn House.
30 ml (1 oz) Pimm's No. 1 Cup
30 ml (1 oz) Plymouth gin
7.5 ml (.25 oz) fresh lemon juice
30 ml (1 oz) Ginger Water*
22.5 ml (.75 oz) Apple Syrup**
Splash Cucumber Soda***
1 cucumber wheel, as garnish.
Shake all ingredients except the cucumber soda over ice and strain into an ice-filled highball glass. Add the garnish.

*Ginger Water: Dissolve 2 teaspoons of ground ginger and 1 cup of granulated sugar (200 g) into 1 quart (about 1 liter) of filtered water.
**Apple Syrup: Melt 8 oz of apple butter in 180 ml (16 oz) apple juice, and cook to attain a syrupy consistency.
***Cucumber Soda: Muddle a chopped cucumber in a mixing glass, and strain through dampened cheesecloth. Mix the cucumber water with three times as much filtered water, add to a siphon, and charge.

London Cup
Adapted from a recipe by Giles Looker, Soul Shakers, London.
This fabulous cocktail won third place in the Martin Miller's Gin Masters, November 9th, 2008. The competition was held at Death & Co, New York.
30 ml (1 oz) Martin Miller's Gin Westbourne Strength gin
30 ml (1 oz) Martini & Rossi sweet vermouth
15 ml (.5 oz) Campari
30 m (1 oz) fresh grapefruit juice
Lemon-lime soda, such as 7-Up
2 slices cucumber, as garnish
1 orange wheel, as garnish
1 slice fresh grapefruit, as garnish
1 mint sprig, as garnish
Pour all the ingredients into an ice-filled collins glass, stir briefly, and add the garnishes.

London Dragon
Adapted from a recipe by Kris Laidlaw, GV Hurley's, Sacramento.
Third place in the Broker's London Dry Gin Contest, 2009.
60 ml (2 oz) Broker's London Dry gin
45 ml (1.5 oz) simple syrup infused with sage and lemon zest
30 ml (1 oz) fresh blood orange juice
30 ml (1 oz) fresh grapefruit juice
1 slice star fruit, as garnish
Shake over ice and pour into an ice-filled old-fashioned glass. Add the garnish.

Londoner No. 1
Adapted from a recipe by Philip Ward, Mayahuel, New York City.
"Maybe it's because I'm a Londoner,
That I love London so.
Maybe it's because I'm a Londoner
That I think of her wherever I go.
I get a funny feeling inside of me
Just walking up and down.
Maybe it's because I'm a Londoner
That I love London Town."
Maybe it's Because I'm a Londoner by Hubert Gregg, 1944.
60 ml (2 oz) Plymouth gin
15 ml (.5 oz) sweet vermouth
15 ml (.5 oz) Grand Marnier
2 to 3 dashes orange bitters
1 flamed orange twist, as garnish
Stir over ice and strain into a chilled cocktail glass. Add the garnish.

Londoner No. 2
Adapted from a recipe by Joe Wood, CocktailStars, England.
"'I can't say whether he'll be in bed,' said the little woman. 'I'm not a Londoner myself, and I don't 'old with the hours some of 'em keeps. But, there, we can but go up and see.' She chuckled a little, as though this were something of an adventure." *A Candidate for Truth by John Davys Beresford.* Published by Little, Brown, and Company, 1912.
2 lime wedges
2 ounce Broker's gin
15 ml (.5 oz) creme de mure
30 ml (1 oz) pink grapefruit juice
7.5 ml (.25 oz) fresh lime juice
Shake over ice and strain into a chilled cocktail glass.

Long Island Iced Tea

Robert Bott, a bartender at the Oak Beach Inn, in Babylon, Long Island, lays claim to this drink's creation, but many years ago an executive at the T.G.I. Friday's chain claimed that it was a Friday's bartender who came up with it.

30 ml (1 oz) gin
30 ml (1 oz) vodka
30 ml (1 oz) light rum
30 ml (1 oz) white tequila
30 ml (1 oz) Cointreau
30 ml (1 oz) fresh lemon juice
20 ml (.75 oz) simple syrup
Cola
1 lemon wedge, as garnish

Shake everything except for the cola over ice, and strain into an ice-filled collins glass. Top with cola. Add the garnish.

Lychee & Lemongrass Fizz

Adapted from a recipe by Julie Reiner, Clover Club, Brooklyn, and Flatiron Lounge, New York City.

If you would like to buy lemongrass in France, ask for *citronnelle*, in Germany you'd be looking for some *zitronengras*, and when in Rome, do as the Romans do, and demand *erba di limone.*

2 lychees
60 ml (2 oz) Tanqueray gin
30 ml (1 oz) lychee juice
20 ml (.75 oz) Belvoir Lime and Lemongrass cordial
15 ml (.5 oz) fresh lime juice
Club soda
1 lime wheel, as garnish
1 lemongrass stalk, as garnish

Muddle the lychees in a mixing glass. Add ice, the gin, lychee juice, Belvoir cordial, and lime juice. Shake over ice and strain into an ice-filled collins glass. Top with club soda. Add the garnishes.

Madam Geneva

Adapted from a recipe by Bob Brunner, The Paragon Restaurant and Bar, Portland, OR.

30 ml (1 oz) Pimm's No. 1 Cup
30 ml (1 oz) gin
180 ml (6 oz) San Pellegrino Aranciata soda
3 slices cucumber, as garnish

Pour all of the ingredients into an ice-filled collins glass, and stir briefly. Float the garnishes on top of the drink.

Maiden's Blush Cocktail

"How can I marry a man who knows that a certain pink is called maiden's blush . . . ?" *Fool for Love* by Eloisa James, 2003.

60 ml (2 oz) gin
20 ml (.75 oz) Cointreau
15 ml (.5 oz) fresh lemon juice
2 dashes grenadine
Shake over ice and strain into a chilled cocktail glass.

Maiden's Prayer Cocktail

"Libby, the unlikely but successful prostitute in Nicky Silver's *Maiden's Prayer*, lets her thoughts drift when she's working. She is with her clients only in the flesh, her mind is with someone else entirely." Ben Brantley, *The New York Times*, February 23, 1998.

30 ml (1 oz) gin
30 ml (1 oz) Cointreau
15 ml (.5 oz) fresh lemon juice
15 ml (.5 oz) fresh orange juice
Shake over ice and strain into a chilled cocktail glass.

Maravel Sling

Created by Gary Regan, 2001, for Trotters, Port of Spain, Trinidad

"At the entrance of the valley of Maravel is a large sugar property, the fields of which were bright with the growing cane . . . The market resounded throughout the day with chaffering and laughter but we saw no disorder nor drunkenness, although two or three rum shops were at hand." *The West Indies: Their Social and Religious Condition* by Edward Bean Underhill, 1862.

60 ml (2 oz) gin
7.5 ml (.25 oz) Benedictine
7.5 ml (.25 oz) mango nectar
15 ml (.5 oz) fresh lemon juice
2 dashes tamarind juice
2 dashes Angostura bitters
Club soda
1 pineapple cube, as garnish
1 maraschino cherry, as garnish
Shake all the ingredients save the club soda over ice and strain into an ice-filled collins glass. Top with club soda. Add the garnishes.

Martinez à la *Imbibe*

Recipe derived from David Wondrich's findings in his wonderful book, *Imbibe*, in which the recipe found in Jerry Thomas's 1887 book, *Bar-Tender's Guide*, is employed as a template for Wondrich's Martinez recipe. The formula here is similar, with a couple of tweaks. Old Tom gin is preferable if you want authenticity, and if you use dry gin instead, you might want to think about adding about 7.5 ml (.25 oz) of simple syrup to the drink. The 1887 recipe calls for Boker's bitters, now defunct, so Angostura bitters has been substituted in this formula. Note: Although this recipe is true to the original to a large extent, the drink works better for most people with twenty-first-century tastes if the ratio of gin to vermouth is around 50:50.

60 ml (2 oz) sweet vermouth
30 ml (1 oz) gin
1 teaspoon maraschino liqueur
1 dash Angostura bitters
Stir over ice and strain into a chilled cocktail glass.

Pieces of the Martini Puzzle

In January, 2002, much as I hated to believe that marketers were responsible for giving the Martini its name, I set out in search of proof that the cocktail was directly tied to the Martini & Rossi vermouth company. I contacted a certain Duncan Horner at Bacardi, the company that distributes the brand in the U.S.A., and in turn Duncan reached out to Martini & Rossi in Italy. Here's what we dug up:

Forwarded by Duncan Horner/BMUSA/Bacardi on 01/08/2002 06:17 PM
Florisa Gatti
01/08/2002 12:38 PM
To: Duncan Horner/BMUSA/Bacardi@BACARDI
Subject: Food for Thought

Dear Duncan,
     please give my personal greetings to Gary [who] I met some years ago in Torino on the occasion of a Bacardi-Martini Grand Prix [a world-class cocktail competition] together with Laura [Baddish, a New York-based marketing maven] and other journalists. As to your questions, I will try to help you with the information I could find in our archives.
     The first Martini & Rossi vermouth was only RED.
     We could find in the old documents the following data:
     M & R started to export the vermouth to USA in 1867: one hundred cases were shipped from the port of Genova to the New York agent, Mr. Manara, by the steamboat "Hermann".

From 1867 to 1889 they exported to USA 51 thousand cases (612,000 litres) of Martini vermouth ("Italian vermouth"). From 1890 to 1910 the cases increased up to 1,226,297 (14,715,564 litres) plus 308,713 litres sent in bulk (drums) to the firm Heublein seated in Hartford, by Mr. Manara approval, to produce a bottled "Martini Cocktail".

In 1876 the Martini vermouth is awarded a gold medal at the Philadelphia International Exhibition. In 1877 a document states that the 3/4 of the vermouth exported to USA is Martini & Rossi Vermouth. In 1883 the "New York Herald" reports the official registration of the "trade mark vino vermouth Martini & Rossi".

Here is the Martini Cocktail's recipe we found in an advertisement on an American paper in 1906 :

"The Original Martini Cocktail"
1/3 Martini & Rossi Vermouth
2/3 Tanqueray or other Dry Gin
Squeeze of Lemon Peel
A dash of Orange Bitters
Stir, but don't shake

The bottle reproduced in the ad was Martini Rosso. On the neck label there was a big wording "ITALY." Sole Agent for the State was W.A. Taylor. 29 Broadway—New York.

In the ad's text you can find the following words: "You cannot make a genuine "Martini" (dry or otherwise) without Martini & Rossi Vermouth. No other cocktail has as big a following, and that of a class that is worth while catering to. Made as above it is the best trade builder we know of."

In 1927, Mr. Taylor, Martini & Rossi agent since 1889 could announce on the "Daily Mirror" a vermouth sales increase of 300%!!

As to the Dry Martini Vermouth: We know that in 1890 the Martini agent in Cuba, Juan Brocchi, asked the company to create a new type of vermouth to win the competition with Noilly Prat that was producing a dryer vermouth, the French one. Ten years later the Dry Martini vermouth was launched on the international markets on the occasion of the celebrations for the New Year 1900.

Toasts to the New Year with Martini Dry were made in Egypt, Turkey and in Cuba.

I hope [that this will] be helpful. Should you need more, please tell me.

Kind regards,

Florisa

I found the fact that Tanqueray gin was mentioned in that 1906 newspaper ad to be pretty fascinating, so I reached out to John Tanqueray in London to find out when Tanqueray was first marketed in the U.S.A. John turned out to be quite the gentleman.

Dear Mr. Regan,

Thank you for email of the 12th regarding Tanqueray Gin in the USA at the turn of the last century. My great-grandfather Charles Waugh Tanqueray, son of the founder, joined forces with Gordon's Gin in 1898. At that time Gordon's was imported in bulk from the UK in barrels and bottled in the USA. It wasn't until the end of Prohibition in the early 1930's that the Company arranged for Gordon's to be distilled in the USA.

Tanqueray Gin in the meantime, founded in 1830, appears according to a bottle in the Archive dept of the company to have been shipped in bulk to the USA and bottled by the Gordon's Dry Gin Co. in the States. Unfortunately I have no record as to the date of the bottle but as it has a glass stopper I assume it must be early 20th C.

I have sent a copy of your email to the Archive Dept of the company from whom you may hear.

Thank you very much for your kind comments regarding our products. No. 10 in particular has been most successful since its launch in the States.

Kind regards.
John Tanqueray

And the archive department did, indeed, come through:

Hi Gary

I have been doing further work on the Tanqueray records here at the Archive and have found a document concerning registration of trademarks that definitely confirms the availability of Tanqueray's Finest Dry Gin in the USA from at least 1900 and also Tanqueray Old Tom from at least 1907. [Incidentally] the Gordon's Boar's Head has been used in the USA from at least 1892.

As you can see this would definitely confirm the availability of Tanqueray for Martini Cocktails in 1906!

The Gordon's Dry Gin Company Ltd. (New York) appears to have been formed around 1913 and after Prohibition, re-formed by 1934.

If I turn up any further information that I think may be useful I will be in touch. Hope this helps.

Best wishes
Sharon Maxwell
Assistant Archivist

Martini (Dry)

The Dry Gin Martini, when it was first created—around the turn of the twentieth century—always called for orange bitters, and they remained an integral part of the drink right up until the 1940s.

"It's absolutely impossible to begin to tell you how to make this one correctly, simply because every Martini-drinking man and woman on the face of the earth has their own version of the drink, and even though mine happen to be the very best Dry Gin Martinis that anyone has ever tasted in the known universe, I'm yet to find anyone who agrees with me. Go figure. Here is a recipe that's not even written in soap, let alone stone. Fiddle with ratios, choose your own gin—Beefeater, Junipero, Plymouth, or Tanqueray—pick whichever dry vermouth you like—Noilly Prat or Dolin—and decide for yourself whether it's an olive or a lemon twist that tickles your fancy. Just don't be silly enough to pick the lemon twist. Do try adding a dash or two or orange bitters, though. They were present when the drink was born, circa 1900, and they stayed there for about half a century, so . . ." Gary Regan, *San Francisco Chronicle*, 2008 (with the addition of the Dolin vermouth which I hadn't tasted when I wrote this.)

75 ml (2.5 oz) gin
15 ml (.5 oz) dry vermouth
1 olive or lemon twist, as garnish

Stir over ice and strain into a chilled cocktail glass. Add the garnish.

The Intoxicating Effect of Sarsaparilla

"And here one must say something about the cocktail. To-day it is bad form at a dinner in a private house to have these refreshers served, and more than bad form to partake of them at restaurants. At least this is what the women think, and, besides, they are supposed to be fattening. However, sometimes an exception may be made, and if so there is no cocktail more delicate than a Martini, made of very dry gin and two kinds of vermouth, the French and the Italian. Much vermouth is being taken these days. It is nothing else than white wine which has been subjected to an infusion of bitter herbs. In Paris and Italy it is used as a mild cocktail, with lime juice and cracked ice and a little mineral water. In this proportion it has about the intoxicating effect of sarsaparilla." *New York Times Magazine*, September 2, 1906.

Martini (Dry) à la *Imbibe*

In his book, *Imbibe*, David Wondrich cites a newspaper article from 1897 wherein a bar owner says that he used to go through a quart of 'gum' (simple syrup) a day in his cocktails, and now he used less than [60 ml or 2 oz] a day, thus helping to pinpoint the time when cocktails got drier and hence, the time when the Dry Martini was ready to emerge. The drink that became the very icon of sophistication in the twentieth century, then, was likely born as the eighteen-hundreds were drawing to a close. You'll note that the proportions of gin to vermouth in this version are far different from the ratios suggested in most mid- to late-twentieth-century books. *Imbibe* suggests using Beefeater or Tanqueray in the drink in order that the gin be strong and aromatic enough to stand up to an equal amount of vermouth which, according to Wondrich, should be Noilly Prat.

45 ml (1.5 oz) Beefeater or Tanqueray gin
45 ml (1.5 oz) Noilly Prat dry vermouth
1 dash orange bitters
1 orange or lemon twist, as garnish
Stir over ice and strain into a chilled cocktail glass. Add the garnish.

In Italy, Though not in Finland

"In Italy (though not in Finland) it is against the law to sell as a Martini Cocktail any beverage not containing vermouth made by the Italian firm of Martini and Rossi." *Time Magazine*, July 18, 1932.

Martini N° 16

"This one is a bit special, as thought by [G'Vine gin producer] Jean Sébastien Robicquet (definitely not a bartender and elaborated at the Georges V in Paris last year for the last time), as a twist around the smoky martini with the Cognac/grape touch. The name comes from the index code of the Cognac's region. I thought you would like the very French touch!" Audrey Forte, Eurowinegate, France.

60 ml (2 oz) G'vine Floraison gin
7.5 ml (.25 oz) Cognac VSOP
1 or 3 (pas deux) fresh grapes, as garnish
Shake over ice and strain into a chilled cocktail glass. Add the garnish.

Maurice Cocktail
Note that the Maurice Cocktail is just a Bronx Cocktail with a couple of dashes of absinthe, but what a difference a couple of dashes of absinthe makes . . .
60 ml (2 oz) gin
7.5 ml (.25 oz) sweet vermouth
7.5 ml (.25 oz) dry vermouth
30 ml (1 oz) fresh orange juice
2 dashes absinthe
1 orange twist, as garnish
Shake over ice and strain into a chilled cocktail glass. Add the garnish.

Mayfair Sour
Adapted from a recipe by Xavier Herit, Daniel, New York City.
60 ml (2 oz) Plymouth gin
22.5 ml (.75 oz) Benedictine
22.5 ml (.75 oz) Apricot Orchard liqueur
22.5 ml (.75 oz) fresh lemon juice
1 egg white
5 dashes peach bitters, as an aromatic garnish
Dry shake, then add ice and shake again. Strain into a chilled cocktail glass, and add the garnish.

Meloncholy Baby
The song "Melancholy Baby" (yes, the drink is spelled to reflect the Midori melon liqueur—how cute is that, huh?) was first performed in public in the Mozart Café in Denver, in 1912, by William Frawley, the guy who played Fred Mertz in the I love Lucy TV series. Aren't you happy to know that?
30 ml (1 oz) gin
30 ml (1 oz) Midori liqueur
20 ml (.75 oz) fresh lemon juice
15 ml (.5 oz) simple syrup
7.5 ml (.25 oz) Cointreau
15 ml (.5 oz) fresh grapefruit juice
1 maraschino cherry, as garnish
Shake over ice and strain into a chilled cocktail glass. Add the garnish.

Midtown Mule

Adapted from a recipe by Marshall Altier, Insieme, New York City.

This is an interesting twist on the Moscow Mule, and although you have to go to the bother of making a cardamom syrup before you can fix the drink, you'll most likely find that it was well worth the effort.

1/6 cucumber, sliced
15 ml (.5 oz) Cardamom Syrup*
60 ml (2 oz) Plymouth gin
1 ounce fresh lime juice
15 ml (.5 oz) Cointreau
Ginger beer
1 lime wedge, as garnish
2 cucumber wheels, as garnish

Muddle the cucumber slices and the cardamom syrup in a mixing glass to form a paste. Add ice and the remaining ingredients, shake for 15 to 20 seconds and strain into a tall ice-filled collins glass. Top with ginger beer, stir briefly, and add the garnishes.

*Cardamom Syrup

1/2 cup cardamom pods
450 g (1 lb) demerara sugar

In a skillet over medium heat, toast the cardamom pods for approximately 30 seconds, stirring constantly. Set aside. In a nonreactive saucepan, heat 475 ml (16 oz) of water to a simmer, add the cardamom to the water and allow to simmer for 3 to 5 minutes. Add the sugar, stir to dissolve, and remove from the heat. Strain through a double layer of dampened cheesecloth, and allow to cool. Bottle and store in the fridge.

Peck's Bad Boy

"Two drinks of gin makes a man or woman look as though they had swallowed a buzz saw." *Peck's Bad Boy Abroad* by George Wilbur Peck. Published by Thompson & Thomas, 1905.

Miller's D.R.Y. Life

Adapted from a recipe by Christine D'Abrosca, Malo Restaurant, Los Angeles.
6 bing cherries
15 ml (.5 oz) 4 Copas 100% organic agave nectar
22.5 ml (.75 oz) fresh lemon juice
15 ml (.5 oz) egg white
15 ml (.5 oz) Cointreau
45 ml (1.5 oz) Martin Miller's Westbourne Strength gin
D.R.Y. Rhubarb Soda
1 thin slice pickled rhubarb, as garnish
Muddle the cherries and agave nectar in a mixing glass. Add ice and remaining ingredients except soda. Shake over ice and strain into a collins glass with 3 ice cubes. Top with soda and add the garnish.

Monarch (London Version)

Adapted from a recipe submitted by Sarah Mitchell, Lab-Townhouse, London, and created by Douglas Ankrah.

"My fave gin drink is one by Douglas Ankrah. Wish it was mine but hey, can't win them all. I know it seems I'm plugging the old master, but it is truly credit where credit is due. What flavours you like depends on what gin you use. Martin Miller's Westbourne for a good punch, Plymouth for something a little more delicate. It's up to the bartender to distinguish for the guest." Sarah Mitchell, Lab-Townhouse, London.

45 ml (1.5 oz) gin (see comments above)
10 ml (.3 oz) elderflower cordial
2 flat barspoons caster sugar (aka superfine sugar)
22.5 ml (.75 oz) fresh lemon juice
5 to 8 mint leaves
Shake really hard over ice and strain into a chilled cocktail glass. "Smells amazing when you bring it to your mouth," Sarah Mitchell.

Monarch (San Francisco Version)

Adapted from a recipe by Neyah White, Nopa, San Francisco.

30 ml (1 oz) gin (light style, such as Bluecoat, Hendrick's, Leopold's or Damkrak)
15 ml (.5 oz) Lillet Blanc
15 ml (.5 oz) Benedictine
15 ml (.5 oz) Aperol
1 large lemon twist, as garnish

Stir over ice and strain into a chilled sherry glass. Add the garnish.

Monkey Gland Cocktail

There are two legitimate Monkey Gland Cocktails, one of which takes absinthe as an accent and was detailed in Harry Craddock's *Savoy Cocktail Book*, 1930. The other, which calls for Benedictine instead of absinthe, is found in Patrick Gavin Duffy's *Official Mixer's Guide*, 1934. Craddock, based in London, had access to absinthe, but Duffy changed the recipe to make it easier on American bartenders since absinthe was banned at the time in the U.S.A. Both versions are well worth trying.

60 ml (2 oz) gin
30 ml (1 oz) fresh orange juice
2 dashes absinthe or Benedictine
2 dashes grenadine

Shake over ice and strain into a chilled cocktail glass.

Montford

Adapted from a recipe by Dan Warner, Beefeater Brand Ambassador.

Styled around a classic martini. Aperitif Trophy Winner, Drinks International Bartender Challenge 2007.

45 ml (1.5 oz) Beefeater gin
22.5 ml (.75 oz) Lillet Blanc
10 ml (.3 oz) Noilly Prat Amber vermouth
2 dashes Regans' Orange Bitters No. 6
1 lemon twist, as garnish

Stir over ice and strain into a chilled champagne coupe. Add the garnish.

Montford Spritz
Adapted from a recipe by Dan Warner, Beefeater Brand Ambassador.
22.5 ml (.75 oz) Beefeater 24 gin
22.5 ml (.75 oz) Noilly Prat Amber vermouth
22.5 ml (.75 oz) Aperol
2 dashes Peychaud's bitters
45 ml (1.5 oz) champagne
1 grapefruit twist, as garnish
Pour all the ingredients into an ice-filled wine goblet and stir briefly. Add the garnish.

Moonlight Cocktail
Created by Gary Regan, Ardent Spirits, NY, 2007.
45 ml (1.5 oz) gin
15 ml (.5 oz) Cointreau
15 ml (.5 oz) creme de violette
15 ml (.5 oz) fresh lime juice
Shake over ice and strain into a chilled champagne flute.

Moonlight Cocktail

"Couple of jiggers of moonlight and add a star,
Pour in the blue of a June night and one guitar,
Mix in a couple of dreamers and there you are:
Lovers hail the Moonlight Cocktail." *Moonlight Cocktail* recorded by Glen Miller, lyrics by Kim Gannon, music by Lucky Roberts.

Morning Dew
Adapted from a recipe by Joshua Haig Harris, 15 Romolo, San Francisco.
3 large chunks honeydew melon
5 to 6 fresh spearmint leaves
60 ml (2 oz) Right gin
22.5 ml (.75 oz) Domaine de Durban muscat
15 ml (.5 oz) simple syrup
15 ml (.5 oz) egg white
1 spearmint blossom, as garnish
Muddle the honeydew and spearmint leaves in a mixing glass. Add the remaining ingredients. Dry shake, then add ice and shake again. Double strain into a chilled cocktail glass. Add the garnish.

Mosel Cocktail
Adapted from a recipe by Thad Vogler, Bar Agricole, San Francisco.
This incredibly complex cocktail won second place in the Martin Miller's Gin Masters, November 9th, 2008. The competition was held at Death & Co, New York.
45 ml (1.5 oz) Martin Miller's Gin Westbourne Strength gin
45 ml (1.5 oz) Mosel Spatlese Riesling
2 dashes cherry bitters*
2 dashes peach bitters*
Stir over ice and strain into a chilled champagne coupe.
*Thad used "homemade biodynamic" bitters in this drink. You will probably have to use a branded bitters such as Fee Brothers.

Myriam
Adapted from a recipe by Wouter Vullings, Bols Bartending Academy/The Fabulous Shaker Boys, Amsterdam.
60 ml (2 oz) Damrak gin
30 ml (1 oz) wild nettle cordial*
10 dashes orange flower water**
1 lemon twist, as garnish
Stir over ice and strain into a chilled cocktail glass. Add the garnish.
*"You may find wild nettle cordial in a health food store, or you can make your own by boiling nettles and some sugar in water," Wouter Vullings.
**Wouter prefers to use Bitter Truth's orange flower water, but if you can't find it . . .

Negroni

I always thought that Count Negroni, the man said to have been the creator of this classic drink, was a myth dreamed up by some marketer or other. It sounded to be too far-fetched to be true. Fact, though, is often stranger than fiction, so it should have come as no surprise when David Wondrich, intrepid researcher and author of *Imbibe*, discovered the story of the birth of the Negroni in an Italian book, *Sulle tracche del Conte: la vera stroria del cocktail "Negroni,"* by Lucca Picchi, head bartender at Caffe Rivoire in Florence, Italy, and yes, there actually was an Italian Count, Camillo Negroni. And just as we'd been told by the good folk at Campari for many a year, he actually was the guy who took the soda out of the Americano—Campari, sweet vermouth, and club soda—and added gin to the mixture to give it more of a kick. The bar he frequented in Florence at the time, circa 1920, was called Bar Casoni, and the bartender there went by the name of Fosco Scarselli. Count Negroni, by the way, had travelled around the U.S.A. and made a living as a rodeo cowboy for a time. We can presume, then, that he was a tough man, so removing the soda from a Negroni and replacing it with gin makes a great deal of sense, right?

The incredible aspect of the Negroni that not everyone understands is that it works every time, no matter what brands of gin or sweet vermouth you use. And you can slap my wrist and call me Deborah if it doesn't also work no matter what ratios you use, too. Seriously. Go up on the gin, go up on the Campari, go up on the vermouth. These three ingredients are soul mates, and they support each other no matter how much you try to fool them.

45 ml (1.5 oz) Campari
45 ml (1.5 oz) sweet vermouth
45 ml (1.5 oz) gin
1 orange twist, as garnish

Pour all of the ingredients into an ice-filled old-fashioned glass and sir briefly. Add the garnish.

New Amsterdam
Adapted from a recipe from Jim Meehan, PDT, New York City.
Genever was hard, if not impossible, to find in the USA at the end of the
twentieth century. Now, though, it's making a comeback, and this is one of the
first twenty-first-century cocktails to call for it as a base.
60 ml (2oz) Bols genever
30 ml (1 oz) Clear Creek kirschwasser
1 barspoon Demerara Syrup*
2 dashes Peychaud's bitters
1 lemon twist, as garnish
Stir over ice and strain into a chilled cocktail glass. Add the garnish.

*Demerara Syrup: combine 120 ml (1/2 cup) of water and 100 grams (1 cup) of
demerara sugar in a small saucepan over medium heat. Stir frequently until the
sugar is dissolved, remove the pan from the heat, allow the mixture to room
temperature, and store in the refrigerator.

New Ideal
Adapted from a recipe by Neyah White, first published in the *San Francisco
Chronicle*, 2008.
"The New Ideal August 19, 1917. America, as she grows more and more sure of
her high destiny, must also grow more modest. She must realize herself as one
of the sister states in the great commonwealth of nations, and the eagle will
take lessons in voice culture. As a quiet voice can make itself heard in a medley
of noises where a screaming voice would be inaudible, so must America's voice
become deep and quiet." *Last Letters from the Living Dead Man* by Elsa Barker,
1919.
30 ml (1 oz) Bluecoat gin
15 ml (.5 oz) Punt e Mes
15 ml (.5 oz) Luxardo maraschino liqueur
60 ml (2 oz) fresh grapefruit juice
4 dashes blackberry root tincture (optional)
1 lemon twist, as garnish
Shake over ice and strain into a chilled cocktail glass. Add the garnish.

Nippon no Mori
Adapted from a recipe by Arnd Henning-Heissen, Sochu Bar, Berlin, Germany.
2 barspoons fennel
45 ml (1.5 oz) G'Vine Nouaison gin
30 ml (1 oz) St. Germain elderflower liqueur
30 ml (1 oz) Martini & Rossi Bianco vermouth
30 ml (1 oz) jasmine tea
3 thin lime wheels, as garnish
Shake over ice and double strain into a highball glass filled with crushed ice. Add the garnish.

North Beach
Adapted from a recipe by Lance J. Mayhew, 50 Plates/Beaker & Flask, Portland, OR.
30 ml (1 oz) Bombay Sapphire gin
30 ml (1 oz) Aperol
30 ml (1 oz) fresh lemon juice
30 ml (1 oz) simple syrup
1 lemon twist, as garnish
Shake over ice and strain into a chilled cocktail glass. Add the garnish.

Old "Oregon" Fashioned
Adapted from a recipe by Ryan Magarian, Portland, OR.
60 ml (2oz) Aviation gin
7.5 ml (.25 oz) simple syrup
2 dashes Regans' Orange Bitters No. 6
1 dash Peychaud's bitters
1 orange wheel, as garnish
Stir over ice and strain into a chilled cocktail glass. Add the garnish.

Old-Timer

Adapted from a recipe by Neyah White, Nopa, San Francisco, 2008.

"Next to being turned down in his first town, the youthful First-tripper encounters no greater discouragement than that of his initial meeting with the professional pessimistic Old-timer, with his perpetual grouch . . . Where is the commercial traveler who has not encountered him and given him a wide berth ? He is to be seen in the hotel lobby, disputing his bill with the clerk because something or other went wrong." *Men who Sell Things* by Walter D Moody. Edition 15, 1919.

60 ml (2 oz) oude genever
4 sprigs of fresh thyme
15 ml (.5 oz) simple syrup
15 ml (.5 oz) fresh lemon juice
60 ml (2 oz) ginger beer
60 ml (2 oz) soda

Slap thyme sprigs to get the oils going (no need to muddle if it is fresh) and toss into a collins glass. Add ice and build, topping with ginger and soda, Stir enough to get the thyme even distributed.

A Drink Fit for the Gods Of Olympus

"A dashing young yachtsman sang a dainty French melody, taught him by a peasant girl at Biarritz; another member of the party told a story with a droll climax. All drank to the life that hurried past. Ultimately, everybody at the table became more or less heated, except Tom Ray. He was cool, contented, unflushed.

"A member of the party called a waiter, then turned to Tom Ray and made this suggestion :

"'I say, dear fellow, invent us a new drink.'

"'Great idea!' said another. 'Make this night historical.'

"'I'll think it over, and send you a suggestion,' Tom Ray replied.

"'No; we want it this minute!'

"'If you insist, I will impart to you a secret I have long cherished; I will give you a friend's inspiration that is infinitely better than any of mine. Let me have a talk with your head-waiter.

"After that conference, a bowl of finely cracked ice was brought and three bottles of liquor—all chilled. The labels had been removed, to highten [sic] the mystery of the concoction. Taking the bottles, one at a time, Tom Ray filled a goblet to the rim and turned the contents into the bowl of ice. Three liquors, in equal proportions. A waiter then stirred the compound until it smoked with cold. The ice was then removed with a strainer and the drink was served in tall cocktail glasses.

"'No questions are to be asked or answered until every glass is drained,' Tom insisted. 'I believe you will like it.'

"Every man stood to his guns.

"'Excellent!' said they all.

"'Superb!' commented Tom Ray. 'I may say this, because it is not my invention. The receipt is: Equal parts of French and Italian Vermouth and Plymouth gin!'

"'Gin?'

"'Yes; the juice of the juniper berry!'

"'Gin!' exclaimed everybody present—in doubt, because the taste was completely hidden. They never had tasted a common drink.

"'Certainly,' replied Tom Ray, firmly. 'What could be more appropriately associated with this wonderful club?'

"'But gin is made for varlets,' somebody stammered.

"'By tradition, yes,' was the answer; 'but a drink like this is fit for the gods of Olympus.' When an opinion was uttered by Tom Ray, the final verdict had been rendered.

"'Give it a name!' shouted several voices when the delicate after-taste began to develop on their palates.

"'I christen it with the name of its inventor, Mr. Oliver, of the Stock Exchange, added Tom Ray, taking up his glass, after all the others had been refilled. 'I name it The Oliver Cocktail! '" *The King of the Lobby* is a chapter from *When Money Talked*, by Julius Chambers, found in *The Gateway: A Magazine for the Great Lake States and Canada*, August, 1905.

Oliver Cocktail

The original formula—detailed in the box above—for the Oliver works well, but truth be told, I chose to put this drink into the book because of the story that goes with it, so I decided to play around with the recipe a little. I added orange bitters to the recipe, and I chose the No. 6 brand specifically because the cardamom plays nicely with the Plymouth gin. And since I was playing around with the drink I went for the Noilly Prat brands of vermouth, too. (For those of you who are bound to ask, I used the "new" N.P. dry bottling made available in the USA in 2009.) The orange twist is an optional aromatic garnish, so if you want a mediocre version of the drink, leave it out.

45 ml (1.5 oz) Plymouth gin
45 ml (1.5 oz) Noilly Prat dry vermouth
45 ml (1.5 oz) Noilly Prat sweet vermouth
2 dashes Regans' Orange Bitters No. 6
1 orange twist, as garnish
Stir over ice and strain into a chilled champagne flute. Add the garnish.

Oliver's Twist

Created by Gary Regan for the *Gourmet* Magazine food-pairing challenge, 2004. This drink was named for Garrett Oliver, brewmaster for the Brooklyn Brewery, and one of the best-loved men in the beverage industry.

30 ml (1 oz) Tanqueray No. TEN gin

15 ml (.5 oz) Cointreau

30 ml (1 oz) pineapple juice

3 dashes Angostura bitters

1 maraschino cherry, as garnish

Shake over ice and strain into a chilled cocktail glass. Add the garnish.

One Hot Cucumber

Adapted from a recipe by Evelyn Hsu, restaurant.mc, Millburn, NJ.

60 ml (2 oz) Hendrick's gin

45 ml (1.5 oz) cucumber water

15 ml (.5 oz) simple syrup

7.5 ml (.25 oz) fresh lime juice

6 mint leaves

3 thinly sliced cucumbers and cayenne pepper, as garnish

Shake over ice and strain into a chilled champagne coupe. Add the garnish.

Pacific Rim Martini

Adapted from a recipe by Ginger DiLello, Philadelphia Fish and Company, Philadelphia.

Ginger, the predominant flavor in this drink, was also the color of the goddess Macha's hair. And you don't want to cross the goddess Macha. Legend has it that she slept with each of her five brothers, then forced them to build her a fort in Ireland. Quite a price to pay, huh?

75 ml (2.5 oz) gin (yes, there's a vodka version, but we don't talk about it)

15 ml (.5 oz) Domain de Canton ginger liqueur

1 small piece crystallized ginger, as garnish

Stir over ice and strain into a chilled cocktail glass. Add the garnish.

Paint it Black

Adapted from a recipe by Chris Tucker, L Wine Lounge, Sacramento
First place in the Broker's London Dry Gin Contest, 2009.
60 ml (2 oz) Broker's London Dry gin
2 tablespoons Blackberry, Ginger and Star Anise Tonic Jelly *
90 ml (3 oz) Blackberry Mint Charged Water **
Lime zest, as garnish
Paint the inside of a collins glass with 1 tablespoon of the jelly, then fill the glass with ice. Add the gin and the remaining tablespoon of jelly to a mixing glass. Add ice, shake, and double strain into the prepared glass. Top with charged water and garnish with lime zest.

*Blackberry, Ginger and Star Anise Tonic Jelly

850 grams (30 oz) blackberries
.5 liter (2 cups) sliced ginger
10 star anise pods
875 grams (4.3 cups) sugar
240 ml (1 cup) boiling water
2 tablespoons quinine powder
2 tablespoons citric acid powder
In a 6-quart saucepot, combine berries, ginger and anise and sweat (heat until droplets appear on berries and spices) over medium heat. Stir occasionally to prevent scalding on bottom of pot. In a heat-proof glass measuring cup, combine quinine, citric acid and boiling water. Whisk until there are no clumps. Add to blackberry pot and continue stirring. Once bubbling, add sugar and continue stirring until all sugar is dissolved. Continue to cook over medium heat for about 30 minutes, reducing fluid by one-third. Strain into sterile preserve jars and screw on caps and lids.

**Blackberry-Mint Charged Water

110 grams (1 cup) blackberries
1 small bunch fresh mint
1 liter (1 quart) fresh, cold water
In sauce pot, combine all items and bring to a boil over high heat. Boil for 90 seconds. Strain and let cool. Add cooled water to soda siphon or seltzer charger and charge. Keep cold.

Palin's Christmas Punch

Adapted from a recipe by Sam Ross, Milk & Honey, New York City.

This fabulous punch won the Martin Miller's Gin Masters, on November 9th, 2008. The competition was held at Death & Co, New York.

Zest from 2 lemons
1 teaspoon granulated sugar
360 ml (12 oz) Martin Miller's Gin Westbourne Strength gin
360 ml (12 oz) fresh lemon juice
300 ml (10 oz) Demerara Date Syrup*
420 ml (14 oz) Zirbenz Stone Pine liqueur
45 ml (1.5 oz) absinthe
45 ml (1.5 oz) Regan's Orange Bitters No. 6
1 bottle (750 ml) dry champagne

In a large pitcher, muddle the lemon zests with the sugar to extract the oils. Pour all of the ingredients except the champagne into the pitcher, add ice, and stir briefly. Strain into a punch bowl, top with champagne, float Lemon Ice** and stir. Serve in punch cups. Garnish with Absinthe Dates.***

*Demerara Date Syrup:** Dissolve 2 cups (400 g) of demerara sugar into 1 cup (240 ml) of water. Add 1 cup of crushed dates, stir briefly, and allow to rest for three days. Strain through a double layer of dampened cheesecloth, and store in the refrigerator.

Lemon Ice: Drop lemon wheels into a small plastic container filled with water and place in freezer—voilà!

***Absinthe Date:** Using an eye dropper, drop 3 to 4 drops of absinthe into the top of a date.

Paradise Cocktail

Loosely based on Harry Craddock's recipe in *The Savoy Cocktail Book*, 1930.
45 ml (1.5 oz) gin
20 ml (.75 oz) apricot brandy
15 ml (.5 oz) fresh orange juice
15 ml (.5 oz) fresh lemon juice

Shake over ice and strain into a chilled cocktail glass.

Peach Fuzz

Adapted from a recipe by Joshua Haig Harris, 15 Romolo, San Francisco.
3/4 white donut peach, cut into chunks
22.5 ml (.75 oz) fresh lemon juice
60 ml (2 oz) Right gin
22.5 ml (.75 oz) light organic agave nectar
15 ml (.5 oz) egg white
4 to 6 dashes Fee Brothers peach bitters
1 white donut peach wedge, as garnish
Muddle the peach chunks and lemon juice in a mixing glass. Add the remaining ingredients. Dry shake, then add ice and shake again. Double strain into a chilled cocktail glass. Add the garnish.

Pearl

Adapted from a recipe by Jon Santer, Bar Agricole, San Francisco.
Pearl Bailey, who has nothing whatsoever to do with this drink, was an African American singer who got herself a degree in theology when she was 67 years old.
45 ml (1.5 oz) Plymouth gin
20 ml (.75 oz) Aperol
15 ml (.5 oz) Lillet Blanc
60 ml (2 oz) Prosecco (or any dry sparkling wine)
1 drop lemon oil
Stir the gin, Aperol, and Lillet over ice and strain into a chilled champagne flute. Add the Prosecco and lemon oil and stir briefly.

Pegu Club Cocktail

The earliest recipe we can find for the Pegu Club Cocktail (after Robert Hess—DrinkBoy.com—pointed the way, that is), is in the 1927 book, *Barflies and Cocktails* by Harry MacElhone, famed owner of Harry's New York Bar in Paris. His recipe called for 4 parts gin, 1 part orange curaçao, a teaspoon of Rose's lime juice, and a dash each of Angostura and orange bitters. In his 1930's *Savoy Cocktail Book,* Harry Craddock noted, "The favourite cocktail of the Pegu Club, Burma, and one that has traveled, and is asked for, round the world."
60 ml (2 oz) gin
30 ml (1 oz) Cointreau
15 ml (.5 oz) fresh lime juice
1 dash Angostura bitters
1 dash orange bitters
Shake over ice and strain into a chilled cocktail glass.

> **"The Broad Bosom of a Friend**
>
> In the Pegu Club I found a friend—a Punjabi—upon whose broad bosom I threw myself and demanded food and entertainment." *From Sea to Sea*, Rudyard Kipling, 1889.

Pegu Club (Redux)
Adapted from a recipe by Thad Vogler, Bar Manager at Jardiniere, San Francisco.
45 ml (1.5 oz) gin
20 ml (.75 oz) Qi White Tea liqueur
20 ml (.75 oz) fresh lime juice
2 dashes Angostura bitters
1 demitasse spoon raw organic sugar
Shake over ice and strain into a chilled cocktail glass.

Peppermelon
Adapted from a recipe by H. Joseph Ehrmann, Elixir, San Francisco.
"The balance of sweet and hot makes this cocktail refreshing, with each sip demanding another. Use organic ingredients wherever possible." H. Joseph Ehrmann.
45 ml (1.5 oz) Bluecoat gin
22.5 ml (.75 oz) Black Pepper Honey Syrup*
30 ml (1 oz) watermelon juice
15 ml (.5oz) lemon juice
1 watermelon cube coated with black pepper, as garnish
Shake well over ice for 10 seconds and strain into a chilled cocktail glass. Add the garnish.

*Black Honey Pepper Syrup:** Boil 2 cups (475 ml) of water and add 4 tablespoons of black peppercorns. Cook for 5 minutes and strain the solids out. Measure the remaining liquid and add enough water to bring it back to two cups. Return to the heat and stir in 2 cups (475 ml) of honey until dissolved. Cool and store in a recycled bottle.

Plymouth Hoe

Adapted from a recipe by Gary Regan, Ardent Spirits, NY.
This drink was created on May 13, 2009, at the World Cocktail Day event in New York City, held at Pranna restaurant.
60 ml (2 oz) Plymouth gin
15 ml (.5 oz) Grand Marnier
7.5 ml (.25 oz) Navan vanilla liqueur
4 to 5 dashes Angostura bitters
1 lemon twist, as garnish
Fill a mixing glass two-thirds full of ice and add all of the ingredients. Stir for approximately 30 seconds, strain into a chilled cocktail glass, and add the garnish.

Pompier Cocktail

Adapted from a recipe by Gary Regan, Ardent Spirits, NY.
This drink was based on the Pompier Highball that's detailed in Charles Baker Jr.'s fabulous book, *The Gentleman's Companion,* 1939. It's fairly low in alcohol, and if you want to you can try making it with just a little more gin, but don't use more than, say, 15 ml (.5 oz) total.
75 ml (2.5 oz) dry vermouth
7.5 ml (.25 oz) creme de cassis
7.5 ml (.25 oz) gin
1 lemon twist, as garnish
Stir over ice and strain into a chilled cocktail glass. Add the garnish.

Prairie Dog

Adapted from a recipe by Gary Regan, Ardent Spirits, NY.
Prairie dogs are related to squirrels, and Richard Modlin, a writer and ecologist who spends time in Maine during the summer, wrote a short story about a squirrel who always appeared "at the time of day when we stopped to enjoy a cocktail" Name of the story? *The Cocktail Squirrel,* of course.
45 ml (1.5 oz) Hendrick's gin
15 ml (.5 oz) Domain de Canton ginger liqueur
7.5 ml (.25 oz) fresh lemon juice
1 lemon twist, as garnish
Shake over ice and strain into a chilled cocktail glass. Add the garnish.

Primavera
Adapted from a recipe by Naren Young, Bobo, New York City.
"Basically a silver fizz variation, but frickin delicious if i do say so . . ." Naren Young.
3 cucumber wheels
3 basil leaves
60 ml (2 oz) Beefeater gin
22.5 ml (.75 oz) St. Germain elderflower liqueur
7.5 ml (.25 oz) absinthe
22.5 ml (.75 oz) fresh lime juice
1 egg white
Club soda, to top
Any spring frippery you desire, as garnish
Muddle the cucumber and basil in a mixing glass. Add the remaining ingredients
and dry shake like a [Naren used an expletive here but we deleted it because we
know how sensitive bartenders ears can be]. Add ice, shake again, and strain into
an ice-filled collins glass. Top with a little soda. Add the garnish.

The Sultana

"Beware of nothing! I'm going to drink cocktails all day and waltz all night.
I'm going to be so civilized that people will talk about me. Pamela, Pammy,
did you ever think you would like to live in a palace and have Sultana printed
on your visiting-cards?" *The Sultan of Sulu: An Original Satire in Two Acts* by
George Ade, 1903.

Pulitzer
Adapted from a recipe by Jonathan Pogash, Hospitality Holdings (The Campbell
Apt, The Carnegie Club, The World Bar, Bookmarks Lounge, Madison & Vine),
New York City.
"This drink is served at Bookmarks Lounge at the Library Hotel in New York City.
All of our drinks are literary themed, and the color of this drink led me to name it
the Pulitzer. It's a deep golden color, and not only satisfies the taste buds but also
the nose. The combination of three senses—taste, sight, and smell—make this
drink a great reminder to enjoy life to the fullest." Jonathan Pogash.
30 ml (1 oz) Plymouth gin
15 ml (.5 oz) St. Germain elderflower liqueur
7.5 ml (.25 oz) Fernet Branca
7.5 ml (.25 oz) fresh lemon juice
1 teaspoon agave nectar
1 nice looking mint sprig that you've slapped around a bit in order to wake it up,
as garnish.
Shake over ice and strain into a chilled cocktail glass. Add the garnish.

Punch and Judy

Adapted from a recipe by Charlotte Voisey, Mixologist, Hendrick's Gin.

Punch, of Punch and Judy puppet show fame, was known as Pulcinella when he started his antics in sixteenth-century Italy, and Pulcinella was a character based on the Lord of Misrule, a person who was appointed annually to preside over the festival of Saturnalia in ancient Rome.

30 ml (1 oz) Martell cognac VSOP
7.5 ml (.25 oz) Old New Orleans Crystal rum
15 ml (.5 oz) Hendrick's gin
15 ml (.5 oz) Bols orange curaçao
60 ml (2 oz) pineapple juice
15 ml (.5 oz) fresh lime juice
15 ml (.5 oz) fresh orange juice
15 ml (.5 oz) Partida agave nectar
2 dashes Angostura bitters
4 mint leaves
1 lime wheel, as garnish
Freshly grated nutmeg, as garnish

Assemble ingredients in a mixing glass with as much love and interest that is healthy (that is to say, not in a obsessive fashion, but certainly with passion and perhaps as if you were preparing the drink for someone you respect, admire and love in a platonic fashion)—no need to muddle the mint, just throw it in—shake properly (hard) and strain over fresh ice in a highball glass. Cut a thinly sliced lime wheel and place on top of the Punch and Judy; add a hearty sprinkle of ground nutmeg directly on the lime wheel.

Purple Heart

Adapted from a recipe by Eric Alperin, The Doheny, Los Angeles.

"It's lovely that gin is on the rise again. This one is a twist on the classic, the French 75." Eric Alperin.

30 ml (1 oz) gin
15 ml (.5 oz) fresh lemon juice
15 ml (.5 oz) simple syrup
Champagne, to top
Cherry Heering, to float
1 skewered Amarena cherry, as garnish

Shake over ice and strain into a chilled champagne flute. Top with champagne and float the Cherry Heering. Add the garnish.

Quintessence

Adapted from a recipe by Jim Wrigley, Brand Ambassador, Whitley Neill Gin, UK.
"The concept for this drink was to create an after-dinner gin drink working with the flavours on a cheese board, and Gubbeen, a soft, creamy cheese from England, was my chef's choice of pairing—it works really well. I originally served the drink on a napkin on a long plate, with a thin slice of the cheese, some thin cheese biscuits and a cheese knife. After seeing the mess that ensues I think it's probably best to serve the cheese already on the crackers!" Jim Wrigley.

1/4. large navel orange
1/4 Seville lemon
1 barspoon quince jam
45 ml (1.5 oz) Whitley Neill gin
22.5 ml (.75 oz) Luxardo maraschino liqueur
10ml (.3 oz) amaretto
1 skewered cape gooseberry and lemon twist, as garnish

Muddle the fruit and jam in a mixing glass. Add ice and the remaining ingredients. Shake and strain into an ice-filled old-fashioned glass. Add the garnish.

Ramos Gin Fizz

Henry Ramos, creator of this Fizz, had his own methods of making sure that the drink was prepared correctly: He hired a bevy of bartenders who passed the shaker from one to the next until the drink reached the desired consistency. In *Famous New Orleans Drinks & How to Mix 'Em*, author Stanley Clisby Arthur states that at Mardi Gras in 1915, "35 shaker boys nearly shook their arms off, but still were unable to keep up with the demand."

Since we have something that Henry Ramos didn't have, there's no longer any need to shake till you arms nigh-on drop off. Using a blender to make the Ramos Gin Fizz is the way to go. It yields a silky cocktail that's ice-cold, and when you use the correct amount of ice—about half as much as you would if you wanted a frozen drink—it's easy to achieve the right amount of dilution, too.

Makes 2 cocktails
60 ml (2 oz) gin
30 ml (1 oz) cream
1 raw egg white (pasteurized)
15 ml (.5 oz) simple syrup
15 ml (.5 oz) fresh lime juice
15 ml (.5 oz) fresh lemon juice
7.5 ml (.25 oz) orange flower water
Club soda
2 half-wheels orange, as garnish

Blend everything except the club soda with enough ice to fill one champagne flute. Divide the mixture between two champagne flutes, and top each drink with a splash of club soda. Add the garnishes.

It Sings Ever So Sweetly

"A famous Chicago poet once said of the Ramos Gin Fizz, 'Ah, my boy, when you have drunk it there is music within you, for it sings ever so sweetly and continues to sing no matter where you may wander, so that the tender recollection of it remains with you forever.'" St. Louis Republic, 9/15/1895. Transcribed by David Wondrich, 6/9/2009. Stolen by gaz regan, later that same day.

Raspberry & Rosemary
Adapted from a recipe by Debbi Peek, Portfolio Mixologist, Bacardi USA
30 ml (1 oz) fresh lemon juice
15 ml (.5 oz) simple syrup
6 to 8 fresh raspberries
6 to 8 fresh rosemary needles
45 ml (1.5 oz) Bombay Sapphire gin
15 ml (.5 oz) raspberry liqueur
Fresh raspberries, as garnish
1 rosemary sprig, as garnish
Muddle the lemon juice, simple syrup, raspberries and rosemary in mixing glass. Add ice and the remaining ingredients. Shake over ice and double strain to remove raspberry seeds into a chilled cocktail glass. Add the garnish.

Raspberry Collins
Adapted from a recipe by David Nepove, Enrico's Sidewalk Cafe, San Francisco.
"Red raspberries are nearly always in good demand. The grower who lives near a small town, where there is not too much competition, and who can depend upon getting from eight to twelve cents a quart for his crop, will have no trouble in making red raspberries pay." *Bush-fruits: A Horticultural Monograph of Raspberries, Blackberries, Dewberries, Currants, Gooseberries, and Other Shrub-like Fruits* by Fred Wallace Card. Edition 5, 1898.
4 fresh raspberries
30 ml (1 oz) fresh lemon juice
22.5 ml (.75 oz) simple syrup
45 ml (1.5 oz) Tanqueray gin
Club soda
1 lemon twist, as garnish
Muddle the raspberries with the lemon juice and simple syrup in a mixing glass. Add ice and the gin. Shake and strain into an ice-filled collins glass. Top with the club soda, stir briefly, and add the garnish.

Red Lion
Adapted from a recipe by Ryan Magarian, Portland, OR.
45 ml (1.5 oz) Aviation gin
22.5 ml (.75 oz) Grand Marnier
15 ml (.5 oz) fresh lemon juice
22.5 ml (.75 oz) fresh orange juice
1 orange wheel, as garnish
Shake over ice and strain into a chilled cocktail glass. Add the garnish.

Gladsome and Refreshing Qualities

"The gin cocktail is known to have certain gladsome and refreshing qualities in those milder states of asthenia which follow a day's work and precede an evening meal. Dr. George T. Maxwell, of Jacksonville, Fla., however, in addition recommends the gin cocktail as closely approaching a specific in yellow fever." *American Homoeopathist*, 1890.

Rembrandt
Adapted from a recipe by Ryan Magarian, Portland, OR.
60 ml (2 oz) genever gin
30 ml (1 oz) dry vermouth
7.5 ml (.25 oz) Drambuie
3 Drambuie-marinated raisins on a cocktail pick, as garnish
Stir over ice and strain into a chilled cocktail glass. Add the garnish.

Renaissance Negroni
Adapted from a recipe by Duggan McDonnell, Cantina, San Francisco.
"In cases where a medical man considers it necessary to prescribe gin in preference to other spirits, we believe the 'Original' Plymouth Gin will be found superior to all others." *The London Medical Recorder*, 1890.
45 ml (1.5 oz) Plymouth gin
30 ml (1 oz) Germain-Robin Liqueur de Poète
20 ml (.75 oz) Campari
1 orange twist, as garnish
Stir over ice and strain into a chilled cocktail glass. Add the garnish.

Right Night

Adapted from a recipe by Joshua Haig Harris, 15 Romolo, San Francisco.

1 brandied cherry
15 ml (.5 oz) Moscato d'Asti
45 ml (1.5 oz) Right gin
7.5 ml (.25 oz) St Germain elderflower liqueur
30 ml (1 oz) fresh lemon juice
15 ml (.5 oz) simple syrup
15 ml (.5 oz) egg white

Place the cherry at the bottom of a cocktail glass, pour in the Moscato d'Asti, and set aside. Dry shake the remaining ingredients, then add ice and shake again. Strain into the cocktail glass.

Riveredge Cocktail

Based on a recipe by James Beard in *Crosby Gaige's Cocktail Guide and Ladies' Companion*, by Crosby Gaige, 1945.

"And now, ladies and gentlemen, I present to you one of man's best friends. No, it's not the dog—It's Jimmy Beard, father and mother of cooking in the open, harbinger of hors d'oeuvre, and creator by royal decree of the canapé. If you do not possess his magnum opus, *Cook it Outdoors,* or his encyclopedia, *Hors d'oeuvre and Canapés*, you are not properly equipped to deal with present-day existence." *Crosby Gaige's Cocktail Guide and Ladies' Companion*, by Crosby Gaige, 1945.

Makes 16 ounces, serves 4
180 ml (6 oz) gin
60 ml (2 oz) dry vermouth
60 ml (2 oz) fresh orange juice
Grated zest of 1 orange
2 dashes orange bitters
4 orange twists, as garnish

Blend with one cup of ice cubes. Pour immediately into four chilled cocktail glasses. Add the garnishes.

Rose Royale

Adapted from a recipe by Xavier Herit, Daniel, New York City.

30 ml (1 oz) Hendrick's gin
15 ml (.5 oz) rose syrup
15 ml (.5 oz) fresh lemon juice
60 ml (2 oz) champagne
1 rose petal, as garnish

Shake the gin, rose syrup, and lemon juice over ice and strain into a chilled champagne flute. Top with champagne and add the garnish.

Rosé the Riveter

Adapted from a recipe by The Fabulous LeNell Smothers, Spirits and Cocktail Paramour of Great Renown, from Brooklyn by way of Alabama.

Rosie the Riveter, a character who starred in a promotional movie for war bonds, and was featured on posters during WWII, was a real riveter who worked at the Willow Run Ford Motor plant in Michigan. Rose Will Monroe, a widow with two children, took the job to help in the war effort and to support her family.

45 ml (1.5 oz) Hendrick's gin
15 ml (.5 oz) PAMA pomegranate liqueur
7.5 ml (.25 oz) Honey Syrup*
90 ml (3 oz) dry rosé
1 lime wheel, as garnish

Shake over ice and strain into a collins glass filled with cracked ice. Add the garnish. Toast all the beautiful and strong women in your life that make this world a better place!

*Honey Syrup: Mix equal parts honey and water. Do not heat—the honey will dissolve naturally.

Ruby Sunday

Adapted from a recipe by Gary Regan, Ardent Spirits, NY, 2008.

Rhubarb was a 1969 movie, written and directed by British comedian, Eric Sykes, in which "rhubarb" was the only word spoken, and every character's last name was Rhubarb. There was also a 1951 movie called *Rhubarb*, and this one was about an eccentric rich guy who left his money, and a baseball team, to his beloved cat, Rhubarb. *Rhubarb Rhubarb*, released in 1980, was a remake of the 1969 *Rhubarb* movie, and again, "rhubarb" was the only word spoken throughout the picture. Oh yes, in case you hadn't noticed, there's a little rhubarb in this drink, too.

60 ml (2 oz) Bombay Sapphire gin
30 ml (1 oz) Domaine de Canton ginger liqueur
30 ml (1 oz) Rhubarb Simple Syrup*
15 ml (.5 oz) fresh lemon juice
6 fresh mint leaves
1 lemon twist, as garnish

Add everything, mint leaves and all, to a shaker full of ice. Shake over ice and strain into a chilled champagne flute. Add the garnish.

*Rhubarb Simple Syrup: Take 4 cups rhubarb that's been cut into 1-inch lengths, cover with water (about 2 cups or 475 ml), add 1/2 cup (100 g) sugar, bring to the boil and simmer for just a couple of minutes until the rhubarb is tender. Strain the water from the rhubarb—that's your simple syrup. Use the rhubarb in a yummy dessert. Gary made this kind of cobbler thing. Well, it wasn't really a cobbler as such, but . . .

Runaway

Adapted from a recipe by Neyah White, Nopa, San Francisco.

This cocktail doesn't have any gin in it. We caught this at the last minute when there was still time to delete it, but we thought, oh hell, let's leave it there and see if anyone notices . . .

45 ml (1.5 oz) Calvados
15 ml (.5 oz) Benedictine
22.5 ml (.75 oz) Croft PINK Porto
15 ml (.5 oz) fresh lemon juice
2 dashes Angostura bitters

Shake over ice and strain into chilled cocktail glass.

Sappho

Adapted from a recipe by Rafael Ballesteros, Spain, circa 2007.

"Vain it is for us to weep
That we all in death must sleep
With man's life ends all the story
Of his wisdom, wit, and glory.
Then enjoy it while we may,
Eat, and drink, and dance, and play
Drain the founts of joy and pleasure,
Fill the goblet without measure."
Sappho: A Tragedy, in Five Acts by Estelle Anna Robinson Lewis, 1878.

Green Chartreuse, to rinse the glass
75 ml (2.5 oz) gin
15 ml (.5 oz) Campari
7.5 ml (.25 oz) Cointreau
1 orange twist, as garnish

Pour the Chartreuse into a chilled cocktail glass, and by tilting the glass and rotating it at the same time, coat the entire interior with the liqueur. Discard the excess Chartreuse. Stir the remaining ingredients over ice and strain into the prepared cocktail glass. Add the garnish.

Satan's Whiskers

There are two formulas for Satan's Whiskers. This one, known as "straight," calls for Grand Marnier, whereas the "curled" potion takes orange curaçao.

15 ml (.5 oz) gin
15 ml (.5 oz) dry vermouth
15 ml (.5 oz) sweet vermouth
15 ml (.5 oz) fresh orange juice
7.5 ml (.25 oz) Grand Marnier
2 dashes orange bitters

Shake over ice and strain into a chilled cocktail glass.

Scottish Pair

Adapted from a recipe by Charlotte Voisey, Mixologist, Hendrick's Gin.

There's some pear nectar in this drink, so you might get the impression that perhaps the creator misspelled the name of the cocktail, but no, it's just a little wordplay on behalf of Ms. Voisey. The "Scottish Pair" refers to the Hendrick's gin and the Glenfiddich single malt scotch called for in the recipe. Both are made in Scotland, you see, and Ms. Voisey enjoys to play with words.

22.5 ml (.75 oz) Hendrick's gin
22.5 ml (.75 oz) Glenfiddich 12-year-old single malt scotch
60 ml (2 oz) pear nectar
15 ml (.5 oz) agave nectar
1 lemon wedge, as garnish
1 pear slice, as garnish
Shake over ice and strain into a chilled cocktail glass. Add the garnishes

Seattle Southside

Adapted from a recipe by Allen Katz, Mixologist for Southern Wine and Spirits, New York City.

The Mathilde poire liqueur used in this recipe won a Gold Medal in the 2009 San Francisco World Spirits Competition. The product is made from Williams Bon Chrétien pears, a variety grown mainly in the orchards of the Anjou region of France, in the Loire valley.

60 ml (2 oz) Citadelle gin
60 ml (2 oz) Mathilde poire liqueur
30 ml (1 oz) fresh lemon juice
1 fresh mint sprig, as garnish.
Shake over ice and strain into a chilled cocktail glass. Add the garnish.

Secret Cocktail

Adapted from a recipe in *Vintage Spirits & Forgotten Cocktails* by Ted Haigh, aka Dr. Cocktail, Los Angeles.

According to Ted Haigh, when this cocktail was created it had a different name from this one but, if it went by that name now, many people would never order it. What's the other name? Afraid you'll have to read Ted's book. We ain't about to incur the wrath of the good Dr. Cocktail!

45 ml (1.5 oz) gin
15 ml (.5 oz) Laird's applejack
15 ml (.5 oz) fresh lemon juice
1 egg white
2 dashes grenadine
1 maraschino cherry, as garnish

Shake over ice and strain into a chilled cocktail glass. Add the garnish.

Sex on a Peach

Adapted from a recipe by Gary Regan, Ardent Spirits, NY, 2007.

The Benedictine Palace, in Fécamp, on the coast of Normandy, has been described as "a subtle blend of extravagance and sobriety." Alexandre Le Grand, the man who built the palace, wanted it to be both the distillery that produced Benedictine liqueur and also a renowned museum with a large collection of art from the fourteenth, fifteenth, and sixteenth centuries. He succeeded on both counts.

15 ml (.5 oz) Benedictine, to rinse the glass
75 ml (2.5 oz) Bombay Sapphire gin
15 ml (.5 oz) Cointreau
15 ml (.5 oz) peach schnapps
15 ml (.5 oz) fresh lemon juice

Rinse a chilled cocktail glass with Benedictine, and discard the excess. Shake the remaining ingredients over ice and strain into the prepared glass.

Shifting Sands

Adapted from a recipe by Sasha Petraske, Milk & Honey, New York City.

45 ml (1.5 oz) Beefeater 24 gin
15 ml (.5 oz) maraschino liqueur
22.5 ml (.75 oz) fresh grapefruit juice
15 ml (.5 oz) fresh lemon juice
Club soda, to top
1 grapefruit wedge, as garnish

Shake over ice and strain into an ice-filled collins glass. Top with a little club soda, stir briefly, and add the garnish.

Shoe Shine Cocktail
Adapted from a recipe by Joe McCanta, S.A.F. Organic Restaurant, Istanbul.
"Influenced obviously by the Martinez and actually the Avenue too . . . I'm really happy with how this drink turns out! Hope you are too." Joe McCanta.
45 ml (1.5 oz) Hayman's Old Tom gin
10 ml (.3 oz) Noilly Prat Amber vermouth
10 ml (.3 oz) Vya sweet vermouth
1 dash Bitter Truth orange flower water
1 dash Cynar
2 dashes Regans' Orange Bitters No. 6
1 flamed lemon twist, as garnish
Stir over ice and strain into a chilled cocktail glass. Add the garnish.

Silk Road Sour
Adapted from a recipe by Timothy Carroll, The East Room in Shoreditch, London.
"For me, Whitley Neill gin is the perfect match for apricot flavours, whilst the Benedictine adds a delicious complexity to the overall flavour profile [of this drink]. If you don't have Whitley Neill to hand it works well with Plymouth, and with Beefeater, but the Whitley Neill really adds a whole dimension." Timothy Carroll.
45 ml (1.5 oz) Whitley Neill London Dry Gin
10 ml (.3 oz) Benedictine
10 ml (.3 oz) apricot brandy
22.5 ml (.75 oz) fresh lime juice
7.5 ml (.25 oz) simple syrup
1 dash Angostura bitters
1 pink grapefruit twist, as garnish
Shake over ice and fine strain into a chilled champagne coupe. Add the garnish.

Singapore Sling: A Discussion

The Singapore Sling is one of those drinks that's long been the topic of debate among bartenders in the wee hours of the morning, and it's probably caused a couple of fisticuff battles, too. It wasn't long ago that we all believed that the Raffles Hotel version was the one and only real McCoy, but then that pesky Ted "Dr. Cocktail" Haigh came along, did a little more research than the rest of us, and deduced that the very first Singapore Sling might have been made with kirschwasser—a cherry eau-de-vie—instead of the Heering cherry liqueur that we find in most recipes. Eau-de-vie, for the record, is a distilled spirit, and liqueurs are distilled spirits that have been sweetened and flavored with various botanical ingredients—these are vastly different products.

David Embury, it seems, agree with Doc. In the second edition of *The Fine Art of Mixing Drinks*—I haven't seen a first edition—he calls specifically for kirsch in his Singapore Gin Sling, stating, "Of all the recipes published for this drink I have never seen any two that were alike." Embury calls for gin, simple syrup, lemon or lime juice, kirsch, and a dash of Angostura, then adds that "some recipes call for the addition of a pony of Benedictine."

Next up we have George Sinclair, the Thinking Bartender, and his nicely-researched article about this drink led me to look again at *The Gentleman's Companion* by Charles H. Baker Jr., 1939. Here we have yet another version, this one named "The Immortal Singapore Raffles Gin Sling" in Baker's book. This formula is somewhat minimalist, and a little on the sweet side, but it's good to record these things, right?

Here, then, are three versions of this drink. The first is said to have been created in the early 1900s at the Raffles Hotel in Singapore by bartender Ngiam Tong Boon, and the second receipt is based on the formula uncovered by Dr. Cocktail in a book dating to 1922—Haigh's discovery was called the Straights Sling, but it was referred to as a "well-known Singapore drink"—and the third recipe is based on Baker's book.

Singapore Sling (Raffles Hotel Style)
The ingredients in this version are listed on a coaster from the Raffles Hotel, but no measurements were given, and the club soda isn't mentioned.
60 ml (2 oz) Beefeater gin
15 ml (.5 oz) Cherry Heering
7.5 ml (.25 oz) Benedictine
15 ml (.5 oz) Cointreau
60 ml (2 oz) pineapple juice
20 ml (.75 oz) fresh lime juice
2 dashes Angostura bitters
Club soda
Shake everything except the club soda and strain into an ice-filled collins glass. Top with club soda.

Singapore Sling (Straights Sling Style)
Adapted from a recipe for a "Straights Sling" found by Ted "Dr. Cocktail" Haigh in a book published in 1922.
This is a dry version of the drink that calls for kirsch, a cherry eau-de-vie, instead of a sweetened cherry brandy.
60 ml (2 oz) gin
15 ml (.5 oz) Benedictine
15 ml (.5 oz) kirschwasser
20 ml (.75 oz) fresh lemon juice
2 dashes orange bitters
2 dashes Angostura bitters
Club soda
Shake everything except the club soda and strain into an ice-filled collins glass. Top with club soda.

Singapore Sling (Charles H. Baker Style)

"The Immortal Singapore Raffles Gin Sling, Met in 1926, and thereafter Never Forgotten . . . The original formula is 1/3 each of dry gin, cherry brandy and Benedictine; shake it for a moment, or stir it in a barglass, with 2 fairly large lumps of ice to chill. Turn into a small 10 oz highball glass with one lump of ice left in and fill up to individual taste with chilled club soda. Garnish with the spiral peel of 1 green lime. In other ports in the Orient drinkers often use C & C ginger ale instead of soda, or even stone bottle ginger beer." *The Gentleman's Companion* by Charles H. Baker Jr., 1939.

30 ml (1 oz) dry gin
30 ml (1 oz) cherry brandy
30 ml (1 oz) Benedictine
Club soda, ginger ale, or ginger beer
1 lime spiral, as garnish

Shake the gin, cherry brandy, and the Benedictine over ice, strain into an ice-filled highball or collins glass, top with the soda, and add the garnish.

"A Delicious, Slow-Acting, Insidious Thing

Just looking around the terrace porch we've seen Frank Buck, the Sultan of Johore, Aimee Semple McPherson, Somerset Maugham, Dick Halliburton, Doug Fairbanks, Bob Ripley, Ruth Elder and Walter Camp . . . When our soft footed Malay boy brings the 4th Sling and finds us peering over the window sill at the cobra-handling snake charmers tootling their confounding flutes below he murmurs 'jaga baik-baik Tuan'—'jaga bye-bye too-wan,' as it is in English—or 'take care master' as it means in English. The Singapore Sling is a delicious, slow-acting, insidious thing." *The Gentleman's Companion* by Charles H. Baker Jr., 1939.

Sin No More Sling

Adapted from a recipe by Philip Greene, Museum of the American Cocktail, Washington, D.C.

60 ml (2 oz) gin
22.5 ml (.75 oz) Domaine de Canton ginger liqueur
15 ml (.5 oz) Cherry Heering
15 ml (.5 oz) fresh lemon juice
1 dash each Angostura and Regans' Orange Bitters No. 6
Club soda

Shake everything except the club soda over ice and strain into an ice-filled collins glass. Top with the soda and stir briefly.

Sleeve

Adapted from a recipe by Neyah White, Nopa, San Francisco, 2008.
30 ml (1 oz) gin (Neyah White likes to use Plymouth or Beefeater in this drink)
30 ml (1 oz) Pineau de Charente
2 dashes orange bitters
1 orange slice, as garnish
Stir gently over ice and strain into a chilled sherry glass. Add the garnish.

South Seas Aviation

Adapted from a recipe by Ryan Magarian, Portland, OR.
"The South Pacific archipelago of Vanuatu is charmingly schizophrenic: some people wear gowns or three-piece suits, others wear only grass skirts or grass sheaths. Some carry gold cigarette lighters, others carry smoldering sticks. Some drink Bordeaux, others drink kava, a local intoxicant with less cachet but more effect." Taken from *Two Worlds in the South Seas,* an article by Nicholas D. Kristof that appeared in *The New York Times*, November 1, 1987.
2 fresh pink grapefruit segments
45 ml (1.5 oz) Tanqueray gin
15 ml (.5 oz) maraschino liqueur
20 ml (.75 oz) fresh lemon juice
20 ml (.75 oz) simple syrup
1 maraschino cherry, as garnish
Muddle the grapefruit segments in a mixing glass. Add ice and the rest of the ingredients. Shake and strain into a chilled cocktail glass. Add the garnish.

Southside Cocktail

Muddy Waters, Chuck Berry, and Bo Diddley all emerged from Chicago's South Side, as did a group of representational artists known as The Chicago Imagists. Their work was known for "grotesquerie, surrealism, and complete un-involvement with New York art world trends," according to the NationMaster on-line encyclopedia.
4 lemon wedges
2 to 3 teaspoons granulated sugar
4 to 5 fresh mint leaves
75 ml (2.5 oz) gin
1 mint sprig, as garnish
Muddle the lemon wedges, sugar, and mint leaves in a mixing glass until the sugar is completely dissolved, all the juice is extracted from the lemons, and the mint is thoroughly integrated into the juice. Add ice and the gin to the mixing glass, then shake and strain into a chilled cocktail glass. Add the garnish.

Southside Fizz
Adapted from a recipe by David Wondrich, author of *Imbibe*, New York City.
4 wedges lemon
2 to 3 teaspoons granulated sugar
6 to 8 fresh mint leaves
75 ml (2.5 oz) gin
Club soda
3 mint sprigs, as garnish
Muddle the lemon wedges, sugar, and mint leaves in a mixing glass until the sugar is completely dissolved, all the juice is extracted from the lemons, and the mint is thoroughly integrated into the juice. Add ice and the gin to the mixing glass, shake over ice, and strain into an ice-filled collins glass. Add the soda, and the garnish.

Spanish Rose
Adapted from a recipe by David Nepove, Enrico's Sidewalk Cafe, San Francisco.
1 rosemary sprig
20 ml (.75 oz) fresh lemon juice
45 ml (1.5 oz) Plymouth gin
20 ml (.75 oz) Licor 43
15 ml (.5 oz) cranberry juice
Strip the leaves from the bottom half of the rosemary sprig and place in them in a mixing glass. Add the lemon juice and muddle well. Add ice, the gin, and the Licor 43 and shake for approximately 15 seconds. Strain into an ice-filled wine goblet, top with the cranberry juice, and garnish with the remaining rosemary sprig.

Stan Lee Sour

Adapted from a recipe by Stan Vadrna, Bartender for Life, Stanislav Vadrna's Analog Bar Institute, and a very dear friend.

This drink was created for the Paparazzi (Bratislava, Slovakia) cocktail menu in 2006, and that menu won 1st Place in the Best Cocktail Menu category at the Cocktail 200 Awards competition in Las Vegas, 2006.

As you sip the Stan Lee Sour, meditate on the Japanese term, *ichigo ichie*, Stan Vadrna's personal mantra. The phrase means "one meeting, one opportunity," and for Stan it represents the opportunity that bartenders have to properly care for their guests upon encountering them for the first time.

5 cm (2 inches) fresh lemongrass
22.5 ml (.75 oz) fresh lemon juice
22.5 ml (.75 oz) simple syrup
60 ml (2 oz) Hibiscus-and-Jasmine-Infused Gin*
1 egg white
2 dashes Regans' Orange Bitters No. 6
1 pinch dried hibiscus, as garnish
1 tiny piece of lemongrass, as garnish

Muddle the lemongrass in a mixing glass with the lemon juice and simple syrup. Add the remaining ingredients and dry shake for 10 seconds to emulsify the egg white. Add ice, shake as though your life depended on it, and strain into a chilled champagne coupe. Sprinkle the dried hibiscus over the center of the drink and hang the tiny piece of lemongrass on the rim of the glass.

Hibiscus-and-Jasmine-Infused Gin: Add 1 tablespoon of dried hibiscus flowers and 2 teaspoons of jasmine tea to 480 ml (2 cups) of gin. Allow the mixture to sit in a dark, cool room for two hours, gently agitating the bottle every 30 minutes, then strain though a double layer of dampened cheesecloth.

Starlight 200

Adapted from a recipe created by Jacques Bezuidenhout for Harry Denton's Starlight Room, San Francisco.

"With no real capital of his own, Denton has leveraged the currency of his personality and party spirit to get other people to put up the money for his opulence. He has no ownership in either Harry Denton's or Harry Denton's Starlight Room. He is a consultant to and employee of the Kimpton Group, though being on the wagon must be cutting into his compensation package. What he brings is a barman's name and look and nature, though he claims his first talent is decorating. `I love interiors,' he says . . ."I think it's the most elegant room in the city to have a cocktail.'" Sam Whiting, Chronicle Staff Writer, *San Francisco Chronicle*, Wednesday, August 23, 1995.

45 ml (1.5 oz) Plymouth gin
20 ml (.75 oz) Leacock's madeira
15 ml (.5 oz) Otima10-year-old tawny port
1 dash Angostura bitters
1 orange twist, as garnish
Stir over ice and strain into a chilled cocktail glass. Add the garnish.

Starry Night Cocktail

Adapted from a recipe by Gary Regan, Ardent Spirits, NY.

Vincent Van Gogh was known to be an absinthe drinker, and it has been said that the reason that the stars in his "Starry Night" painting appear to have their own swirling halos is because that's what absinthe does to one's eyesight. We've experimented with this and it hasn't worked so far . . .

75 ml (2.5 oz) Van Gogh gin
30 ml (1 oz) Goldschläger cinnamon schnapps
Stir over ice and strain into a chilled cocktail glass.

Strawberry Southside

Adapted from a recipe by Jonathan Pogash, Hospitality Holdings (The Campbell Apt, The Carnegie Club, The World Bar, Bookmarks Lounge, Madison & Vine), New York City.

"This is a refreshing take on the classic Southside Fizz that we serve at The Carnegie Club and the Campbell Apartment Terrace. The ingredients blend very nicely, and even though it's a gin-based drink, some guests think that they're drinking a Strawberry Mojito." Jonathan Pogash.

60 ml (2 oz) Beefeater gin
22.5 ml (.75 oz) fresh lemon juice
30 ml (1 oz) simple syrup
1 large strawberry, sliced
1 handful of mint leaves
1 mint sprig, as garnish
1 strawberry slice, as garnish
60 ml (2 oz) Moet & Chandon champagne

Muddle the strawberry in the lemon juice and simple syrup in a mixing glass,. Add ice, the mint and gin and shake very well. Strain into an ice-filled collins glass. Top off with the champagne and add the garnishes.

Sunset

Adapted from a recipe by Neyah White, Nopa, San Francisco, 2008.

"'I'll give you all you ask . . . and your life shall be one long cocktail of orange blossoms, ocean beaches and Spring street.' And verily thus it came to pass." *Sunset, The Pacific Monthly*, published by the Southern Pacific Company Passenger Dept., 1913.

60 ml (2 oz) Croft PINK Porto
30 ml (1 oz) Tanqueray Rangpur Gin
2 dashes Regans' Orange Bitters No. 6
90 ml (3 oz) ginger beer
1 mint sprig, as garnish
Fresh fruit in season, as garnish

Pour all the ingredients into an ice-filled highball glass, stir briefly, and add the garnishes.

Sunset on Dunnigan

Adapted from a recipe by H. Joseph Ehrmann, Elixir, San Francisco.

"A romantic cocktail that will brighten your day, the Sunset on Dunnigan complements the citrusy herbal qualities of the Night Harvest Sauvignon Blanc with the same notes in the gin, while simultaneously adding the botanical dryness of a crisp gin. Elderflower liqueur lends a summery, floral aspect that balances the drink nicely with its light sweetness. The slight bitterness of a spritz of grapefruit zest ties it all together." H. Joseph Ehrmann.

60 ml (2 oz) Night Harvest Sauvignon Blanc
30 ml (1 oz) gin (light juniper, citrus forward)
15 ml (.5 oz) elderflower liqueur
Grapefruit zest, as garnish

Stir over ice and strain into a chilled cocktail glass. Garnish with a twist of fresh grapefruit, zested directly over the cocktail so as to spray the oils over the surface of the cocktail. Drop the zest into the drink.

Tailspin

"There are two different versions of the 'Tailspin.' The most commonly found, is the one which is essentially a 'Bijou.' On DrinkBoy.com, however, I list one which uses a dash of Campari instead of orange bitters. Where I got this version from I have no idea . . . I have gone through all of the books in my collection and haven't uncovered the 'Campari' version, so I am clueless as to from whence it comes, but frankly I like it better than the Bijou version. The Tailspin in the 1935 edition of Mr. Boston's is the 'Bijou' version (i.e. Orange Bitters), and the original Mr. Boston's pamphlet from 1934 doesn't have the Tailspin listed." Robert Hess, April, 2009.

22.5 ml (.75 oz) gin
22.5 ml (.75 oz) sweet vermouth
22.5 ml (.75 oz) green Chartreuse
1 dash Campari
1 maraschino cherry, as garnish
1 lemon twist, as garnish

Stir over ice and strain into a chilled cocktail glass. Add the garnishes.

Tarragon and Back Again
Adapted from a recipe by Chris Schatzmana, Stingaree, San Diego, CA.
20 tarragon leaves
2 strawberries
30 ml (1 oz) Bombay Sapphire gin
30 ml (1 oz) PAMA pomegranate liqueur
30 ml (1 oz) club soda
Muddle the tarragon and strawberries in a mixing glass. Add ice and the gin and liqueur. Shake and strain into an ice-filled collins glass. Top with club soda and stir briefly.

Tart Gin Cooler
Adapted from a recipe by Mardee Haidin Regan and Gary Regan, Ardent Spirits, NY, circa 1996.
Bitter lemon soda can be approximated by adding fresh lemon juice to tonic water, and the Regans were experimenting with this concept by substituting different fruit juices for the lemon juice when they came up with this drink. It works very well as a hot-weather drink, and it makes for a good brunch drink, too.
60 ml (2 oz) gin
60 ml (2 oz) fresh pink grapefruit juice
60 ml (2 oz) tonic water
2 to 3 Peychaud's bitters
Pour the ingredients into an ice-filled collins glass and stir briefly.

Tea with the Brokers
Adapted from a recipe by Gary Regan, Ardent Spirits, NY.
60 ml (2 oz) Broker's Gin (the 47% abv bottling)
60 ml (2 oz) peach tea
30 ml (1 oz) Domain de Canton ginger liqueur
15 ml (.5 oz) fresh lemon juice
2 dashes orange bitters
1 lemon twist, as garnish
Shake over ice and strain into a chilled champagne flute. Add the garnish.

Thai Fizz

Adapted from a recipe by Gregor de Gruyther, Ronnie Scott's, London.
Note: Gregor passed away in June, 2009. He will be missed by many, and remembered for a long, long, time.
60 ml (2 oz) Bombay Sapphire gin
10 ml (.3 oz) fresh lemon juice
15 ml (.5 oz) fresh lime juice
15 ml (.5 oz) kaffir lime leaf-infused gomme syrup
Club soda
2 to 3 coriander sprigs, as garnish
Shake over ice and strain into a beer tankard or a highball glass over cubed ice. Top with soda and add the garnish.

Thai Lady

Adapted from a recipe by Jamie Terrell when he worked at Lab Bar, London.
45 ml (1.5 oz) Plymouth gin
15 ml (.5 oz) Cointreau
30 ml (1 oz) fresh lemon juice
15 ml (.5 oz) Lemongrass Syrup*
Shake over ice and strain into a chilled cocktail glass.

*Lemongrass Syrup: Over a medium heat, dissolve 1 cup (200 g) of granulated sugar into 1 cup (240 ml) of water. Allow to cool to room temperature, and pour the syrup into a blender with 4 stalks of lemongrass. Blend the mixture and strain through a double layer of dampened cheesecloth. Store in the refrigerator.

The Siam Society

"Next there was that question of drink. He had never himself tasted alcohol in his life, until he arrived in Bangkok, and he found in 20 years' experience that the men and the women who died of cholera or dysentery were teetotallers." *The Journal of the Siam Society*, 1904.

Third Degree

The proportions given in this recipe are based on those given in *The Savoy Cocktail Book*, 1930. The book also specified that Plymouth gin be used, that the drink be shaken, not stirred, and that it should be served straight up in an old-fashioned glass.

In the early 1900s the "Martini with a Spot," a drink similar to this one, was served at British gentlemen's clubs (the kind of gentlemen's clubs with overstuffed armchairs, not the clubs with poles for dancing girls).

60 ml (2 oz) Plymouth gin

30 ml (1 oz) dry vermouth

4 dashes absinthe

Shake over ice and strain into a chilled old-fashioned glass.

Tillicum Cocktail

Adapted from a recipe by Robert Hess, DrinkBoy.com, Seattle.

Tillicum Village, about eight miles from Downtown Seattle, is the place to go if you want to sample fresh salmon that's cooked in the style of the local Native Americans—the fish are held on cedar stakes above alderwood fires for about an hour. Visitors to Tillicum can also sample clams cooked in water that's brought to a boil when heated rocks are dropped into the pan—another traditional Native American cooking method. Note that this drink calls for a garnish of smoked salmon.

67.5 ml (2.25 oz) gin

22.5 ml (.75 oz) dry vermouth

2 dashes Peychaud's bitters

1 small slice smoked salmon, skewered on a cocktail pick, as garnish

Stir over ice and strain into a chilled cocktail glass. Add the garnish.

Tipsy Parson

Adapted from a recipe by Jim Ryan, Hendrick's Gin Brand Ambassador, New York City.

This was one of the drinks served at the Hendrick's Bartender's Croquet Tourney in New York City on May 12, 2009. It's outrageously fabulous, and immensely quaffable in its incredible enormity.

30 ml (1 oz) Hendrick's gin
30 ml (1 oz) Pimm's No. 1 Cup
45 ml (1.5 oz) Strawberry-Rhubarb Compote*
4 fresh mint leaves
1 sprig fresh mint, as garnish
1 cucumber spear, as garnish
Shake over ice and strain into an ice-filled collins glass. Add the garnishes. Smile.

*Strawberry-Rhubarb Compote: Clean, hull, and halve 80 strawberries. Clean and chop up 6 rhubarb stalks. Throw everything into a large nonreactive saucepan and add 1 liter (34 oz) fresh orange juice. Heat on medium to low until the fruit starts to break down into a mush. Add 2 cups (400 g) turbinado sugar (aka sugar in the raw). Stir well and continue heating until the liquid is reduced to about 1.5 liters (6.3 cups). Remove the pan from the heat, allow the mixture to come to room temperature, and puree it in a blender. Store in the refrigerator.

Tom Collins

Old Tom, a sweetened gin, was first used in this drink, and now dry gin is commonly used. If you use Old Tom, cut back on the simple syrup a little.

75 ml (2.5 oz) gin
30 ml (1 oz) fresh lemon juice
20 ml (.75 oz) simple syrup
Club soda
1 maraschino cherry, as garnish
1 1/2 orange wheel, as garnish
Shake everything except the club soda over ice and strain into an ice-filled collins glass. Top with club soda. Add the garnishes.

Tom Collins and John Collins: A Discussion

Much has been written about the origins of the Tom Collins, and it was George Sinclair, bartender, drink historian, blogger, and all-around mischief-maker, who uncovered some previously unknown the facts about it in a 2006 article that he penned for *Class* magazine in the UK. The drink, according to George, was seemingly named after a practical joke, and the joke, which was the talk of the town in New York and other cities in 1874, had grown men roaming the streets looking for Tom Collins, a fictitious character who, they were told by pranksters of the nineteenth century, had been saying nasty things about them. Strange how things such as a sense of humor, things that we think of as being basic and ingrained, change over the years, right? This, though, was the great Tom Collins Hoax of 1874, and the drink known as the Tom Collins began to appear in cocktail books shortly after this.

Prior to the Sinclair article, everyone thought that the Tom Collins was a drink that was born of John Collins, a drink seemingly named for the head waiter at Limmer's, a joint in London. John Collins was, in fact, the narrator of the following verse from a poem by Frank and Charles Sheridan:

"My name is John Collins, head waiter at Limmer's,
Corner of Conduit Street, Hanover Square,
My chief occupation is filling brimmers
For all the young gentlemen frequenters there."

Later in the poem gin punch is mentioned: "Mr. Frank always drinks my gin punch when he smokes." So it's long been presumed that the John Collins gin punch originated at Limmer's in London, but Sinclair's findings seemed to put paid to this theory. Indeed, Sinclair as much as dismissed the theory, and more than a few people were inclined to agree with him at the time. But it seems that he was wrong, after all. When *Imbibe*, David Wondrich's book, was released in 2007, things got a little clearer.

While the Tom Collins Hoax of 1874 seemed feasible to some folk as being responsible for the name change, it just ain't so. The Tom Collins seems most definitely to have gotten its name when Old Tom gin replaced the genever in the John Collins. Wondrich cites a gin punch known as John Collins as being introduced to bartenders in New York in the 1850s, and although the recipe is lost to history, if it was anything like the gin punches served at other London clubs—specifically The Garrick Club—during the first half of the nineteenth century, Wondrich says that it would have called for gin, lemon juice, chilled soda water, and maraschino liqueur.

Wondrich is a little evasive in his book, but when asked flat out, "Do you know for sure that a gin punch known as John Collins was around prior to the 1870s?," his reply was, "Yeah, it's in the 1869 *Steward & Barkeeper's Manual*, and George Augustus Sala [a well respected British writer/reporter/editor] found people drinking it here during the Civil War," he told us. A few weeks later, dear David came up with a quote from a Canadian publication, dated 1865, that goes like this: "The last time I saw [John Wilkes Booth] was at Montreal, in October, 1864, at a place called 'Dolly's,' next door to the St. Lawrence Hall, and much frequented by the amateurs of 'Mint Juleps' and 'John Collinses.'"

In 1904, an article entitled "The Last of Limmer's," written by John Morley, a British journalist and politician, appeared in *Macmillan's Magazine*, and here we find a little more information about the drink: "Through the bustle and confusion of Limmer's John Collins trotted serenely in his noiseless pumps . . . mixing pick-me-ups of the kind named after him for the dejected revelers . . . This world-renowned beverage, still popular in America, and not forgotten on this side of the Atlantic, was compounded of gin, soda-water, ice, lemon and sugar," he wrote. Later in this piece Morley mentions that after Collins retired from Limmer's, Dickens visited him in Hempstead. Collins was quite an important man, it seems.

So where does all that leave us? Well, since the first printed recipe found at the time of writing for the Tom Collins turned up in Jerry Thomas' 1876 book, *The Bar-Tender's Guide or How to Mix all Kinds of Plain and Fancy Drinks*, and Thomas called specifically for Old Tom gin, the name change—from John to Tom—seems appropriate. This theory also makes sense when you see that Louis Muckensturm gave recipes for both drinks, calling for Hollands—genever—in the John Collins, and Old Tom in the Tom Collins, in his 1906 book, *Louis' Mixed Drinks*.

In conclusion, then, it seems incontrovertible that the John Collins was named for the head waiter at Limmer's in London, and that the Tom Collins is the same drink but made with Old Tom gin rather than genever. Q.E.D. Now let the matter rest, please.

Tom Hagen Cocktail
Adapted from a recipe by Joshua Haig Harris, 15 Romolo, San Francisco.
15 ml (.5 oz) Dubonnet Blanc
45 ml (1.5 oz) Right gin
30 ml (1 oz) St Germain elderflower liqueur
7.5 ml (.25 oz) Batavia Arrack
1 flamed orange twist, as garnish
Rinse a cocktail glass with the Dubonnet and pour the excess into a mixing glass. Add ice and the remaining ingredients. Stir and strain into the cocktail glass. Add the garnish.

Toulouse-Lautrec
Adapted from a recipe by Timothy Lacey, Drawing Room at Le Passage, Chicago.
1 egg white
30 ml (1 oz) North Shore No. 6 gin
30 ml (1 oz) Atholl Brose (or Drambuie)
15 ml (.5 oz) absinthe
15 ml (.5 oz) cane syrup
22.5 ml (.75 oz) fresh lemon juice
Angostura bitters, as garnish
Combine all ingredients in a shaker and dry shake. Add ice and shake the hell out of it. Strain into a chilled champagne coupe and garnish with a few drops of Angostura bitters, drawing a cocktail stirrer through them to create a lovely pattern.

Track 11
Adapted from a recipe by Joshua Haig Harris, 15 Romolo, San Francisco.
Created for the James Beard Foundation Gala, 2008.
60 ml (2 oz) Right gin
30 ml (1 oz) fresh lemon juice
15 ml (.5 oz) simple syrup
Half of a pasteurized egg white
60 ml (2 oz) apple juice
5 basil leaves
1 sprig fresh basil, as garnish.
Dry shake the egg white, then add ice and all the other ingredients. Shake and double-strain into a chilled cocktail glass. Add the garnish.

Twentieth Century Cocktail

Detailed in *Café Royal Cocktail Book*, 1937, this drink was created by a certain C. A. Tuck.

45 ml (1.5 oz) gin
15 ml (.5 oz) Lillet Blanc
15 ml (.5 oz) white creme de cacao
15 ml (.5 oz) fresh lemon juice

Shake over ice and strain into a chilled cocktail glass.

Proceedings Go Crooked

"In the morning the merchant, the lawyer, or the Methodist deacon takes his cocktail. Suppose it is not properly compounded? The whole day's proceedings go crooked because the man himself feels wrong from the effects of an unskillfully mixed drink." *Café Royal Cocktail Book*, 1937.

---

24 Sour

Adapted from a recipe by Dre Masso, London.

45 ml (1.5 oz) Beefeater 24 gin
22.5 ml (.75 oz) fresh lemon juice
10 ml (.3 oz) Benedictine
10 ml (.3 oz) simple syrup
2 dashes Angostura bitters
22.5 ml (.75 oz) egg white
1 orange slice, as garnish
1 maraschino cherry, as garnish

Shake over ice and strain into an ice-filled old-fashioned glass. Add the garnishes.

21 Hayes

Adapted from a recipe by Rob Schwartz, circa 2004, when he worked at Absinthe Brasserie and Bar, San Francisco.

"21 Hayes is the MUNI bus line that goes past our restaurant every 10 or 15 minutes. I'm sure last time you were in SF you noticed the beautiful orange/ reddish/brownish color of our busses. That's the color the 21 Hayes reminded me of. It tastes a whole lot better though. Also my wife's grandmother was the first female MUNI driver (during WWII), and I wanted to pay her a bit of tribute." Rob Schwartz.

3 slices cucumber, about 1/4" thick
7.5 ml (.25 oz) Pimm's No. 1 Cup
45 ml (1.5 oz) gin
7.5 ml (.25 oz) fresh lemon juice
1 splash simple syrup

Muddle together 4 or 5 small ice cubes with 2 slices of the cucumber and the Pimm's in a large mixing glass using a wooden muddler. Muddle until the cucumber is almost liquid—some of the skin will be left. Add ice and the gin, lemon juice, and simple syrup. Shake well and strain into a chilled cocktail glass. Garnish with the remaining cucumber slice.

Unusual Negroni

Adapted from a recipe by Charlotte Voisey, Mixologist, Hendrick's Gin.

This is an unusual Negroni, and it was created by an unusual sort of a lass, Charlotte Voisey (pronounced Voice-y, not Vwassy). Known as "Miss Pink" to many—though nobody can quite remember how or why she got the name—Charlotte is recognized as a world-class cocktailian who, in 2004-2005, was named Bartender of the Year in the UK. She hails from Essex. We try to forget that . . .

30 ml (1 oz) Hendrick's gin
30 ml (1 oz) Aperol
30 ml (1 oz) Lillet Blanc
1 orange twist, as garnish

Stir over ice and strain into a chilled cocktail glass. Spritz and drop in the twist.

Uva Bella

Adapted from a recipe by Ryan Magarian, Portland, OR.
6 white grapes (1 of which will serve as garnish)
60 ml (2oz) Aviation gin
15 ml (.5 oz) St. Germain elderflower liqueur
22.5 ml (.75 oz) fresh lemon juice
15 ml (.5 oz) simple syrup
1 dash Regans' Orange Bitters No. 6
Muddle 5 of the grapes in a mixing glass. Add ice and the remaining ingredients, and shake. Strain into a chilled cocktail glass and add the remaining grape by slotting it onto the rim of the glass as garnish.

Valentino

A play on the Negroni created by Mardee Haidin Regan and Gary Regan in February 1999, for the Valentine's Day issue of Ardent Spirits e-letter.
The Negroni, made with equal amounts of the same ingredients in the Valentino, is an interesting potion to play with, and no matter what ratios you use when you put this trio together, the drink always seems to work in one way or another.
60 ml (2 oz) gin
15 ml (.5 oz) Campari
15 ml (.5 oz) sweet vermouth
1 orange twist, as garnish
Stir over ice and strain into a chilled cocktail glass. Add the garnish.

Verbena Sour

Adapted from a recipe by Xavier Herit, Daniel, New York City.
60 ml (2 oz) verbena sour-infused Boodles gin*
30 ml (1 oz) fresh lemon juice
15 ml (.5 oz) simple syrup
1 lemon twist, as garnish
Shake over ice and strain into a chilled cocktail glass. Add the garnish.

* **Verbena Sour-Infused Boodles Gin:** Steep 1 liter of Boodles gin with 4 lemon verbena tea bags for 4 hours. Remove the tea bags.

Veruca Fizz
Adapted from a recipe by Christine D'Abrosca, Malo Restaurant, Los Angeles.
1 handful blueberries
7.5 ml (.25 oz) Monin raspberry syrup
15 ml (.5 oz) Cointreau
22.5 ml (.75 oz) fresh lemon juice
45 ml (1.5 oz) Plymouth gin
Izze blueberry soda
3 skewered blueberries, as garnish
Muddle the blueberries and raspberry syrup in a mixing glass. Add ice and the remaining ingredients except blueberry soda. Shake over ice and strain into highball glass fill with crushed ice. Top with blueberry soda. Add the garnish.

Vesper Martini
Named for Vesper Lynd, a character in Ian Fleming's *Casino Royale*, James Bond insisted that this Martini be shaken, and he preferred Lillet to vermouth. The bartender from whom he ordered the drink suggested that a grain-based vodka worked better than a potato vodka.
45 ml (1.5 oz) gin
15 ml (.5 oz) vodka
7.5 ml (.25 oz) Lillet Blanc
1 lemon twist, as garnish
Shake over ice and strain into a chilled cocktail glass. Add the garnish.

The Origin of the Vesper

"'A dry martini,' he said. 'One. In a deep champagne goblet.'
'Oui, monsieur.'
'Just a moment. Three measures of Gordon's, one of vodka, half a measure of Kina Lillet. Shake it very well until it's ice-cold, then add a large thin slice of lemon-peel. Got it?'
'Certainly, monsieur.' The barman seemed pleased with the idea."
Casino Royale, by Ian Fleming, 1953.

Victory Shot
Adapted from a recipe by Gary Regan, Ardent Spirits, NY.
Regan created this one on the eve of the 2008 Presidential election and instructed that red or blue curaçao could be employed, depending on the outcome. Blue won out. Thank God for that.
45 ml (1 oz) dry vermouth
7.5 ml (.25 oz) gin
7.5 ml (.25 oz) blue curaçao
Stir over ice and strain into a shot glass.

VIRGIN Sapphire
Adapted from a recipe created by Jamie Walker when he was Global Brand Ambassador for Bombay Sapphire.
According to a footnote found in *The Divina Commedia and Canzoniere* by Dante Alighieri, the sapphire is a "symbol at once of purity and of the divine glory," and therefore, "in mediæval art the Virgin is commonly painted with a robe of sapphire-blue."
30 ml (1 oz) Bombay Sapphire gin
60 ml (2 oz) pineapple juice
1 splash creme de cassis
1 fresh raspberry, as garnish
Shake everything except for the cassis over ice and strain into a chilled cocktail glass. Pour the creme de cassis down the side of the glass so that it settles at the bottom. Add the garnish.

Waterloo Sunset
Adapted from a recipe by Dan Warner, Beefeater Brand Ambassador.
This cocktail needs to be stirred before drinking. After Dinner Gold Winner, Drinks International Bartender Challenge 2007.
22.5 ml (.75 oz)) Beefeater gin
10 ml (.3 oz) elderflower cordial
Brut champagne
5 ml (.15 oz) raspberry liqueur
1 diagonally speared raspberry, as garnish
Stir the gin and cordial over ice. Strain into a chilled champagne flute. Layer the champagne and liqueur using a barspoon. Add the garnish.

Wicked Old School
Adapted from a recipe by Timothy Lacey, Drawing Room at Le Passage, Chicago.
60 ml (2 oz) genever
30 ml (1 oz) fresh blood orange juice
4 drops Angostura bitters
1 splash simple syrup
Build in an old-fashioned glass with 2 ice cubes, and stir briefly.

Wild Blossom Sour
Adapted from a recipe by Timothy Lacey, Drawing Room at Le Passage, Chicago.
60 ml (2 oz) Martin Miller's Westbourne Strength gin
22.5 ml (.75 oz) elderflower liqueur
10 ml (.3 oz) cane syrup
15 ml (.5 oz) dry vermouth
1 long lemon twist tied in a knot, as garnish
Shake over ice and strain into a collins glass. Add the garnish.

Xanadu
Adapted from a recipe by Ted Kilgore, Monarch, Maplewood, MO.
60 ml (2 oz) Hendrick's gin
22.5 ml (.75 oz) creme de cassis
22.5 ml (.75 oz) pomegranate juice
7.5 ml (.25 oz) fresh lime juice
Shake over ice and strain into a chilled cocktail glass.

Chapter 12

Various Rules and Regulations Surrounding Gin Production

U. S. A.: Alcohol and Tobacco Tax and Trade Bureau (T. T. B.)

Information provided by The Distilled Spirits Council of the U. S. A., 2009.

"Gin" is a product obtained by original distillation from mash, or by redistillation of distilled spirits, or by mixing neutral spirits, with or over juniper berries and other aromatics, or with or over extracts derived from infusions, percolations, or maceration of such materials, and includes mixtures of gin' and neutral spirits. It shall derive its main characteristic flavor from juniper berries and be bottled at not less than 80-proof. Gin produced exclusively by original distillation or by redistillation may be further designated as "distilled". "Dry gin" (London dry gin), "Geneva gin" (Hollands gin), and "Old Tom gin" (Tom gin) are types of gin known under such designations.

European Union Gin Definitions

All gins are made with ethyl alcohol flavoured with juniper berries (juniperus communis) and other flavourings. The ethyl alcohol used must be distilled to the minimum standards stated in the EU Spirit Drink Regulations. In all types of gin, the predominant flavour must be juniper, and they must have a minimum retail strength of 37.5 per cent abv.

There are three definitions of gin: Gin, Distilled Gin and London Gin.

Gin

This made from: a Suitable ethyl alcohol and flavourings b The ethyl alcohol does not have to be re-distilled c The flavouring can be either approved natural or artificial d The flavourings can be simply mixed together with the ethyl alcohol to form the gin (compounded) e There is no restriction on the addition of other approved additives such as sweetening f Water is added to reduce the gin's strength to the desired retail level, but not below 37.5 per cent abv.

G There is no restriction on the colouring of gin with an approved colouring

Distilled gin

Distilled gin is made in a traditional still by: a Redistilling neutral alcohol in the presence of natural flavourings b There is no minimum strength laid down for the resultant distillate c After distillation, further ethyl alcohol of the same composition may be added d Additional flavourings may be added after distillation and these can be either natural or artificial flavourings e The distillate can be further changed by the addition of other approved additives since there is no prohibition on their use in the definition f Water may be added to reduce the strength to the desired retail level g There is no restriction on the colouring of distilled gin with approved colourings

London Gin

London Gin is made in a traditional still by re-distilling ethyl alcohol in the presence of all natural flavourings used. a The ethyl alcohol used to distil London Gin must be of a higher quality than the standard laid down for ethyl alcohol. The methanol level in the ethyl alcohol must not exceed 5 g per litre of pure alcohol b The flavourings used must all be approved natural flavourings and they must impart the flavour during the distillation process c The use of artificial flavourings is not permitted d The resultant distillate must have a minimum strength of 70 per cent abv e No flavourings can be added after distillation f Further ethyl alcohol may be added after distillation provided it is of the same standard g A small amount of sweetening may be added after distillation provided the sugars do not exceed 0.5 g per litre of finished product (the sugar is not discernible and is added to some products purely for brand protection purposes) h The only other substance that may be added is water i London Gin cannot be coloured

INDEX

Z